JBoss ESB
Beginner's Guide

A comprehensive, practical guide to developing service-based applications using the Open Source JBoss Enterprise Service Bus

Kevin Conner

Tom Cunningham

Len DiMaggio

Magesh Kumar B

[PACKT] open source*
PUBLISHING   community experience distilled

BIRMINGHAM - MUMBAI

JBoss ESB
Beginner's Guide

First published: January 2012

Production Reference: 1180112

Published by Packt Publishing Ltd.
Livery Place
35 Livery Street
Birmingham B3 2PB, UK.

ISBN 978-1-84951-658-7

www.packtpub.com

Cover Image by Rakesh Shejwal (shejwal.rakesh@gmail.com)

Credits

Authors
Kevin Conner

Tom Cunningham

Len DiMaggio

Magesh Kumar B

Reviewers
Ty Lim

Mark Little

Naveen Malik

Martin Večeřa

Acquisition Editor
Sarah Cullington

Lead Technical Editors
Chris Rodrigues

Pallavi Iyengar

Technical Editor
Vanjeet D'souza

Project Coordinator
Vishal Bodwani

Proofreader
Kevin McGowan

Indexers
Rekha Nair

Monica Ajmera Mehta

Graphics
Manu Joseph

Production Coordinator
Shantanu Zagade

Cover Work
Shantanu Zagade

About the Authors

Kevin Conner is the Platform Architect for the SOA platform within JBoss, a division of Red Hat. After graduating from Newcastle University, Kevin worked as a kernel programmer with Integrated Micro Products, developing fault tolerant network drivers. IMP was later acquired by Sun Microsystems where he was to discover Java. He has over 15 years, experience of Java, predominately Enterprise technologies, which he has used to develop software for technical, financial, and local government clients. Before joining JBoss he was a Senior Engineer with Arjuna Technologies, working on transaction products.

I would like to thank everyone at Packt Publishing for giving me the opportunity to write this book. Special thanks to Sarah Cullington for guiding us through the initial work, Pallavi Iyengar and Chris Rodrigues for continuing her work, Vishal Bodwani for his enthusiasm and encouragement and all the technical reviewers.

I would also like to thank all my colleagues at Red Hat for providing a rich and fertile environment in which ideas are encouraged to flourish, without which this book would be rather brief. It is truly an inspiring place to work.

A big thank you must also go to my family and friends who, having heard about this project, encouraged me to go forward with enthusiasm.

Finally my biggest thanks are reserved for those who are most important to me, my wife and children. They have been patient and encouraging throughout this process, allowing me to work late through the night and on weekends in order to catch up with the schedule, all the while having to deal with one of the most disruptive events any family can undertake— emigration to a distant country. I began this process while planning to leave one country, finishing it while setting up a home in a second. I love you all very much.

Tom Cunningham is currently the project lead for JBoss ESB and has worked for Red Hat since 2007 on JBoss ESB and SwitchYard. He is an active committer on the Apache jUDDI and Apache Scout projects. Tom received a B.S. in Computer Science from Georgetown University and an M.S. in Computer Science from Arizona State University and has worked in software development for over 14 years.

I'd like to thank my sons Ben and Nate, my wife Sonia, and my parents for their support in writing this book.

Len DiMaggio stumbled onto computer programming while studying Business Administration and has never looked back. Len is a Graduate of Bentley University and has worked for some of the better known pioneering technical companies such as DEC, BBN, GTE, Rational, IBM, and now JBoss by Red Hat. He is the software test team lead for the open source JBoss Service Oriented Architecture Platform (SOAP) which is built on JBoss ESB.

This is Len's first book. He is a "Most Valuable Blogger" at *Dzone* where he is a frequent contributor. Len has also written over 50 articles for *Dzone*, *Red Hat Magazine*, *Dr. Dobbs' Journal*, and other publications. Len writes a blog that is (mostly) dedicated to software testing subjects (`http://swqetesting.blogspot.com/`). He is a proud member of the JBoss community (`http://community.jboss.org/people/ldimaggio`) and, when he is not testing software, is a frequent contributor to Fotopedia (`http://www.fotopedia.com/`).

I'd like to thank my wife Maria for her understanding and support during many late night writing and editing sessions, and Mary and Robert for their frequent (and extremely important!) interruptions for hockey, dancing, baseball, soccer, and softball as they kept what's truly important in life in perspective.

I'd also like to thank way too many current and former co-workers to mention for everything I learned from them, my co-authors Kevin, Tom, and Magesh, my mates' in Geordie Land and přátelé in Brno and the open source communities that make JBoss ESB and all the other JBoss projects possible. And finally, I'd like to thank Sarah, Chris, Vishal, Vanjeet, and everyone else at Packt for giving us the opportunity to write this book!

Magesh Kumar B. is a Senior Software Engineer at JBoss, a division of Red Hat. He has a Masters in Computer Applications from Coimbatore Institute of Technology. His passion is coding in Java and has architected many enterprise applications prior to Red Hat. His project contributions include JBoss WS and JBoss Portal. His current projects are JBoss ESB and SwitchYard.

He hails from Ooty and lives in Bangalore, India with his wife, three kids and his parents. You can reach him at mageshbk@gmail.com. This is his first book.

I would first like to thank Kevin Conner for introducing me to JBoss ESB. Without him I wouldn't have been part of this book. I would like to thank Len and Tom for those delightful days while we wrote this book.

Next I would like to thank Sarah Cullington from Packt for her initial review when we started this book. I would like to thank my parents, my wife Charu, my sons Lavesh and Shashwath for being so patient while they missed my time with them. Lastly to my little daughter Yashtika for showing her godly smile when the times were tough.

About the Reviewers

Ty Lim has been in the IT Industry for over 15 years. He has worked for several start-up companies in the mid 1990s and found himself working at several major large corporations after his stint in Silicon Valley. He has worked in the following industries: Software Development, Consulting, Healthcare, Telecommunications, and Financial. He has experience utilizing JBoss, Tomcat, and WebSphere middleware technologies.

He holds a Bachelor of Science degree in Computer Science from the University of the Pacific, and is currently pursuing a Master of Science degree in CIS from Boston University.

He has worked on the *IBM WebSphere Application Server v7.0 Security* book.

I would like to thank all my friends and family for their continued support. I am truly blessed to have such a great support system. It is because of all of you that I consider myself a very happy man.

Dr Mark Little is CTO of the JBoss Division in Red Hat. Prior to this he was Technical Development Manager for the Red Hat SOA Platform. Mark has extensive experience in the areas of SOA and distributed systems, specializing in fault tolerance. Over the years he has led various efforts including ESB and transactions. He has been a Distinguished Engineer at Hewlett Packard, and author of many standards in the areas of Web Services, Java, CORBA, and elsewhere.

He co-authored many books including *Java 2 Enterprise Edition 1.4 (J2EE 1.4) Bible* (Wiley), *Java Transaction Processing: Design and Implementation* (Prentice Hall), *Enterprise Service Oriented Architectures: Concepts, Challenges, Recommendations* (Springer), and *Service-Oriented Infrastructure: On-Premise and in the Cloud* (Prentice Hall).

I'd like to thank my wife and family for putting up with my workloads over the years. It can't have been easy and I value their support immeasurably. I'd like to especially thank my nine year old son, Adam.

Martin Večeřa is a software quality engineer for JBoss by Red Hat interested in bleeding-edge projects and technologies. His main area of interest is Java middleware where he has seven years of experience. Previously he developed information systems for power plants and medical companies. Martin publishes articles on Java middleware to various international and local web magazines. Other main areas of his interest are data mining, business intelligence, and rule-based systems.

www.PacktPub.com

Support files, eBooks, discount offers and more

You might want to visit www.PacktPub.com for support files and downloads related to your book.

Did you know that Packt offers eBook versions of every book published, with PDF and ePub files available? You can upgrade to the eBook version at www.PacktPub.com and as a print book customer, you are entitled to a discount on the eBook copy. Get in touch with us at service@packtpub.com for more details.

At www.PacktPub.com, you can also read a collection of free technical articles, sign up for a range of free newsletters and receive exclusive discounts and offers on Packt books and eBooks.

http://PacktLib.PacktPub.com

Do you need instant solutions to your IT questions? PacktLib is Packt's online digital book library. Here, you can access, read and search across Packt's entire library of books.

Why Subscribe?

- Fully searchable across every book published by Packt
- Copy and paste, print and bookmark content
- On demand and accessible via web browser

Free Access for Packt account holders

If you have an account with Packt at www.PacktPub.com, you can use this to access PacktLib today and view nine entirely free books. Simply use your login credentials for immediate access.

Table of Contents

Prologue—the need for an ESB   1

Preface   3
  What is "JBoss"?   3
    JBoss is also a community   4
  What is Open Source and what are its advantages?   4
  What is middleware?   6
  What is an SOA? What is an ESB?   8
  What is JBoss ESB?   9
  What capabilities does JBoss ESB have?   10
  Why JBoss ESB?   11
  What is JBoss ESB's relationship with SOA?   12
  What resources does the JBoss ESB community provide?   12
    Online forums with a difference   12
      The user forum   13
      The developer forum   13
    Other useful documents   13
    Mailing lists   14
    JIRA announcements and bugs   14
    Live chat   15
  What are the JBoss project and product models?   15
  What this book covers   15
  Chapter bibliography   18

Chapter 1: Getting Started   23
  Downloading JBoss ESB   23
  Downloading and installing an application server   25
  Time for action – downloading and installing JBoss AS   25
  Choosing which JBoss ESB distribution is right for you   28

Time for action – downloading and installing jbossesb-4.10.zip	**29**
Reviewing the contents of jbossesb-4.10.zip	30
Time for action – deploying JBoss ESB to JBoss AS	**30**
Keeping things slim	**33**
Time for action – modifying a profile	**33**
Deployable Java archives	33
Testing the installation	**34**
Time for action – testing the installation	**34**
Looking at logs	**35**
Finding the logs	35
Time for action – viewing the deployment of an application in the server.log	**36**
Consoles	**37**
Time for action – examining an MBean	**38**
What do you do if you see an error?	**39**
Summary	**40**
Chapter 2: Deploying your Services to the ESB	**41**
The quickstarts	**41**
Anatomy of a deployment	**43**
Defining the providers, services, and listeners	44
Other deployment files	46
Helloworld quickstart	47
Time for action – deploying the quickstart	**48**
Deploying a JBoss ESB archive remotely	**50**
Time for action – accessing the admin console	**50**
Time for action – performing the deployment	**51**
Introduction to JBDS	**54**
Time for action – downloading JBDS	**54**
Time for action – installing JBDS	**55**
Running JBDS	**60**
Time for action – setting up the ESB runtime in JBDS	**63**
Time for action – using JBDS to run the quickstart	**68**
Deploying the quickstart in JBDS	**70**
Time for action – deploying the quickstart	**71**
Summary	**75**
Chapter 3: Understanding Services	**77**
Preparing JBoss Developer Studio	**78**
Time for action – opening the Chapter3 app	**78**
Examining the structure of ESB messages	**80**
Examining the message	80

Time for action – printing the message structure	**81**
Message implementations	84
The body	84
Time for action – examining the main payload	**85**
The header	89
Routing information	89
Message identity and correlation	90
Service action	91
Time for action – examining the header	**91**
The context	93
Message validation	94
Configuring through the ConfigTree	**95**
Configuring properties in the jboss-esb.xml file	95
Traversing the ConfigTree hierarchy	96
Accessing attributes	96
Time for action – examining configuration properties	**97**
Service pipeline and service invocation	**99**
Lifecycle methods	99
Processing methods	101
Time for action – examining exceptions	**103**
Dynamic methods	105
MEP (Message Exchange Pattern) and responses	106
ServiceInvoker	108
Synchronous delivery	109
Asynchronous delivery	109
Time for action – examining exceptions	**110**
Composite services	**112**
Service Chaining	112
Service Continuations	114
Transactions	**115**
Security context	**117**
Summary	**118**
Chapter 4: JBoss ESB Service Actions	**119**
Understanding actions	**119**
What is an action class?	**120**
The action chain	**121**
Custom actions	**123**
Lifecycle actions	123
JavaBean actions	126
Custom actions using annotations	127
Lifecycle annotations	128
Processing annotations	129

Out-of-the-box (OOTB) actions—how and when to use them   **131**

Scripting   132

Services—invoking EJBs   133

Web services/SOAP   134

Time for action – running the quickstart   **134**

Transformers/converters   135

Smooks message fragment processing   136

Time for action – running the quickstart   **138**

Routers   140

Time for action – implementing content-based routing   **142**

Notifiers   144

Time for action – let's see how notifiers work   **144**

Business Process Management   145

Drools   146

BPEL processes   146

Chapter bibliography   **148**

Summary   **148**

Chapter 5: Message Delivery on the Service Bus   **149**

The bus   **150**

Preparing JBoss Developer Studio   **151**

Time for action – creating File Filters   **151**

Time for action – opening the Chapter5 app   **152**

Transport providers   **154**

Time for action – using a File provider   **155**

InVM transport   157

Transactions with InVM transport   158

Time for action – testing InVM transactions   **159**

InVM message optimization   162

Controlling InVM message delivery   164

Time for action – using lock-step delivery   **165**

InVM threads   168

Time for action – increasing listener threads   **168**

Provider configurations   **170**

JMS provider   171

FTP provider   171

SQL provider   172

File provider   173

Summary   **174**

Chapter 6: Gateways and Integrating with External Clients   **175**

  What is a gateway and a notifier?   **176**

    How do we compose messages?   177

      Simple composer example   178

  Preparing JBoss Developer Studio   **179**

  The JMS gateway   **180**

  Time for action – using the JMS gateway   **180**

  The File gateway   **182**

  Time for action – using the File gateway   **182**

  The HTTP gateway   **184**

  Time for action – using the HTTP gateway   **185**

    The HTTP bus and HTTP provider   187

  The Camel gateway   **188**

  The FTP gateway   **189**

  The UDP gateway   **189**

  Time for action – using the UDP gateway   **190**

  The JBoss Remoting gateway   **192**

  Time for action – using the JBR gateway   **193**

  The Groovy gateway   **194**

  The SQL gateway   **195**

  Time for action – using the SQL gateway   **195**

  The JCA gateway   **198**

  Summary   **199**

Chapter 7: How ESB Uses the Registry to Keep Track of Services   **201**

  The registry—what, how, and why?   **202**

  UDDI—the registry's specification   **203**

  jUDDI—JBoss ESB's default registry   **205**

    Configuring jUDDI for different protocols   205

    Looking at jUDDI's database   206

  Time for action – looking at the jUDDI registry database   **208**

  Other supported UDDI providers   **209**

  Custom registry solutions   **209**

  End-point reference   **209**

  Time for action – looking at EPRs   **210**

  JAXR—introducing the Java API for XML registries   **212**

  Federation   **212**

  Load balancing   **213**

  Registry maintenance and performance   **213**

  Registry interceptors   **214**

Monitoring	**214**
Examining jUDDI query counts	215
Time for action – querying the UDDI server	**216**
Chapter bibliography	**220**
Summary	**220**
Chapter 8: Integrating Web Services with ESB	**221**
Preparing JBoss Developer Studio	**222**
Time for action – preparing the Chapter8 application	**222**
Time for action – switching consoles	**224**
Exporting ESB services as a web service	**225**
Time for action – running the sample	**226**
Action implementation	228
Securing EBWS	229
Time for action – securing the sample	**230**
Other security mechanisms	233
ESB web service client	**234**
soapUI client	234
Time for action – ESB SOAP client	**234**
Request processing	236
Response processing	238
The Wise SOAPClient	239
Time for action – Incorporating the Wise SOAP Client	**240**
Request and response processing	241
Custom handlers	243
Co-located web services	**244**
SOAPProcessor	245
Time for action – incorporating a SOAPProcessor client	**245**
Web service proxies	**248**
SOAPProxy	248
Time for action – incorporating SOAPProxy into the application	**248**
Tweaking HttpClient	**250**
SOAPClient	250
SOAPProxy	251
Sample properties	251
Custom configurator	252
SOAPProxy security pass through	**253**
Cleaning up deployments	254
Time for action – SOAPProxy security pass through	**255**
Summary	**257**

Appendix A: Where to go Next with JBoss ESB?   **259**

  Creating service definitions with the JBDS ESB editor   **259**

  Using other UDDI providers (HP Systinet and SOA Software Service Manager)   **262**

  Using other JBoss project technologies   **263**

    JBoss Drools and rules-based services   263

    JBoss Riftsaw and BPEL services   268

    JBoss jBPM and Business Process Management   272

  Using Maven with JBoss ESB   **274**

    Compiling with Maven   275

    ESB packaging with Maven   276

  How to test your ESB services   **278**

    Testing a single action   279

    AbstractTestRunner   280

    TestMessageStore   282

    Arquillian   283

    Cargo   285

  Chapter bibliography   **286**

Appendix B: Pop-quiz Answers   **287**

Index   **289**

Prologue—the need for an ESB

It's 9AM Monday. After weeks of work, your team has almost completed a difficult systems integration project. Your system was entirely based on a Java Messaging System (JMS) interface, and you had to integrate it with a different team's web services based system. It meant that your team had to write "glue code" to handle data translation between the two systems, but all that was behind you now, so you could get back to concentrating on finishing up the actual business logic code for the integrated system.

And then, your boss appears at your office door and casually announces that there is one more integration needed for the system. But this time, you have to integrate the system with an older legacy system that is text file and FTP based. Text files! Suddenly you see weeks of writing more new glue code to handle data transformation, protocol conversion, and who knows what else.

How long would it be until you would be able to get back to being able to focus on your "real job" of working on the business logic challenges that your system was intended to solve? What you need is a tool that will enable you to connect these systems together.

Preface

In this preface, we'll introduce JBoss, Open Source, and, of course, JBoss ESB. We'll also introduce thinking in Service Oriented Architecture terms, how JBoss ESB can help you, and why JBoss ESB is the best choice for your SOA needs.

This preface is organized into a series of questions and answers. We'll begin at the beginning, the beginning of JBoss, that is.

What is "JBoss"?

In 1999, Marc Fleury (http://www.thedelphicfuture.org/) started an open source project that he named "EJBoss" (for "Enterprise Java Beans open source software"). The goal of the project was to provide an open source server implementation of the EJB specification.

The server quickly became popular due to its low cost and ease of use. In 2001, the name was changed to "JBoss" due to Sun Microsystem's legal concerns over the use of the term "EJB". (http://community.jboss.org/thread/69613).The JBoss Group was first incorporated in 2001. In 2006, JBoss was acquired by the world's leading open source software company, Red Hat (http://www.redhat.com). JBoss is currently known as "JBoss by Red Hat" (http://www.jboss.org/).

As Javid Jamae and Peter Johnson point out in their 2009 book, *JBoss in Action* (http://www.amazon.com/JBoss-Action-Configuring-Application-Server/dp/1933988029), the word "JBoss" is often used to describe the company, its application server, and other JBoss technologies, including JBoss ESB. The full list of JBoss open source technologies and projects can be found at http://www.jboss.org/projects/matrix.

JBoss is also a community

One aspect of JBoss that is especially striking is the significant market and market mind share presence that it has, given its relatively small size. The number of JBoss employees who lead, develop, test, and document all the JBoss open source projects is very small, especially when compared to industry giants such as IBM and Oracle. So, how does JBoss do it? It takes a community.

It's really misleading to look at the small number of JBoss employees relative to the large shadow that JBoss casts, as behind JBoss the company; there's JBoss the community. "JBoss" is also the open source community that supports and contributes to the development, testing, and documentation of JBoss projects. Literally tens of thousands of people (as of this writing, over 80,000 people have registered as members of the JBoss community `http://community.jboss.org`) all around the world have contributed in one way or another to JBoss projects. Some of them have contributed actual code, while others have contributed documentation, feedback on design or bugs, or have promoted JBoss projects in their personal and commercial blogs.

What is Open Source and what are its advantages?

In its simplest terms, "open source" describes software where the source code, that is, the human readable source from which the software is built, is freely available.

Why is this important?

If you can see the source code of software, you can study and review not just the outward behavior of the software, but also its internal functioning and logic. You can understand how it works, how it fails, and how it can be improved.

Let's take a step back and think about just what software is. It's not a physical medium like steel or concrete (in his book, *The Art of Software Testing*, Glenford Myers refers to software being "malleable" in comparison to physical media). Rather, it is a manifestation of human logic, packaged into a form that can be used to accomplish specific tasks. These tasks can take the form of executing business processes, spacecraft navigation, or even just tools to enable us to waste time surfing the web. Software is, effectively, a bunch of ideas.

Now, how can you improve an idea? You subject it to a rigorous review that is also public, so that the idea must stand on its own merits. Where's a better place to have a review like this, in a cathedral, or a bazaar?

Eric Raymond contrasted the differences between closed source and open source software development with the analogy that is the title of his book, *The Cathedral and the Bazaar* (Raymond, Eric Steven, `http://www.catb.org/~esr/writings/homesteading/cathedral-bazaar`)

In the bazaar there is a free exchange of ideas. Those ideas, and criticisms of those ideas, can come from many sources and a wide number of people. The bazaar may seem to be chaotic, but it also allows for freedom and innovation and the unfettered filtering out of bad ideas. Think about it, if you are trying to design a complex system, wouldn't it be more successful if the design process includes a review by the widest possible audience?

In contrast, in the cathedral, only the members of a small, closed society are able to participate in the review of an idea and influence its ultimate design. The ideas are held secret from the outside world. The members of this closed society may be skilled, but they will be few in number and their actions are constrained by the rules of cathedral life.

These two worlds parallel these software development models:

- In the closed source model, the ideas are secrets:
  - Only a small, select number of people can see the inner workings behind these ideas. They review, refine, debug, and correct the software that represent these ideas, and release them to the public in a closed form.
  - Design and security flaws, unless they are caught by the holders of the secrets, are built into the software.
  - Bad decisions can be hidden from the consumers of the software. These consumers see only the external form and output from the software. The consumers can ask for changes to be made to the software, but do not have a way to make the changes themselves. The consumers are often locked into complex, expensive, and restrictive license agreements with the software producers.

- In the open source model, the ideas are open:
  - Anyone can review them, critique them, attempt to improve them, and even look for ways to exploit them. A large community of people participate in the conversion of these ideas into software. These people bring their own experiences, outlooks and their "many eyes" to the task of building the software.
  - Design and security flaws are often uncovered by people other than the original designers.
  - Bad decisions are often held up to public ridicule by members of the community, until the decisions are corrected.
  - The consumers of the software see both the external form and output from the software as well as its inner workings. These consumers are able to both request changes to the software, and can make those changes themselves, within the framework of flexible license agreements. The consumers can even retain the use of the software after their licenses expire.

❑ Closed source leads to more bloat-ware as there is no community to weed this out. In large closed source companies more complexity is viewed as good. In an open source community, this bloat will be exposed to the light of day and removed.

What is middleware?

Like many technology terms "middleware" can be difficult to define. One interesting definition is:

> *Middleware: The kind of word that software industry insiders love to spew. Vague enough to mean just about any software program that functions as a link between two other programs, such as a Web server and a database program. Middleware also has a more specific meaning as a program that exists between a "network" and an "application" and carries out such tasks as authentication. But middleware functionality is often incorporated in application or network software, so precise definitions can get all messy. Avoid using at all costs.*

`http://www.salon.com/technology/fsp/glossary/index.html`

That's not a very informative definition. Let's define what middleware is in terms of where it resides in a software system's architecture and the functions that it performs.

The "where" is easy. Middleware occupies the "middle," in between the operating system and your applications.

One of its primary tasks is to connect systems, applications, and databases together in a secure and reliable way. For example, let's say you bought a sweater at a store web site last night. What happened? You looked through various sweaters' images, selected color and size, entered a charge card number, and that was it, right? Well, behind the scenes, middleware made sure that the store's inventory database showed that sweater in stock, connected to the charge card company's database to make sure that your card wasn't maxed out, and connected to the shipping company database to verify a delivery date. Additionally, it made sure that hundreds or thousands of people could all shop on that site at the same time. Also, while it looked to you like you were looking at one web site, middleware tied together many different computers, each in a different location, all running the store's e-commerce application, into a cluster. Why is this important? To make sure that you can always get to the store online, even if some of these computers are down due to maintenance or power failures.

Before we move on, let's look at middleware in terms of a real-world analogy:

Middleware is plumbing.

There are four ways that this is true.

First, it's mostly invisible.
You don't generally see much of the plumbing in your house. What you see is the water. As a consumer, you don't see middleware. You see the web sites and the information flow that middleware makes possible. This is part of why middleware is hard to define. If you live and work with software, and if you're reading this you probably do, then you're very aware of software packages at the top level in a logical view, such as e-commerce web applications, and packages that exist at the bottom level, such as databases and the operating system. The middle part, that plumbing that ties everything together, can seem less concrete and identifiable.

Second, as a developer, you rely on middleware to provide a standard way of doing things.
If you wanted to build your own plumbing from scratch, you could. But it's much easier to just buy plumbing fixtures. You, as a software developer, could design and build your own application servers, database connection drivers, authentication handlers, messaging systems, etc. But these wouldn't be easy to build and maintain. It's much easier to make use of middleware components that are built according to established (and especially open!) standards. In middleware, these standards take the form of libraries of functions that your applications use through well-defined application programming interfaces (APIs). You call these functions instead of having to invent your own to handle tasks such as accessing databases or executing transactions.

Third, it ties together parts of complex systems.
There's another similarity about your household plumbing and middleware; tying systems together. They both enable you to tie together systems that were built by different people, at different times, without your having to reconstruct everything from scratch. Think about your house for a minute. If your house is older, you probably have several generations of plumbing all working together. You didn't have to upgrade your washing machine with multiple service packs when you installed a new hot water heater. In middleware, one of the most powerful approaches is Service-oriented Architecture (SOA) based on an Enterprise Service Bus (ESB). As its name implies, an ESB provides a server, messaging, and APIs that function like a hardware bus. In order to integrate enterprise software applications developed at different times, by different organizations, and even communicating via different protocols, you don't have to rewrite them to speak one consistent language. The ESB enables you

to "plug" these applications as services into the bus. The ESB takes care of
transforming messages between the protocols and routing the messages to
the correct services.

Fourth and finally, it lets you worry about other things.
When you put an addition onto a house, what do you worry about? Bathroom
fixtures, kitchen appliances, flooring, colors, and how to pay for it all. It's a very
stressful process. The last thing you want to worry about is whether you want
3/4-inch or half-inch pipe, copper or PVC connectors, #9 or #17 solder, etc.
With middleware taking care of all the invisible functions, you, as a software
developer, can concentrate on building software to solve your business
problems and fulfill your customers' needs.

```
http://magazine.redhat.com/2008/03/11/what-is-middleware-in-plain-
english-please/
```

What is an SOA? What is an ESB?

Service Oriented Architecture (SOA) is not a single program or technology. It's really a
matter of software architecture or design. Some of the basic principles of SOA are:

- **Based on inter-operable services**: Instead of building an application from a huge
  monolithic program, SOA design calls for breaking systems into multiple services.
  These services are not rigidly coded together, but interact by sending and receiving
  messages.

- **Software reuse**: By dividing large applications into services, individual services, or
  groups of services can be reused.

- **Loose coupling**: Services are not rigidly coded together, but rather interact through
  "loose coupling" where services communicate by sending and receiving messages.

- **Abstraction**: The messages sent between services follow a well-defined contract. No
  information on the internal implementation of the services is needed.

- **Location**: Clients and services don't store the network or server location of target
  services. The information is made discoverable in a registry.

In hardware terms, a "bus" is a physical connector that ties together multiple systems or subsystems. Instead of having a large number of point-to-point connectors between pairs of systems, you connect each system to the bus once.

An **Enterprise Service Bus (ESB)** does the same thing, logically, in software. Instead of passing electric current or data over the bus to and from the connections (or "endpoints") on the ESB, the ESB logically sits in the architectural layer above a messaging system. The messaging system allows for asynchronous communications between services over the ESB. In fact, when you are working with an ESB, everything is either a service (which in this context is your application software) or a message being sent between services. It's important to note that a "service" is not automatically a web service. Other types of applications, using transports such as FTP or JMS, can also be services.

For more information on what an ESB is, a great resource is *Enterprise Service Bus: Theory in Practice* by David Chappell.

What is JBoss ESB?

JBoss ESB is JBoss' open source Enterprise Service Bus.

One of the main goals of JBoss ESB is to enable you to knit together disparate systems. JBoss ESB does this by abstracting the differences between these systems by treating each of them as a logical service on the ESB. The services communicate via messages, as on the bus, everything is either a message or a service. As a result, regardless of the inner workings/architecture of any service, you can "plug" them into the ESB and connect them without having to write system-specific "glue code".

JBoss ESB does not dictate to you specific integration patterns for any types of legacy systems. They are all treated as logical services on the ESB. This approach ensures that JBoss ESB itself does not become one more legacy system that you have to compensate for by writing integration "glue code".

What capabilities does JBoss ESB have?

Some of the main capabilities of JBoss ESB are as follows:

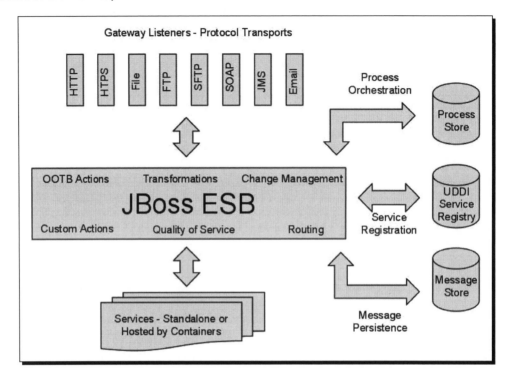

- ◆ **Service registration and hosting:** We'll talk a lot about services in this book, and after all, the ESB is the vehicle to host the service, and the services are what we use to implement our business logic. A registry is used to look up service endpoints at runtime. **UDDI (Universal Description, Discovery and Integration—** http://uddi.xml.org) is a registry standard. JBoss ESB provides jUDDI (http://juddi.apache.org) as a registry implementation; it stores internal ESB Endpoint References (EPRs) in the jUDDI registry. Without the registry, your client application won't be able to locate its target services. Don't worry about the location of the services, you can find them through the registry. We will discuss the registry in *Chapter 7*.

- ◆ **Protocol translation through Adapters:** In order to support connecting legacy applications over the ESB, JBoss ESB must be able to translate data submitted from various protocols to a format that can be transmitted over the ESB. JBoss ESB manages this translation using Adapters (for JMS, FTP, files, and so on) to "on-board" messages onto the ESB. JBoss ESB translates the messages into a format referred to as "ESB-aware" when the messages are on-boarded onto the ESB. We'll discuss messages' "ESB awareness" in *Chapter 6*.

- **Process orchestration**: "Orchestration" refers to the control of multiple processes by a central process (sort of like an orchestra conductor). JBoss ESB supports service orchestration through its integrations with JBoss jBPM (for business process orchestration) and JBoss RiftSaw for web service orchestration using BPEL (Business Process Execution Language—http://docs.oasis-open.org/wsbpel/2.0/ wsbpel-specification-draft.html).

- **Change management**: It's rare that a service will be deployed to the ESB only once. The service will have to change over time and be updated. JBoss ESB handles this by supporting the hot deployment of services and versioning services, and monitoring/ managing deployed services through administrative consoles.

- **Quality of service**: Bad things can always happen to good services and servers. JBoss ESB supports transactions to ensure that services are reliable.

- **Rich set of out-of-the-box actions**: Creating a custom service is that much easier as one of JBoss ESB's features is an extensive set of predefined ("out of the box") actions that can be incorporated into your services. These actions support a wide variety of tasks including:

  - **Transformers and converters**: converting message data from one form to another.

  - **Business Process Management**: integrating with JBoss jBPM.

  - **Scripting**: automating tasks in supported scripting languages.

  - **Services**: integration with EJBs Routing—moving message data to the correct services.

  - **Notifier**: sending data to ESB-unaware destinations.

  - **Webservices/SOAP**: support for web services as service endpoints.

Why JBoss ESB?

Why should you choose JBoss ESB? Well, in addition to the rich feature set we just listed in the previous section (and also making the authors of this book very happy), here are some other good reasons:

- **Low entry cost**: It's free. You can download, evaluate, and use JBoss ESB at no cost.

- **It's open**: You can see the code, the documents, the bugs, and even the e-mails and IRC chat between members of the development team.

- **You won't be alone**: Thousands of individuals and organizations have downloaded and are using JBoss ESB. It's supported by a vibrant user community. We'll discuss the full set of community resources in a bit.

- ◆ **It's easy to get started**: Included in the JBoss ESB distributions are over 80 example programs referred to as "quickstarts." Each quickstart is a fully operational JBoss ESB service that can be used as a learning tool, or can be extended to service as the basis for your own custom services.

- ◆ **It's Standards Based**: JBoss ESB supports such standards as JMS and UDDI. In addition, all of the configuration files used by JBoss ESB and ESB serve are written in XML.

What is JBoss ESB's relationship with SOA?

Is an ESB the same thing as SOA? Not exactly. An ESB does not provide a Service Oriented Architecture, but it does provide the tools than can be used to build one—especially loose-coupling and asynchronous message passing. SOA is a series of principles, patterns, and best practices. JBoss ESB is the base SOA infrastructure that JBoss has contributed to the community which can be used to develop SOA applications.

In middleware, one of the most powerful approaches is SOA based on an ESB. In order to integrate enterprise software applications developed at different times, by different organizations, and even communicating via different protocols, you don't have to rewrite them to speak one consistent language. JBoss ESB enables you to "plug" these applications as services into the bus. JBoss ESB takes care of transforming messages between the protocols and routing the messages to the correct services.

What resources does the JBoss ESB community provide?

We mentioned previously that JBoss ESB, just like other JBoss open source projects, is a community project. It's free for you to use, but it is not supported with a service level agreement (SLA). You don't get a 1-800 number to call for help at 2AM on a Sunday.

Remember, you're a member of a community, and you are not alone. You have access to multiple resources.

Online forums with a difference

You can ask questions, and review questions that have been asked in the past in online forums.

At first glance, being told to search a user forum for an answer to a problem that you are having with software may sound like a brush in the same league as RTFM ("read the fine manual") After all, every commercial software product has a user forum these days. Actually, every product of any kind has a forum these days.

There are, however, very important differences between JBoss project forums and forums for closed software products. In forums dedicated to closed source software, you can often see conversations between users where they share experiences and attempt to discern the root causes of problems, where the inner workings and designs of the software is a black box. They, in effect, pool their ignorance in the hope of solving a puzzle from the outside in. Also, In JBoss forums, the community members who respond to forum questions are either the people who have designed and built the software, or are other users who all share one common characteristic; they all have access to the source code.

There are actually two separate forums.

The user forum

This forum (`http://community.jboss.org/en/jbossesb?view=discussions`) is intended to handle all problems using JBoss ESB. For example, if you have a problem with an installation, or cannot find a specific resource, or have any type of question on your initial experiences, you should ask it in the user forum. But, as literally thousands of people have used JBoss ESB before you, there is a good chance that whatever question you are asking has already been asked before. So, before you post a new question, search the forum to see if it's really an old question that has already been asked (and answered) before.

The developer forum

This forum (`http://community.jboss.org/en/jbossesb/dev?view=discussions`) is intended for questions related to the development of JBoss ESB. You should try to make sure to ask your questions related to the use of JBoss ESB on the user forum, which is higher traffic and has a higher participation rate from members of the community in the User Forum. You can also subscribe to RSS feeds for these forums, so that you can see new questions as they are asked and answers to new and old questions.

Other useful documents

In addition to the forums you also have access to the JBoss ESB project wiki and blog. The wiki (`http://community.jboss.org/wiki/JBoss ESB`) contains hundreds of useful articles on configuring and using specific features of JBoss ESB. The JBoss ESB blog (`http://jbossesb.blogspot.com/`) has a lower level of traffic, and tends to cover new announcements and more time-critical subjects.

Mailing lists

The JBoss ESB project has multiple active mailing lists (`http://www.jboss.org/jbossesb/lists`). All of these are open for anyone to subscribe to. It's a good idea to look at the archive of these lists before you subscribe so you can get an idea of the type of information communicated through the lists, and the frequency of the mail messages:

- **esb-announce** (`https://lists.jboss.org/mailman/listinfo/esb-announce`): This list is used for general announcements, such as when a new release of JBoss ESB is available.

- **esb-users** (`https://lists.jboss.org/mailman/listinfo/esb-users`): This list is intended to complement the user forum, not duplicate or replace it. It's intended to provide a way for users and the JBoss ESB development team to communicate. If you are tempted to use this list to ask basic, newbie type questions, please don't! Questions of that type are better asked in the user forum.

- **esb-commits** (`https://lists.jboss.org/mailman/listinfo/esb-commits`): This list is used for svn (subversion) commit announcements. You probably don't want to subscribe to this list unless you are actively involved in making changes to JBoss ESB project code.

- **esb-dev** (`https://lists.jboss.org/mailman/listinfo/esb-dev`): This list is intended to complement the development forum by providing a way for the developers to communicate.

- **esb-issues** (`https://lists.jboss.org/mailman/listinfo/esb-issues`): JBoss ESB uses JIRA for bug and issue tracking. When a JIRA is logged or modified, an announcement is sent to this list.

JIRA announcements and bugs

There's one aspect of closed source software that can make systems integration work difficult. Just as the source is closed, so are the bugs. When you purchase a closed source product, you may receive a list of resolved problems, but it is likely that this list is incomplete and sanitized so as to present a positive view of the product.

With JBoss open source software, in contrast, the bug tracking database is as open as the code. You can see all the bugs, tasks related to the project, and the feature requests at `http://jira.jboss.org`. Now, it may at first appear as though JBoss projects are plagued with alarmingly large numbers of bugs. It's important to keep in mind that since ALL the bugs are logged in JIRA, some of the bugs are actually user errors, duplicates, problems with the samples or documentation, or even problems that have already been resolved.

Remember, you're not looking at a carefully screened Potemkin Village-like (`http://en.wikipedia.org/wiki/Potemkin_village`) view of the bug database, you're looking at all of them. Note that the only bugs that are not publicly viewable are related to security issues. These issues are generally kept private until they are resolved so as to not put users of the software at risk. And, if the number of bugs in JIRA for an open source project does seem too large, just try asking your closed source software suppliers for full and open access to their bug tracking systems. It's doubtful that any access that you receive will be full and open.

Live chat

Finally, you can talk to live people! The JBoss ESB project has an IRC (Internet Relay Chat), channel at irc.freenode.net **#jbossesb**. You can use this channel to direct questions to JBoss ESB project community members. Check this out when you get a chance. Regardless of your timezone, you'll find someone online in the **#jbossesb** channel.

What are the JBoss project and product models?

You've probably noticed that we have consistently referred to JBoss software as "projects" and not as "products." We've done this intentionally as in the JBoss model, while all the software is open source, there are definite differences between JBoss projects and products. The major differences are:

The JBoss Enterprise Platforms (`http://www.redhat.com/jboss/platforms/`) combines multiple projects, into an integrated, certified package. The JBoss Application Server (JBoss AS) is the core of "Enterprise Application Platform" (`http://www.jboss.com/products/platforms/application/`) and JBoss ESB is the core of the SOA Platform (`http://www.jboss.com/products/platforms/soa/`).

You could assemble platforms like these on your own, but this would be a complex task. And, you would then be faced with the need to maintain the packages over time and ensure that you located and correctly integrated all new bug fixes, functional updates, and security updates. Or, you can buy a product subscription and have JBoss do this for you.

It's a common model for organizations to start with JBoss software by using one or more projects, and then "graduate" to purchasing products as their use of the projects expands.

What this book covers

Congratulations! You now have an understanding of JBoss's history, open source software and JBoss projects and products, Service Oriented Architecture and the role of an ESB in it, as well as a good idea of how JBoss ESB fits into SOA, and the level and types of support that are provided to you in the JBoss ESB community.

The chapters in this book will enable you to work hands-on with JBoss ESB as you learn how to build, deploy, and administer your own ESB services. Each chapter builds on what you learned in the previous chapter.

The chapters cover the following subjects:

Chapter 1, Getting Started
In this chapter, you begin to get hands-on with JBoss ESB. When you complete this chapter, you'll have JBoss ESB downloaded, deployed to an application server, and running. This chapter describes the JBoss ESB distributions that are available, how you decide which distribution is right for you and how you can download it. After you download JBoss ESB, this chapter walks you through the steps you take to deploy JBoss ESB to a JBoss AS server, and how to start the server. Once you have the server running, this chapter shows you how to verify that the server is running correctly with JBoss ESB. And, if there are problems with the server or the deployment of JBoss ESB to that server, this chapter shows you how to debug these problems.

Chapter 2, Deploying your Applications to the ESB
Once you have JBoss ESB deployed to an application server and running, it's time to learn how to deploy and manage deployed services. You'll learn how to do that in this chapter by using one of JBoss ESB's "quickstart" example programs. This chapter starts by reviewing the core components of JBoss ESB, how they work and how your services can use them. The chapter then describes "ESB-awareness." This concept is important to understand as it defines how you can "onboard" messages onto the ESB through gateways from external sources. After this, you get hands on with the JBoss ESB quickstart example programs; how you build, deploy, and run the quickstarts, and how they illustrate JBoss ESB features. Finally, this chapter introduces the eclipse based JBoss Developer Studio (JBDS). JBDS makes service development easier for you through its IDE-based ESB editor and makes it easier for you to deploy and administer deployed services.

Chapter 3, Understanding Services
Running a simple service is a useful first step, but in this chapter, you'll expand on that by learning in-depth about services and how they perform tasks with the actions pipeline, and how services are able to support transactions. The chapter also shows how services can be made secure by using authentication and authorization, and how services can be executed based on schedules that you define. You'll also learn how to make your services more robust with load-balancing, fail-over and fault-tolerance configuration.

Chapter 4, Understanding Actions
Actions enable your services to perform simple and complex tasks. This chapter shows you how to use the built-in actions provided with JBoss ESB. These actions support JBoss ESB's core functions of transformation, routing, and support for web services, and JBoss ESB's integrations to use Business Process Management with jBPM, Rules services with Drools, BPEL processes with Riftsaw, and virtual databases with Teiid. The chapter also shows you how to create and debug your own custom actions.

Chapter 5, Preparing for Message Delivery on the Service Bus
One of the major features of JBoss ESB is how it is able to deliver messages to services. In this chapter you'll learn how to use connectors to get messages onto and off of the JBoss ESB bus. You'll also learn how JBoss ESB uses message transport providers and how to configure them. This chapter describes how you use the transports that the ESB supports in your services, and how transactions, security, pass-by-value and pass-by-reference get affected with such transports. The transports covered include JMS, JCA, file, ftp, sftp, ftps, sql.

Chapter 6, Gateways and how to integrate with External Clients
In addition to moving messages over the ESB between services, it's important for the ESB to be able to "on-board" messages from external sources. JBoss ESB does this with Gateways. This chapter shows you how to write clients and then use gateways to enable your services to receive ESB unaware messages through gateways from those clients. The chapter also shows you how to use notifiers to send messages off the JBoss ESB bus to external ESB unaware destinations.

Chapter 7, How the ESB Uses the Registry to Keep Track of Services
How does JBoss ESB keep track of deployed services? In a registry. In this chapter you'll learn how the registry works, and how to extend the the default operations performed by the service registry. This chapter introduces you to the UDDI (Universal Description Discovery and Integration) protocol and shows how your clients can use it to locate services. The chapter also introduces you to federated registries, where you can segment your services into hierarchical groupings, and shows you steps that you can take to maintain your service registry to keep it running reliably.

Chapter 8, Integrating Web Services with the ESB
In this chapter you'll learn how to take your ESB services and export them over SOAP/HTTP and about the choices available for invoking local and remote web services. This chapter shows you how to automatically expose ESB services through a web service with EBWS, invoking co-located web services with `SOAPProcessor`, invoking remote web services with `SOAPClient`, and dynamic proxying of web services with `SOAPProxy`. This chapter concludes by showing you how to integrate web service security with JBoss ESB.

Appendix A, Where to Go Next with JBoss ESB?
This appendix looks into topics like using the JBDS Editor and other UDDI Providers (HP Systinet, SOA Software Service Manager). We will also see Drools and Rules Based Services, RiftSaw and BPEL-based services, jBPM and Business Process Management. Other topics covered include using Maven with JBoss ESB—creating a project from scratch with Maven archetype and using the JBoss Maven plugin and testing ESB Services (`TestMessageStore` and Arquillian).

Appendix B, Pop-quiz Answers
Check how well you scored in the quizzes.

Chapter bibliography

JBoss in Action by Javid Jamae and Peter Johnson (`http://www.amazon.com/JBoss-Action-Configuring-Application-Server/dp/1933988029/ref=sr_1_1?s=books&ie=UTF8&qid=1325764563&sr=1-1`).

"Middleware." Smart Environments by Eric Steven Raymond and G. Michael, Addison-Wesley: New York. 101-127. 2004 (`http://serenity.uncc.edu/youngblood-old/publications.html`)

The Art of Software Testing by Glenford Myers (`http://www.amazon.com/Art-Software-Testing-Second/dp/0471469122`)

Conventions

In this book, you will find several headings appearing frequently. To give clear instructions of how to complete a procedure or task, we use:

Time for action – heading

Action 1

Action 2

Action 3

Instructions often need some extra explanation so that they make sense, so they are followed with:

What just happened?

This heading explains the working of tasks or instructions that you have just completed.

You will also find some other learning aids in the book, including:

Pop quiz – heading

These are short multiple choice questions intended to help you test your own understanding.

Have a go hero – heading

These set practical challenges and give you ideas for experimenting with what you have learned.

You will also find a number of styles of text that distinguish between different kinds of information. Here are some examples of these styles, and an explanation of their meaning.

Code words in text are shown as follows: "The decompose method also has access to the original request".

A block of code is set as follows:

```java
public void readReply() throws JMSException {
    QueueReceiver receiver = session.createReceiver(replyQueue);
    Message msg = receiver.receive();
    if (msg instanceof TextMessage) {
        System.out.println(((TextMessage) msg).getText());
    }
```

When we wish to draw your attention to a particular part of a code block, the relevant lines or items are set in bold:

```java
public void readReply() throws JMSException {
    QueueReceiver receiver = session.createReceiver(replyQueue);
    Message msg = receiver.receive();
    if (msg instanceof TextMessage) {
        System.out.println(((TextMessage) msg).getText());
    }
```

Any command-line input or output is written as follows:

```
# cp /usr/src/asterisk-addons/configs/cdr_mysql.conf.sample
    /etc/asterisk/cdr_mysql.conf
```

New terms and **important words** are shown in bold. Words that you see on the screen, in menus or dialog boxes for example, appear in the text like this: "Now click **Run | Run As | Java Application**".

Warnings or important notes appear in a box like this.

Tips and tricks appear like this.

Reader feedback

Feedback from our readers is always welcome. Let us know what you think about this book—what you liked or may have disliked. Reader feedback is important for us to develop titles that you really get the most out of.

To send us general feedback, simply send an e-mail to feedback@packtpub.com, and mention the book title through the subject of your message.

If there is a topic that you have expertise in and you are interested in either writing or contributing to a book, see our author guide on www.packtpub.com/authors.

Customer support

Now that you are the proud owner of a Packt book, we have a number of things to help you to get the most from your purchase.

Downloading the example code

You can download the example code files for all Packt books you have purchased from your account at http://www.packtpub.com. If you purchased this book elsewhere, you can visit http://www.packtpub.com/support and register to have the files e-mailed directly to you.

Errata

Although we have taken every care to ensure the accuracy of our content, mistakes do happen. If you find a mistake in one of our books—maybe a mistake in the text or the code—we would be grateful if you would report this to us. By doing so, you can save other readers from frustration and help us improve subsequent versions of this book. If you find any errata, please report them by visiting http://www.packtpub.com/support, selecting your book, clicking on the **errata submission form** link, and entering the details of your errata. Once your errata are verified, your submission will be accepted and the errata will be uploaded to our website, or added to any list of existing errata, under the Errata section of that title.

Piracy

Piracy of copyright material on the Internet is an ongoing problem across all media. At Packt, we take the protection of our copyright and licenses very seriously. If you come across any illegal copies of our works, in any form, on the Internet, please provide us with the location address or website name immediately so that we can pursue a remedy.

Please contact us at copyright@packtpub.com with a link to the suspected pirated material.

We appreciate your help in protecting our authors, and our ability to bring you valuable content.

Questions

You can contact us at questions@packtpub.com if you are having a problem with any aspect of the book, and we will do our best to address it.

1
Getting Started

As we stated in the Preface, JBoss ESB is JBoss' open source Enterprise Service Bus. JBoss ESB enables you to quickly integrate new and legacy systems, exposing their combined functionality through services "plugged" into the service bus. JBoss ESB takes care of routing and processing service requests while you concentrate on your system's design and development.

In this chapter we will:

- ◆ Discuss the choices that you have for which distribution of JBoss ESB to run
- ◆ Show where you can find the distributions, and how to install them
- ◆ We'll also introduce you to the ESB's Administrative Console
- ◆ Walk you through how to locate services in the console
- ◆ Show you how to debug server errors

In short, you'll learn how to get JBoss ESB up and running. Okay, it's time to get hands-on with JBoss ESB!

Downloading JBoss ESB

One of the ways in which JBoss projects make it easy to get started is that they are easy to install and get running. In most cases, you simply download a ZIP file, and remember, since these are Java projects, you can use the same ZIP project file on any supported operating system and with any supported JVM. Unzip the file to a directory, and run a shell script or .bat file coincidentally named run, and you're off and, well, running. You can install JBoss ESB into any directory that you choose. You can even have multiple installations on the same system.

Please note that in the examples and illustrations in this book, we will download to, and install software into the /opt directory, which is a standard Unix directory for optional software packages. All references to download and installation directories will be relative to /opt. Please note that you may install the JBoss Application Server and JBoss ESB into any directory you want.

Let's begin by looking at how you can download the bits for JBoss ESB.

At the time of this writing, the download page for JBoss ESB was aptly named `http://www.jboss.org/jbossesb/downloads`. The webpage is as follows:

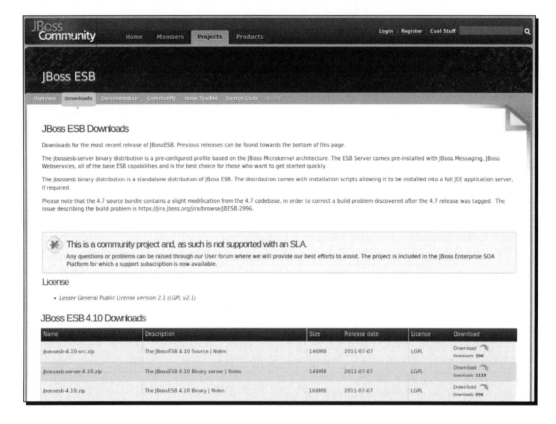

If you explore around this page, you'll find several older releases of JBoss ESB. The newest releases are always displayed at the top of the page. This is the release (4.10) that we'll install and use throughout the remainder of the book. We'll use the 4.10 release as, at the time of this writing, it was the most up-to-date release, and it includes many features and bug fixes that were not present in earlier releases.

Before we go any further with JBoss ESB, we have to download the application server on which JBoss ESB will run. It's really something of a misnomer to say that you *run* a JBoss ESB server. What you really do is *deploy* JBoss ESB to an application server and then deploy your services to JBoss ESB.

So, let's get ourselves an application server.

Downloading and installing an application server

Application servers provide many functions, such as clustering, supporting resource pooling and sharing (for example database connections), caching, transaction support, and persistence. We'll use **JBoss Application Server** (**JBoss AS**) as the application server onto which we'll deploy JBoss ESB.

The version of JBoss AS that we will use in this book is version 5.1.0.GA. We'll use this version of JBoss AS as it has been widely used and tested with JBoss ESB 4.10.

Time for action – downloading and installing JBoss AS

Follow these steps to download and install JBoss AS release 5.1.0.GA:

1. Go to the following page: `http://www.jboss.org/jbossas/downloads`. Go to **Projects | Servers | Application Server**. Click on **Download**, and you should reach the following page:

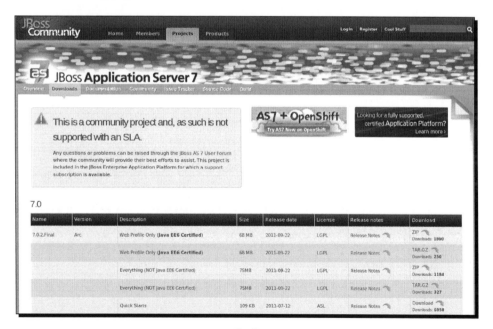

2. Scroll down and select **5.1.0**.

3. When the download is finished, move the `jboss-5.1.0.GA.zip` file to the directory where you want to install and run the server. For the remainder of the book, we'll use the `/opt` directory.

4. Unzip the `jboss-5.1.0.GA-jdk6.zip` file. Unzipping the file will create a directory named `jboss-5.1.0.GA-jdk6`. Under this directory, you'll see the following directories:

   ❑ `conf`: Configuration files are stored here.

   ❑ `data*`: Information used by the server, such as references to deployed service endpoints are stored here.

   ❑ `deploy`: We've already seen this directory, this is where deployed archives are kept.

   ❑ `deployers`: These are the deployer binaries that initialize the deployed archives and services.

- ❑ `deploy-hasingleton`: You're probably already noticing files with a prefix of "ha". In this context, "ha" indicates "high availability". In other words, something to do with running your server and applications in a cluster. A clustered singleton service is deployed to servers in a cluster, but is only available on one of those servers. These "ha-singleton" services are deployed in this directory.

- ❑ `farm`: The clustered services that are available on multiple servers in a cluster are deployed in this directory.

- ❑ `lib`: The server's `.jar` files are kept here.

- ❑ `log*`: The logs are kept here.

- ❑ `tmp*` and `work*`: Temporary files used by the server are kept in these directories.

5. In a terminal/shell window, go to that directory, and then the `bin` sub-directory, and execute `run.sh`. (Note that on Windows, you would execute a file named `run.bat` in the same directory.) The server will start up and write logging information to the screen. When you see a message that looks like this, then the server is up and running:

```
19:52:22,708 INFO  [ServerImpl] JBoss (Microcontainer) [5.1.0.GA
(build: SVNTag=JBoss_5_1_0_GA date=200905221634)] Started in
44s:251ms
```

6. You can check that the server has started successfully by going to `http://localhost:8080/`. Here you'll see the top-level JBoss AS server page:

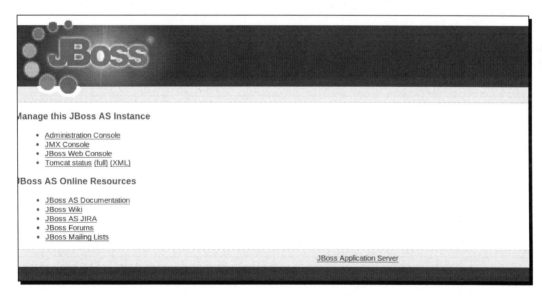

A complete description of JBoss AS and all its capabilities is beyond the scope of this book. Our primary interest in the server is as a platform where we can deploy JBoss ESB. For additional information on JBoss AS see `http://www.jboss.org/jbossas/`

7. Stop the server by pressing *Ctrl + C*.

What just happened?

As we discussed earlier in this chapter, you don't really "run" a JBoss ESB server. You deploy it to an application server. Therefore, before we could do anything with JBoss ESB, we needed an application server. Based on its wide adoption and its integration with JBoss ESB, we choose JBoss AS as our application server. Now, it's time for us to select a JBoss ESB distribution, download, and install it.

Choosing which JBoss ESB distribution is right for you

There are a number of different choices for the distribution you may use for JBoss ESB. We'll discuss those now to give you a better idea what you may want to start with.

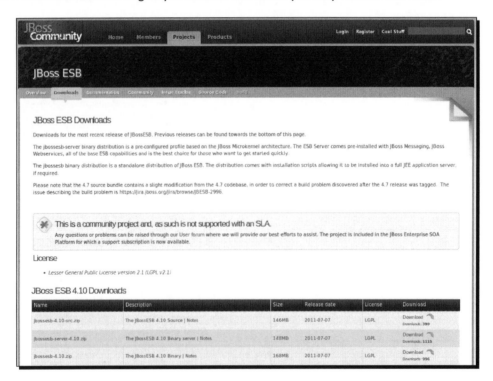

- ◆ `jbossesb-server-4.10.zip`: The `jbossesb-server` binary distribution is a pre-configured JBoss AS server distribution. The ESB Server comes pre-installed with JBoss Messaging, JBoss Webservices, all of the base ESB capabilities and is the best choice for those who want to get started quickly.

   Note that the ESB server is configured with version 4.2.3 of JBoss AS. While this distribution makes it easy to get started, we won't spend much time with it as this configuration is based on an older version of JBoss AS. What's not in this distribution? Well, this is not a full-blown Java EE server. As such, this distribution does not include support for clustered configurations, hibernate, or transactions and is probably not suited to being run in a large production environment.

- ◆ `jbossesb-4.10-src.zip`: This is the next distribution you might want to consider and it is the source code distribution for JBoss ESB. You can use this distribution to build your own copy of `jbossesb-server-4.10.zip`. Because JBoss ESB, like all the other JBoss projects, is open source, you can examine all the source code, learn from it, modify it, and even make contributions to it.

   As you've probably already guessed, we're following the Goldilocks principle here. The first one was the simplest to get started with, but was limited. The second one didn't have those limitations, but is more complicated to get started with.

- ◆ `jbossesb-4.10.zip`: (This is referred to on the download page as the "binary" distribution), it is a standalone distribution of JBoss ESB. The binary distribution comes with installation scripts allowing it to be installed into a full JEE application server. We'll install this distribution into our JBoss AS 5.1.0.GA server and use it for the bulk of work in this book.

Time for action – downloading and installing jbossesb-4.10.zip

Okay. Enough with the preliminaries. It's time for the main event. Let's look at the `jbossesb` binary distribution. This is the distribution that we'll use for the remainder of the book.

As was the case with our installation of JBoss AS, to install JBoss ESB 4.10, simply select the file for download, save the file, and then unzip it.

What just happened?

Unzipping the `jbossesb-4.10.zip` file creates a directory named `jbossesb-4.10` under our current directory. (Remember that we are using the `/opt` directory for our work with JBoss ESB.)

Reviewing the contents of jbossesb-4.10.zip

When you unzip the `jbossesb-4.10.zip` file, you'll see the following directory tree under the `jbossesb-4.10` directory:

◆ `Contributors.txt`: These are the names of the people who have contributed to JBoss ESB.

◆ `docs`: The user, programmer, and admin docs for JBoss ESB.

◆ `install`: This is the directory from which you'll install JBoss ESB into the JBoss AS server. We'll get back to this directory in a minute.

◆ `javadocs`: The code is open source, so here are the javadocs so that you can easily view the classes and methods.

◆ `JBossEULA.txt`: What's an EULA? The acronym stands for "End User License Agreement". These are the rules that govern how you can use or repackage JBoss ESB, and its supporting software, for commercial use.

◆ `lib`: This directory contains all the Java `.jar` files needed by JBoss ESB.

◆ `README_FIRST.txt`: The title says it all. This file includes a brief introduction to JBoss ESB, and a pointer to the community user forum.

◆ `samples`: These are the "quickstart" example programs. We'll describe the quickstarts in detail, and walk through how to run them, later in the book.

◆ `xml`: This directory deserves a closer look. If you look in this directory, you'll see a number of XSD (XML Schema Definition) files. These files define the elements used to construct JBoss ESB services.

The files named `jbossesb-<version number>.xsd` are especially interesting as these define the full set of JBoss ESB service configuration attributes. We'll explore these attributes, such as service providers, gateways, IDs for services, and so on in the next chapter when we take a close look at a JBoss ESB service. We'll also revisit these files when we start to use the ESB editor in **JBoss Developer Studio (JBDS)**.

Time for action – deploying JBoss ESB to JBoss AS

Okay, now it's time to install JBoss ESB into the JBoss AS server we installed previously. But, wait. Before we do that, let's examine just what it means to "deploy" JBoss ESB to an application server. "Deploying" something to the application server means putting it in a location where the application server can recognize it, control it, and start the application's lifecycle. Follow these steps to deploy JBoss ESB:

1. The first step is to set our current directory to the `install` directory under the `jbossesb-4.10` directory:

```
cd install
```

2. Before we deploy JBoss ESB, we need to tell it where it will be deployed. You'll find a file named `deployment.properties-example` in the install directory. Copy this file to a file named `deployment.properties`:

```
cp deployment.properties-example deployment.properties
```

3. Next, we have to define the location of the JBoss AS server directory in the `deployment.properties` file. Open up your favorite text editor and define these properties in that file:

```
org.jboss.esb.server.home=/opt/jboss-5.1.0.GA-jdk6
org.jboss.esb.server.config=all
```

You probably noticed that we just referenced a property named `org.jboss.esb.server.config`. What's a server config?

Each JBoss server profile consists of a set of server configurations (to control the level of logging detail, server start up memory requirements, and so on) and the set of services to install. JBoss AS 5.1.0.GA is shipped with these profiles:

♦ `all`: starts all available services

♦ `default`: a base Java EE server

♦ `minimal`: a bare, slimmed down configuration, the minimum for starting the application server

♦ `production`: a profile designed for use in production environments

♦ `standard`: a Java EE certified configuration of services

♦ `web`: a small set of services designed to mimic a web profile

We'll use either the `default` or `all` profile for most of our work in this book.

4. Before we actually deploy JBoss ESB to our JBoss AS server, it's a good idea to save a copy of the server, in the event that we ever want to reset the server to its original configuration. There's another useful aspect of the server profiles that's important to keep in mind; they are very easy to copy. To save a copy of the original `all` configuration, just copy its directory tree:

```
cp -pR all all.original
```

5. Apache Ant is used for many JBoss AS and JBoss ESB deployment tasks. This book assumes you use Apache Ant version 1.8.1 with JBoss ESB 4.10. The `ant` command to deploy JBoss ESB to JBoss AS is very simple:

```
ant deploy
```

What just happened?

We accomplished two tasks in this section, namely:

◆ We protected ourselves from any problems that we might inadvertently introduce in modifying a JBoss AS server's configuration profile by making and saving a copy of that profile. This is an easy thing to do as it only requires a copy command. You might never need to use the copy, but as a backup system for your PC, it's a nice (and easy) insurance policy.

◆ We deployed JBoss ESB to our JBoss AS server, and in the process, made our first use of Apache Ant to administer JBoss ESB. We'll make a lot more use of `ant` later in the book, when we work with the JBoss ESB quickstarts and other example code.

But, what exactly does this invocation of `ant deploy` actually do? In the context of this installation, just what JBoss ESB bits are installed? The installed JBoss ESB bits are:

◆ `server/default/deployers/esb.deployer`: The name is a dead giveaway here. This component enables the server to deploy `.esb` archives.

◆ `server/default/deploy/jbossesb-registry.sar`: This service archive contains ESB's integration to its service registry. A registry is used to look up service endpoints at runtime; a repository is used to store and manage the life cycle of services. We'll describe the registry, how it works, and how you use it in a subsequent chapter.

◆ `server/default/deploy/jbossesb.esb`: This ESB archive contains internal support for messages and message redelivery.

◆ `server/default/deploy/jbpm.esb`: This ESB archive contains the JBoss ESB integration to the jBPM Business Process Management system.

◆ `server/default/deploy/jbrules.esb`: This ESB archive contains the JBoss ESB integration to JBoss Rules for building rules-based services.

◆ `server/default/deploy/smooks.esb`: This ESB archive contains the JBoss ESB integration to the Smooks message transformation and routing engine.

◆ `server/default/deploy/soap.esb`: This ESB archive contains the JBoss ESB support for hosting Web Services.

◆ `server/default/deploy/spring.esb`: This ESB archive contains the JBoss ESB support for applications built with the Spring framework.

Keeping things slim

You may want to experiment with a "slimmed" configuration where you can reduce the server's memory use by removing services. The ability to modify the configuration of a JBoss server is actually one of its most important features. You can remove features that you don't use to save memory, or CPU resources, or to enhance the security of your installation by reducing complexity and the number of features. But, before you start modifying a profile, you should make a copy of it, so, in the event you make some mistakes in your modifications, you can easily restore the original profile.

Time for action – modifying a profile

For example, to modify the `default` profile, just make a copy of it first:

```
cp -pR server/default server/default_original
```

Then hack away at the `default` profile, secure in the knowledge that you can easily restore it.

Deployable Java archives

What types of artifacts are deployable to application servers?

There are several, namely:

- `.jar`: This is a Java archive. A JAR file is used to distribute multiple Java classes in one file.

- `.war`: This is a web application archive. A WAR file* is used to deploy web applications such as JavaServer Pages (JSPs) and Servlets.

- `.ear`: This is an enterprise application archive. An EAR file is used to deploy enterprise applications which include such assets as EJBs.

- `.sar`: This is a JBoss service archive. A SAR file is used to deploy a service to a JBoss application server.

- `.esb`: This is a JBoss ESB service archive. An ESB file is used to deploy a JBoss ESB service to an application server that has JBoss ESB deployed.

  * WAR, EAR, SAR, and ESB can be deployed either as files where the file format is actually a compressed file, or as a directory with the same `.war`, or other extension in its name. If the compressed file has been uncompressed into a directory, it is referred to as an "exploded" WAR, EAR, and so on.

In a nutshell, the act of deploying JBoss ESB to an application server deploys these archives to the server.

Testing the installation

Okay, after you've deployed JBoss ESB to the application server, what's next? Let's start the server and make sure there are no problems.

Time for action – testing the installation

The following steps will demonstrate how to start our server allowing us to test the installation:

1. We'll start by running the JBoss AS server `all` profile. Change to the `bin` directory and enter the following command to start the server using the `all` server profile:

    ```
    sh ./run.sh -c all
    ```

2. At this point, many, many lines of logging information are written to the screen. Near the end of the display, you should see lines that look like this:

    ```
    19:52:20,592 INFO  [TomcatDeployment] deploy, ctxPath=/admin-
    console

    19:52:20,670 INFO  [config] Initializing Mojarra (1.2_12-b01-FCS)
    for context '/admin-console'

    19:52:22,410 INFO  [TomcatDeployment] deploy, ctxPath=/

    19:52:22,452 INFO  [TomcatDeployment] deploy, ctxPath=/jmx-console

    19:52:22,672 INFO  [Http11Protocol] Starting Coyote HTTP/1.1 on
    http-127.0.0.1-8080

    19:52:22,697 INFO  [AjpProtocol] Starting Coyote AJP/1.3 on ajp-
    127.0.0.1-8009

    19:52:22,708 INFO  [ServerImpl] JBoss (Microcontainer) [5.1.0.GA
    (build: SVNTag=JBoss_5_1_0_GA date=200905221634)] Started in
    44s:251ms
    ```

    (If you are not seeing this, but you are seeing lots of lines of text that include ERROR, then skip ahead a few sections to the section named *And what to do if you see an error.*)

What just happened?

We had previously started the JBoss AS server without specifying a server profile. This time, we used the `-c` option to select the server profile into which we had deployed JBoss ESB.

So far, so good. The server seems to be running, based on a quick look—correct at the surface. Now, let's look a little deeper and see what you can do to verify that the JBoss ESB installation is correct and that you will be able to use it for the remainder of the book.

Looking at logs

You might be tempted to think about server logs with the same enthusiasm that you would have approached a college course in financial accounting: probably useful, but definitely boring.

Don't fall into this trap. The server logs are a gold mine of useful information. You'll see in the logs the results of both successful and failed operations. We'll be examining server logs in detail as we work through the examples in this book.

Let's start by finding the logs.

Finding the logs

You saw a lot of logging information displayed on the screen when you started the server a few minutes ago. The problem with this information, however, is that it scrolled by faster than anyone could read and analyze it. Fear not. The same information, and actually, more information, was also written to log files.

Within the `all` server profile, you'll see a `log` directory. This directory contains the following log files:

- ◆ `boot.log`: This shows the actual boot sequence followed by the server.
- ◆ `server.log`: The primary server log file which tracks the lifecycle of managed resources as well as output and error messages written from those resources. The JBoss ESB logger is based on Apache log4j (`http://logging.apache.org/log4j/`). The level of detail written to the server.log is configurable in each server's `jboss-log4j.xml` file.

The degree of detail of information that is written to the logs is defined in the `server/[profile]/conf/jboss-log4j.xml` file as JBoss AS and ESB make use of the Java Log4J library. Log4J defines:

- Appenders that enable you to have logging messages sent to a console or different files
- Log message levels such as `INFO`, `WARNING`, `ERROR`, `DEBUG`, and `FATAL`
- Categories that enable you to filter log messages based on a package

We found the logs. Well, this was pretty easy, seeing as how they are in the `logs` directory. But, seriously, make a mental note as to the location of the logs as you will be returning to them frequently to diagnose problems, or to confirm that your server is running as expected.

What sort of things can you see in the `server.log`? Here's a simple example. Remember how we described the `.esb` archives that were added to the server when we deployed JBoss ESB? Let's look to see if they were initialized successfully when the server was started.

Time for action – viewing the deployment of an application in the server.log

The following steps will show the deployment of an application in the `server.log`:

1. Let's look for errors in the `server.log` file:

   ```
   grep ERROR server.log
   ```

   Good, no `ERROR`. (Yes, the logs are case-sensitive.)

2. Let's move on and look for logging information related to JBoss ESB by "grepping" the `server.log`:

   ```
   grep ESB server.log
   ```

What just happened?

There they are, the very `.esb` archives that we discussed earlier:

```
2011-04-14 21:21:40,998 INFO  [org.jboss.resource.connectionmanager.
ConnectionFactoryBindingService] (main) Bound ConnectionManager
'jboss.jca:service=DataSourceBinding,name=JBossESBDS' to JNDI name
'java:JBossESBDS'

2011-04-14 21:21:41,009 INFO  [org.jboss.internal.soa.esb.dependencies.
DatabaseInitializer] (main) Initializing java:/JBossESBDS from listed sql
files

2011-04-14 21:21:41,132 INFO  [org.jboss.soa.esb.listeners.deployers.
mc.EsbDeployment] (main) Starting ESB Deployment 'jbossesb.esb'
```

```
2011-04-14 21:21:42,788 INFO   [org.quartz.impl.StdSchedulerFactory]
(main) Quartz scheduler 'ESBScheduler:jbossesb.esb' initialized from an
externally provided properties instance.

2011-04-14 21:21:42,789 INFO   [org.quartz.core.QuartzScheduler] (main)
Scheduler ESBScheduler:jbossesb.esb_$_NON_CLUSTERED started.

2011-04-14 21:21:45,645 INFO   [org.jboss.soa.esb.listeners.deployers.
mc.EsbDeployment] (main) Starting ESB Deployment 'jbpm.esb'

2011-04-14 21:21:52,498 INFO   [org.jboss.soa.esb.listeners.deployers.
mc.EsbDeployment] (main) Starting ESB Deployment 'jbrules.esb'

2011-04-14 21:21:53,567 INFO   [org.jboss.soa.esb.listeners.deployers.
mc.EsbDeployment] (main) Starting ESB Deployment 'slsb.esb'

2011-04-14 21:21:53,614 INFO   [org.jboss.soa.esb.listeners.deployers.
mc.EsbDeployment] (main) Starting ESB Deployment 'smooks.esb'

2011-04-14 21:21:56,000 INFO   [org.jboss.soa.esb.listeners.deployers.
mc.EsbDeployment] (main) Starting ESB Deployment 'soap.esb'

2011-04-14 21:22:07,005 INFO   [org.jboss.soa.esb.listeners.deployers.
mc.EsbDeployment] (main) Starting ESB Deployment 'spring.esb'
```

Consoles

The main goal of this book is to help you to create your own JBoss ESB services. At this point in the book, however, we haven't done that yet, so we'll look at some of the ESB's services to verify that the server is running and that the deployment of JBoss ESB was successful. Let's start by looking at the server's **Java Management Extension (JMX)** console. You access the console here: `http://localhost:8080/jmx-console/` JMX Console JMX Console

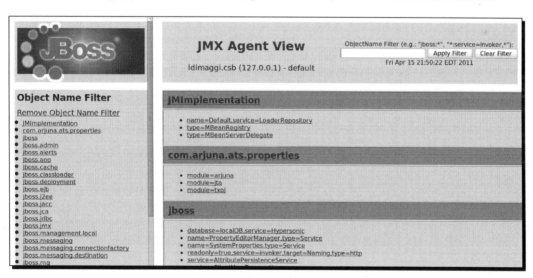

JMX is a Java technology that makes it possible to monitor and administer assets such as servers or software. You do this with JMX by defining **Managed Beans (MBeans)** that abstract/represent the managed objects.

How do they help us? MBeans monitor and control many attributes of the services and actions you will be building and using. They are a wonderful diagnostic tool in situations where you want to track what is happening on your server, and help you examine and control your deployments.

Time for action – examining an MBean

Let's look at one service that is accessed through an MBean. JBoss AS also has an administration console. This console is part of the JBoss "RHQ" project (http://www.jboss.org/jopr) and is the newest administrative tool for JBoss AS. This console provides a system and server-level interface and enables you to monitor and manage resources such as deployed applications, JMS queues and topics, and the server system itself (for example, memory use).

1. Start your server and browse to http://localhost:8080/admin-console/.

2. Log on as the default user (username "admin", password "admin").

3. Browse through the different trees under **Applications**. Note all of the different types of applications which can be controlled and monitored:

For more information on the admin console, see:

`http://community.jboss.org/en/jbossas/embjopr`

`http://community.jboss.org/thread/145880`

What do you do if you see an error?

Problems can happen in the best of families, and software is no exception. If you see an error when you start the server, or when you deploy your own JBoss ESB service what should you do? Here's a set of steps that you should take: an easy way to start is to try to reconstruct the steps that you took before the error occurred. It may be that the root cause of the error was a configuration change or some other form of action that you performed. Remember that if you made a copy of the server profile before you started making changes, you can easily restore it.

If you can't easily identify or remember the cause of the error, then it's time to do some investigation of the logs.

First, examine the server log. Look at the messages that were displayed before or after the error occurred. What sort of things might be in the log? The following are a few examples:

* **"Class not found" (CNF) exceptions:** These problems may be caused by a missing `.jar`, or an incomplete deployment. The root cause of this may be that the `CLASSPATH` environment is not set correctly. Note that, in order to start the server, you don't have to have `CLASSPATH` pre-defined. The start-up scripts will do it for you.

* **"Java not found" exceptions:** The root cause of this problem may be that the `PATH` environment variable is not set correctly. Try to verify that you can invoke the Java runtime from the command line and check its version (`java -version`).

* **"Address already in use" exceptions:** The root cause of this problem is that another server is already running on the port that the server you are starting is trying to use. By default, JBoss AS, with or without JBoss ESB deployed, runs on port 8080. If you see this error when you are trying to start the server, it's because another server is already running.

* **"Illegal state" exceptions:** These problems may be caused by an invalid configuration file. Examine the error in the log and if it specifies an ESB validation error, check your `jboss-esb.xml` file for errors.

If the error that you see doesn't make sense to you, you can always use a search engine to query pertinent information about your error, or ask a question on the user forum and attach your `server.log` to the post.

Pop quiz

Before we move on, it's time to see what you've learned. Pencils ready? Let's begin!

1. JBossESB can run in standalone mode, without being deployed to an application server. True or false?

2. Name the (3) JBossESB distributions.

3. You can always get 24/7 support for all JBoss community projects simply by calling a super secret 1-800 telephone number. True or false?

4. The best way to get help on a question you have on JBoss community projects is to immediately make a vague post to the projects' forum. True or false?

5. What is a server "profile"?

6. How do you make a copy of a server profile, and why would you want to have a copy if the software is free?

7. The server logs are a waste of disk space. You should always delete the log files. True or false?

8. What is an MBean? And how does the JBoss JMX make it easy for you to use them?

Summary

Congratulations! You're off to a great start. You have a running JBoss AS with JBoss ESB installed. Application servers are very cool things. But, what makes them even more cool is that they are the vehicle on which you can build and run your own applications and servers.

In the next chapter, we'll take a close look at what a running service looks like and how you can start to build your own. Can you say "helloworld"?

2
Deploying your Services to the ESB

In the previous chapter we learned some basics about how to set up JBoss ESB in conjunction with JBoss AS. In this chapter we'll go a little deeper and start to learn what you can do with the JBoss ESB deployed to the server you have just configured.

In this chapter you will:

◆ Learn about the core components of JBoss ESB, how they work, and what it means for your services.

◆ Get hands on with a sample application, one of the JBoss ESB quickstarts. Using this quickstart as a live example, you'll explore deploying and administering services.

◆ Learn how to develop, deploy, and administer your services by using the eclipse-based JBoss Developer Studio.

The quickstarts

In this section we'll examine the "quickstart" example programs that are packaged with JBoss ESB. You'll find these in the `/samples/quickstarts` directory of the JBoss ESB installation.

For a writer starting a new assignment, facing a blank piece of paper (or word processing screen) can be an intimidating prospect. As a programmer, facing a blank editor or IDE window can be an equally intimidating prospect when you are learning a new technology. It's common for software development packages to make learning a new technology easier by including a few examples, but these can be either too small or too simple to illustrate key concepts, or may combine so many features into a single example that it becomes confusing.

JBoss ESB takes a different approach with its "quickstart" example programs. There are a large number of individual quickstarts, each of which illustrates one or more JBoss ESB features. It is also an explicit goal of the quickstarts for them to be usable both as educational examples and as the starting point for your own custom applications. As the name "quickstart" indicates, these programs are intended to give you an understanding of JBoss ESB and help you build your own applications quickly. At the time of this writing, there are over 80 quickstarts included with JBoss ESB in the `samples/quickstarts` directory. These quickstarts demonstrate JBoss ESB features such as listeners, routing, data transformations with JBoss Smooks, JBoss ESB integrations with JBoss jBPM and JBoss Rules, and many other features.

While they all demonstrate different features and technologies, the quickstarts share some common characteristics in that they are all built, deployed, and run with a small number of simple Apache Ant commands. The quickstarts also include a readme file that explains the features that each quickstart demonstrates, as well as the steps to run the quickstart. Note that each quickstart includes its own ant `build.xml` file. These ant files are used to define quickstart-specific tasks. A common build task file (this file is named `samples/quickstarts/conf/base-build.xml`) is used to define tasks common to all the quickstarts, such as quickstart deployment.

For the most part, you can run the JBoss project software with no changes after a download, but the quickstarts require you to define some environmental variables. While each quickstart includes its own `build.xml` ant file, all the quickstarts make use of a set of common environmental variables. As a prerequisite before you run any quickstart, you have to configure these common variables. The quickstarts expect these variables to be defined in a file named `quickstarts.properties`. The easiest way to set these variables' values is by copying the file in the `samples/quickstarts` directory named `quickstarts.properties-examples` to `quickstarts.properties` and then editing the `quickstarts.properties` file you just created to set the variables to match your server configuration.

The environment variables are as follows:

- `org.jboss.esb.server.home`: Set this to the home directory of your JBoss AS server installation. In the case of the configuration that we are using in this book, this would be set to `/opt/jboss-5.1.0.GA`.

- `org.jboss.esb.server.config`: Set this to the server profile to which JBoss ESB has been deployed. In the case of the configuration that we are using in this book, this would be set to `all`.

- ◆ `jbpm.console.username` and `jbpm.console.password`: These two variables are used by the jBPM-related quickstarts. Both of these should be set to "admin" unless you have defined security settings different from the out-of-the-box configuration. Obviously, "admin/admin" is not a very secure username and password for a production. We'll talk about the options that JBoss ESB supports for production level password security later in the book in *Chapter7*. For now, we'll keep things simple and stick with "admin/admin".

- ◆ `jbossesb.ftp.hostname`, `jbossesb.ftp.username`, `jbossesb.ftp.password`, and `jbossesb.ftp.directory`: Some of the quickstarts demonstrate aspects of JBoss ESB's support for the FTP protocol (for example, the FTP gateway listener), so you will have to define these environment variables to be able to have your services access an FTP server.

Additionally, the quickstarts all have one more thing in common; whether they are small or large, they are all fully-functioning and deployable JBoss ESB applications. You can take any of them and use it as a starting point to develop your own custom application. A great way to begin is to take a quickstart, make some small changes, deploy it, verify that it works as intended, then rinse and repeat, and extend it. We'll build, deploy, and run a quickstart later in this chapter. Later, in *Chapter 4*, we'll extend a quickstart.

Anatomy of a deployment

Before we take an in-depth look at one quickstart, it's important to understand the deployment requirements for any JBoss ESB service-based application. When we discussed the types of archives that are deployable to the JBoss AS servers in the first chapter, we briefly talked how in addition to WAR files (`.war`), EAR files (`.ear`), and SAR files (`.sar`), JBoss ESB added the `.esb` archive. Let's now take a look at just what has to be in a `.esb` archive, in order for it to be deployed.

Note that the quickstarts all create complete and deployable `.esb` archives. The `base-build.xml` file includes the definition of the "deploy" task and this creates the deployable `.esb` archives.

If you look inside a JBoss ESB .esb archive, you'll see a similar directory tree of files and directories:

```
jar -tvf Quickstart_helloworld.esb
     0 Mon May 30 18:09:52 EDT 2011 META-INF/
   102 Mon May 30 18:09:50 EDT 2011 META-INF/MANIFEST.MF
     0 Mon May 30 18:09:50 EDT 2011 org/
     0 Mon May 30 18:09:50 EDT 2011 org/jboss/
     0 Mon May 30 18:09:50 EDT 2011 org/jboss/soa/
     0 Mon May 30 18:09:50 EDT 2011 org/jboss/soa/esb/
     0 Mon May 30 18:09:50 EDT 2011 org/jboss/soa/esb/samples/
     0 Mon May 30 18:09:50 EDT 2011 org/jboss/soa/esb/samples/quickstart/
     0 Mon May 30 18:09:50 EDT 2011 org/jboss/soa/esb/samples/quickstart/helloworld/
     0 Mon May 30 18:09:50 EDT 2011 org/jboss/soa/esb/samples/quickstart/helloworld/test/
  1438 Mon May 30 18:09:50 EDT 2011 org/jboss/soa/esb/samples/quickstart/helloworld/MyJMSListenerAction.class
  1614 Mon May 30 18:09:50 EDT 2011 org/jboss/soa/esb/samples/quickstart/helloworld/test/SendEsbMessage.class
  2834 Mon May 30 18:09:50 EDT 2011 org/jboss/soa/esb/samples/quickstart/helloworld/test/SendJMSMessage.class
   295 Mon May 30 18:09:50 EDT 2011 META-INF/deployment.xml
  2000 Mon May 30 18:09:50 EDT 2011 META-INF/jboss-esb.xml
   776 Mon Aug 09 17:03:32 EDT 2010 jbm-queue-service.xml
```

Defining the providers, services, and listeners

The most important part of the configuration file for an .esb archive is jboss-esb.xml. Depending upon the complexity of your application, jboss-esb.xml can be an intimidating file to edit, but if you keep in mind that despite the complexity of any application, the goals of this file are to define the application's providers, listeners, and services.

We've discussed services already in this book, but who are these providers? And, what do they provide?

Providers are servers or packages that exist outside of JBoss ESB that—for the lack of a better word—"provide" resources to the services defined in the .esb archive. You define the endpoints through which the services access these resources in jboss-esb.xml. Some examples of the types of resources that providers make available are JMS topics and queues, FTP servers, or SQL access to a database.

Let's take a high-level look at what a jboss-esb.xml file looks like. We'll take a much more in depth look at a specific quickstart's jboss-esb.xml, and other configuration files, in the next section of this chapter. For now, we'll ease into the water and save the detailed XML for a later chapter. The following image describes the connection of the services contained within the jboss-esb.xml file:

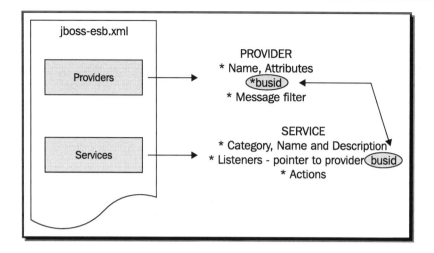

The file is divided into two main sections: **Providers** and **Services**.

Each provider definition includes:

- A **Name**, and, depending on the type of the provider, **Attributes**. For example, FTP providers will include the FTP server name as an attribute.

- A **busid** that is important to make note of, as this ID will be used in the service and listener definitions later in the `jboss-esb.xml` file. This ID is used to reference the endpoint that the provider defines, and is used instead of the provider name, to reference that endpoint.

> As its name implies, the `busid` is the ID of the service and listener endpoints on the bus (the ESB). A service or listener finds its providers using the `busid`.

- A **Message filter** is used to specify details about the resource made available by the provider. For example, for a JMS provider, the filter will reference the JMS queue provided, and for an FTP provider, the filter will reference the FTP server, directories, and so on.

- For schedule-related providers, you define the details of the schedule, such as `cron` settings.

Each service definition includes:

- **Category**, **Name**, and **Description**, the combination of these are used in the service registry.
- **Listeners**; a service definition contains one or more listeners. What's interesting to note here is that just as the providers must define ESB-aware providers to correspond to non-aware providers, the listeners must also define ESB-aware listeners to correspond to the non-aware providers.

What does it mean to be "ESB-aware?"

It refers to being able to handle messages in the format used by the ESB as opposed to any message format such as JMS or HTTP. The providers that you define work in pairs. The ESB-unaware provider helps you to bring messages "onboard" onto the ESB, and the ESB-aware provider handles messages once they are on the ESB. The ESB-unaware providers work with processes that we refer to as "gateways" to "onboard" messages onto the ESB. We'll discuss this in detail in *Chapter 5* and *Chapter 6* when we look at message delivery and gateways.

- In the event that a listener is a gateway listener and corresponds to a provider, then the listener will include this property `is-gateway="true"`.
- Each listener will cross reference the `busid` of the provider on which it relies.
- **Actions**; the sequential action pipeline. These are the actions that are performed by the service.

Other deployment files

In addition to `jboss-esb.xml`, some quickstarts include other deployment-related files, for example, `deployment.xml`.

When an `.esb` archive is deployed, the sequence of actions is that message queues are deployed first, then ESB-aware services, and finally the gateways. This sequence is important so the application services are always running before any clients can push data to them. After this, the registry is updated, so that clients and other services can find the deployed services (`http://community.jboss.org/wiki/JBossESBDeploymentStrategies`). This requirement is specified by the `deployment.xml` file. This file defines the exact order in which the message queues are deployed. In addition, you can use this file to make your `.esb` deployment dependent on other deployments. In this way you can be sure that your `.esb` will have all the resources that it needs to run when it is deployed.

Depending on the types of resources that your `.esb` requires, there may be additional configuration files. One type of file that you'll see with many of the quickstarts is used to define the service dependencies needed by JMS queues. These files are named `jbm-queue-service.xml` (where "jbm" stands for JBoss Messaging).

Let's stop looking at quickstarts in the abstract and examine a quickstart in detail. The tasks that the quickstart performs are very simple, but every configuration and operational characteristic of the quickstart is used and expanded upon by the other quickstarts or custom applications that you build. The quickstart that we'll look at is the ESB version of the classic programming example; *helloworld*.

Helloworld quickstart

In this section, we'll walk through running a quickstart. This will give you hands on experience in deploying, running, reviewing the operations that the quickstart performs, and then undeploying an `.esb` archive.

In keeping with programming tradition, the simplest of the quickstarts is "helloworld". It's a small program, but there are those who love it!

Apologies to Daniel Webster

"It is, as I have said, a small college, and yet there are those who love it."

`http://www.dartmouth.edu/~dwebster/speeches/dartmouth-peroration.html`

What does this quickstart do? It performs one of two functions, depending on how the quickstart is invoked. It either receives a message through a JMS gateway listener and passes that message to the gateway's corresponding ESB-aware listener, or it skips the gateway and receives the message directly at an ESB-aware listener. After that, the quickstart writes the message to the server log and exits.

While, at first glance, the helloworld quickstart may appear too simple to serve as an useful example of a `.esb` archive, it is a fully functioning and deployable `.esb`. As it is simple, it will let us concentrate on the configuration, deployment, and execution of `.esb` archives, without being distracted by examples of JBoss ESB many features or integrations.

Let's start with the deployment.

Time for action – deploying the quickstart

As we discussed earlier in this chapter, a .esb archive is deployed by copying it to the target server profile's deploy/ directory. The best way to do this is to use the quickstart's "deploy" ant target with this command:

cd samples/quickstarts/helloworld

ant deploy

What just happened?

There's quite a bit of output from this command. It's worthwhile looking at some of this in detail so that you understand what's happening here, as you may want to re-use some of either the base-build.xml ant script shared by all the quickstarts, or the ant build.xml script used by this quickstart.

Some of the highlights are listed as follows:

1. First, the programs that are used to send the ESB-aware and unaware messages, and the custom action that will write the received message to the server log are compiled:

   ```
   compile:

   [mkdir] Created dir: /jboss/local/book_downloads/
   jbossesb-4.9/samples/quickstarts/helloworld/build/
   classes [javac] Compiling 3 source files to /jboss/
   local/book_downloads/jbossesb-4.9/samples/
   quickstarts/helloworld/build/classes
   ```

2. Next, remember how we talked about the deployment.xml file being used to specify the JMS queues that the quickstart needs? One of the JBossESB's features is that it can be used with multiple JMS providers. By default, it's configured to use JBoss Messaging, but it also supports other JMS providers such as HornetQ. This XML transformation is performed to generate a deployment.xml file that is specific to the correct JMS provider for your configuration.

   ```
   transformDeploymentXml:

   [xslt] Processing /jboss/local/book_downloads/jbossesb-4.9/
   samples/quickstarts/helloworld/build/META-INF/
   deployment.xml to /jboss/local/book_downloads/jbossesb-4.9/
   samples/quickstarts/helloworld/build/META-INF/
   deployment.xml.transformed

   [xslt] Loading stylesheet /jboss/local/book_downloads/
   jbossesb-4.9/samples/quickstarts/conf/deployment-xml.xsl
   ```

```
[delete] Deleting: /jboss/local/book_downloads/jbossesb-4.9/
samples/quickstarts/helloworld/build/META-INF/deployment.xml

[move] Moving 1 file to /jboss/local/book_downloads/
jbossesb-4.9/samples/quickstarts/helloworld/build/META-INF
```

3. Here is where the `.esb` archive is created:

```
package-deployment:

[jar] Building jar: /jboss/local/book_downloads/jbossesb-4.9/
samples/quickstarts/helloworld/build/Quickstart_helloworld.esb
```

4. And, here is the actual deployment to the server:

```
deploy-esb:

[copy] Copying 1 file to /opt/local/jboss-5.1.0.GA/
server/all/deploy
```

5. Finally, the quickstart is deployed:

```
display-instructions:

[echo] Quickstart deployed to target JBoss ESB/App Server at '/
opt/local/jboss-5.1.0.GA/server/all/deploy'.

[echo] 1. Check your ESB Server console to make sure
 the deployment was executed without errors.

[echo] 2. Run 'ant runtest' to run the Quickstart.

[echo] 3. Check your ESB Server console again.
 The Quickstart should have produced some output.

deploy: BUILD SUCCESSFUL Total time: 2 seconds
```

Now, let's run it and trace through the actions that it performs.

When you run the quickstart, you have two options:

◆ ant `runtest`: generates a JMS message and inserts it into a JMS queue. This causes a JMS gateway listener to wake up, wrap the message in an ESBMessage (thereby making the message ESB-aware), and pass the message to an ESB-aware listener. After that, a custom action prints the message to the server log.

◆ ant `sendesb`: generates an ESB-aware message, and sends it directly to the ESB-aware listener. After that, the same custom action prints the message to the server log.

The server log shows the result, as follows:

```
2011-05-29 23:20:36,599 INFO [STDOUT] (pool-23-thread-1) &&&&&&&&&&&&
&&&&&&&&&&&&&&&&&&&&&&&&&&&&&&&&&&&&
2011-05-29 23:20:36,602 INFO [STDOUT] (pool-23-thread-1) Body: Hello
World
2011-05-29 23:20:36,602 INFO [STDOUT] (pool-23-thread-1) &&&&&&&&&&&&
&&&&&&&&&&&&&&&&&&&&&&&&&&&&&&&&&&&&
```

Quickstart-specific help

While we have been reviewing one of the simpler quickstarts, some of the other quickstarts are more complicated and require a number of steps on the part of the user in order to demonstrate the functionality of the quickstart. A quickstart like `simple_cbr` requires that the user set up two extra terminal processes that will receive messages. Each quickstart contains a readme.txt (or in some cases a readme.html) that explains how to run that specific quickstart. Just follow along the steps of the readme, which also should explain what the purpose of the quickstart is, the functionality that is being demonstrated, and the output you may expect to see.

When you are finished running a quickstart, you can undeploy it from your current server by running the following command in the quickstart's directory:

ant undeploy

That will remove the ESB archive and any additional custom deployments that may have been installed while deploying the quickstart.

Deploying a JBoss ESB archive remotely

What happens when you want to deploy a JBoss ESB archive to a machine you have a server on, but do not have command line access to? The easiest way to deploy a JBoss ESB archive is to copy it into the `/deploy` directory, whether by SSH or a shared network drive, but if you don't have either of those luxuries, JBoss provides a console which allows you to upload a deployment directly onto the server.

Time for action – accessing the admin console

To access the admin console, follow these steps:

1. We'll use JBoss ESB's admin console at this URL: `http://localhost:8080/admin-console` (or whatever the equivalent for your machine might be for the server to which JBoss ESB is deployed.

2. Use `admin` as the username and `admin` as the password and login.

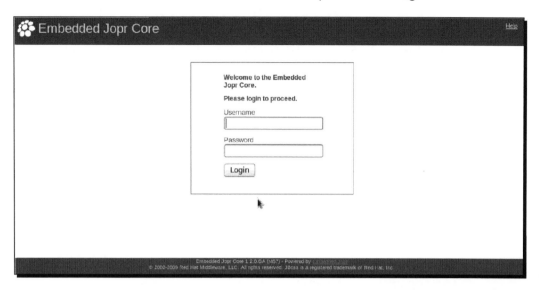

Time for action – performing the deployment

Follow these steps to perform the deployment:

1. Once you are successfully logged in, click on the **JBoss ESB** link in the directory tree. You should see something like the following:

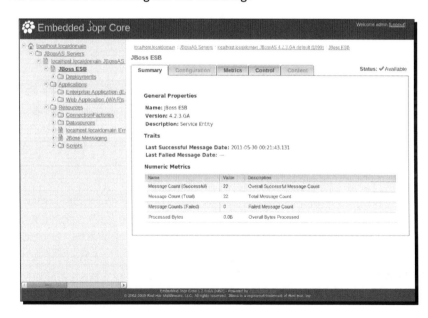

The summary on the right-hand side of the previous screenshot shows the total message count and bytes processed by your JBoss ESB server—we will dive more deeply into that information in a later chapter

2. Click on **Deployments** below the **JBoss ESB** link in the directory. The screen you see should show a list of the JBoss ESB archives that are deployed. If you are wondering where these came from, these deployments are standard internal deployments for a JBoss ESB server.

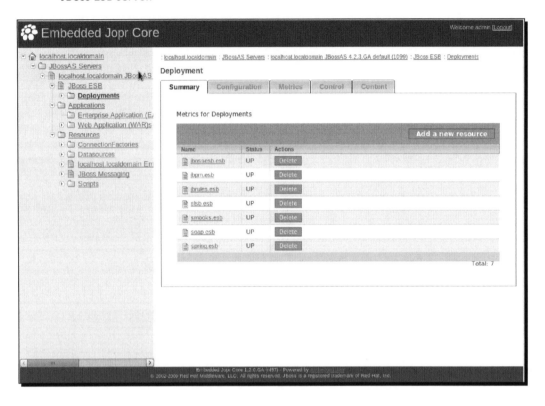

3. Click on **Add a New Resource**. You should be given a screen which allows you to browse and choose an ESB deployment file from your file system.

4. Browse and select your archive and choose whether you would like to deploy it compressed or uncompressed and then click **Continue**.

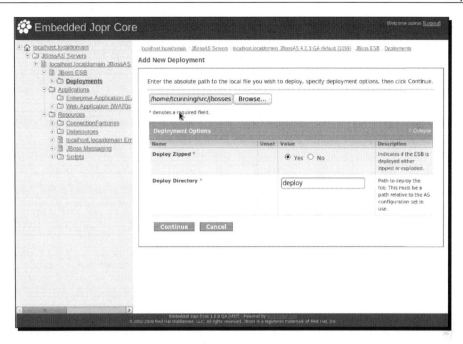

If your deployment was successful, you should see something like the screenshot that follows—if not, you will see the same type of error messages that are written to the server log. The console makes it easier to examine these messages as you can view them without leaving the browser.

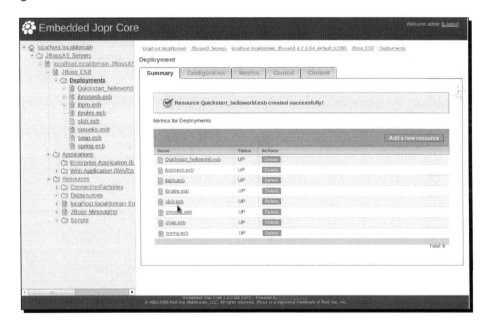

Introduction to JBDS

So far in this book we've been working with JBoss ESB from a command shell, and our tools have been ant and your favorite text editor. This is a valid and usable approach, but it has its limits. When you start working with more and more complex applications, editing .esb configuration files' raw XML can become difficult and error prone. Likewise, deploying .esb archives with ant, while straightforward, forces you to start the server manually, and remember to deploy and re-deploy as you perform development and testing.

Happily, there is another approach available to you. You can use **JBoss Developer Studio** (**JBDS**). JBDS is an eclipse-based integrated development environment. JBDS is fully integrated with JBoss AS, and includes a forms-based editor that makes it easier to read and edit jboss-esb.xml files. Additionally, it's free!

There is another version of JBDS that is bundled with **Red Hat Enterprise Linux** (**RHEL**) JBoss' Enterprise Application Platform that is for sale. We'll use the free version throughout this book.

Time for action – downloading JBDS

Let's get our copy of JBDS. Follow these steps:

1. Go to the download page at http://devstudio.jboss.com/download/.

2. Before you can actually download JBDS, you have to register. Just select **Register for Free Here**.

3. Select **Sign Up** and then select **Create a personal Red Hat login**. At this point you may be asked to confirm your e-mail address. And finally, you'll see the download page, as shown:

4. Select the download that matches your computer system and architecture and save the download file. The file name will look something like jbdevstudio-`product-`
`linux-gtk-x86_64-4.1.0.v201108011413R-H647-GA.jar`.

Time for action – installing JBDS

Once the download is complete, you can start the JBDS installation. Note that unlike JBoss AS or JBoss ESB, JBDS is installed by means of a GUI-based installer. Follow these steps:

1. In a command shell window, move to the directory to which the JBDS distribution file was downloaded.

2. Run the installer by locating the JBDS file that you downloaded and running it with Java. For example, on a 64-bit Linux system, you'd use the following command:

```
java -jar jbdevstudio-product-linux-gtk-x86_64-
4.1.0.v201108011413R-H647-GA.jar
```

3. The installer now presents the following nine steps to you. Step 1 is an introduction and step 2 asks you to accept the license terms (we promise that nothing bad will happen).

4. In step 3 of the installer, you specify the directory where you want JBDS to be installed. We'll use /opt/devstudio/ as our installation directory. If you specify a directory that does not exist, the installer will create that directory for you. Click **Next** to continue.

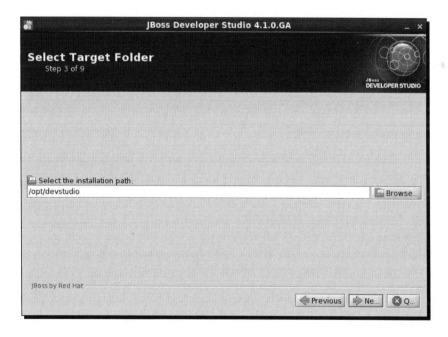

5. Select the Java JVM that you want to use. Remember how we said that Java 6 was a prerequisite? You should simply select the Java 6 JVM that you have installed on your computer. Then, click **Next** to continue:

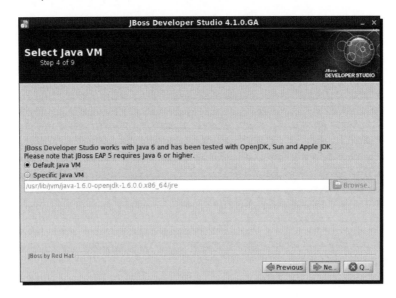

6. IDE stands for Integrated Development Environment. In JBDS, this integration includes enabling you to run a server without leaving JBDS. Select **Add** and we'll configure our JBoss AS server:

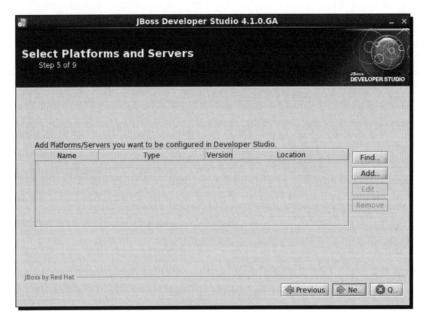

7. Select **Application Server** and specify the directory where our JBoss AS server is installed. Then click **Ok**.

8. Verify that the name and location are correct, and click **Next**. You should then see a screen which summarizes the status of the installation.

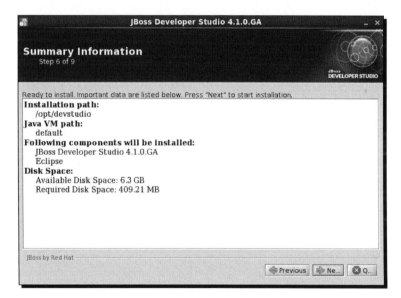

9. At this point, you have supplied all the information that the installer needs, so click **Next** to start the installation.

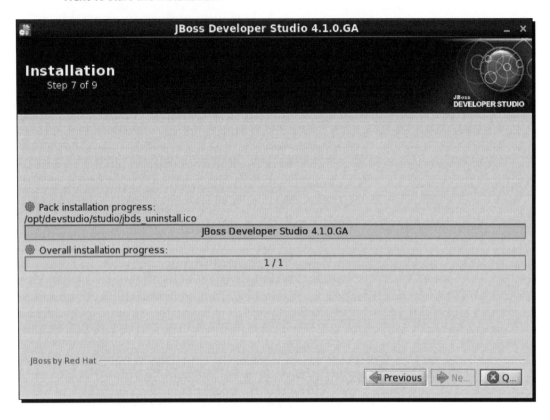

As the installer works, it will display progress information.

10. When it completes, it will give you the option to create shortcuts. These make it easier for you to start JBDS. It's very helpful to have a shortcut on your desktop and **Start** menu, so check both of them and click **Next**.

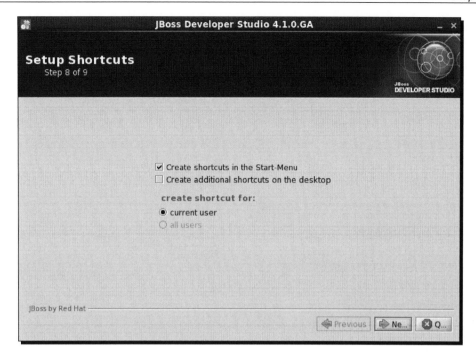

11. When you see the following screen, you'll know that you're done!

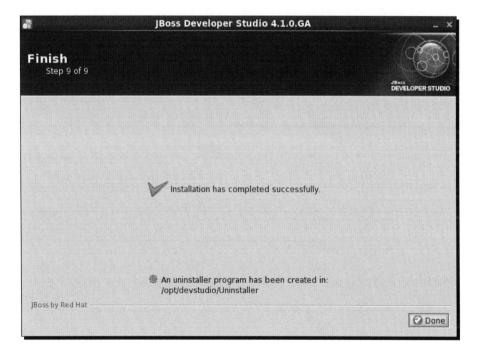

12. Select **Done** to close the installer. You should see the following shortcut on your desktop:

13. Double-click on the shortcut and we'll finish setting up JBDS.

What just happened?

OK, let's recap before moving on. At this point, we have JBDS fully configured with the JBoss AS server and JBoss ESB. Additionally, we can control these without having to exit JBDS. What's next? Let's run that quickstart from inside JBDS.

Running JBDS

When you open JBDS, the first thing that you see is a dialog to select the workspace (the directory tree) that you want to use. If the workspace that you select does not exist, JBDS will create it for you.

It's a good idea to keep your workspace separate from the directory in which you installed JBDS so that there is no chance of updates to JBDS affecting your workspace or vice versa. For our work in this book, we'll use /opt/workspace.

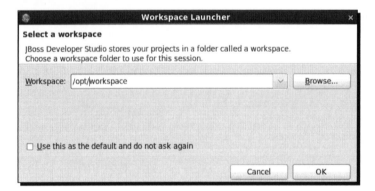

At this point, JBDS displays its **welcome** screen. You can select any of the icons displayed here for general tutorial/introductory information on JBDS. Note that the welcome screen is only displayed by default the first time that you run JBDS. However, it doesn't go away. It's always available under the JBDS help menu. For now, close the welcome screen by selecting the **x** icon next to the screen's **Welcome** title.

JBDS is organized into eclipse "perspectives". Each perspective consists of a set of tools and visual layouts to assist you in specific tasks. The default perspective when you open JBDS is the SEAM (`http://seamframework.org/`) perspective.

For our work with JBDS, we want to use the Java perspective. Select **Window | Open Perspective | Java**:

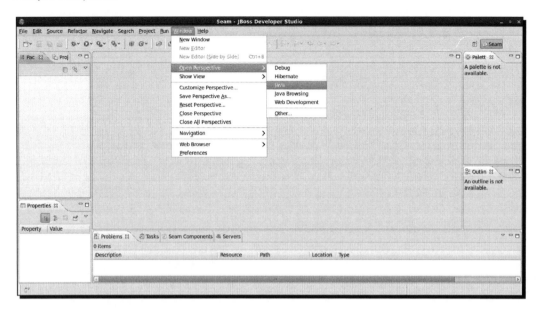

Here's what the the Java perspective looks like:

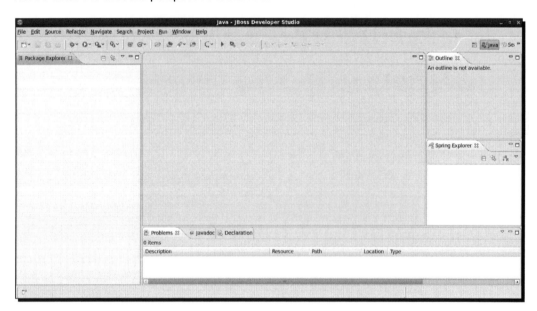

Now it's time to set up the JBoss ESB runtime in JBDS. This is a one-time task.

Time for action – setting up the ESB runtime in JBDS

In order to be able to create and run JBoss ESB applications, JBDS must be configured to access a JBoss ESB runtime. We've already installed JBoss ESB on the JBoss AS server, so all we have to do now is to set the configuration in JBDS. Follow these steps:

1. To set the runtime, select **Window** | **Preferences** | **JBoss ESB Runtime** and you'll see the following dialog:

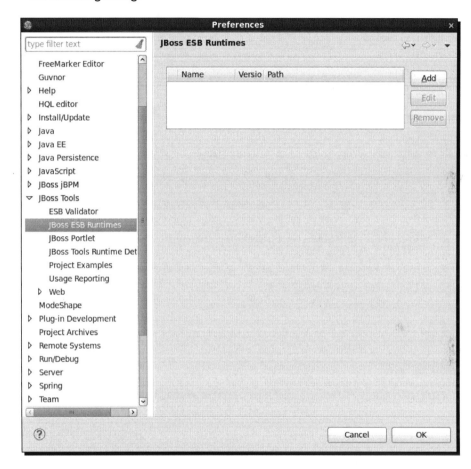

2. Click **Add** to define the ESB runtime and the following dialog is displayed. For **Home Folder** be sure to enter the directory of the JBoss AS server into which you previously deployed JBoss ESB. Also, remember to select the "all" server profile.

Note that as of this writing, JBDS supported the configuration of JBoss ESB releases up to release 4.9. You can safely configure the 4.10 runtime to have a version of 4.9 in this dialog. By the time that this book is published, this dialog will support setting the version to 4.10.

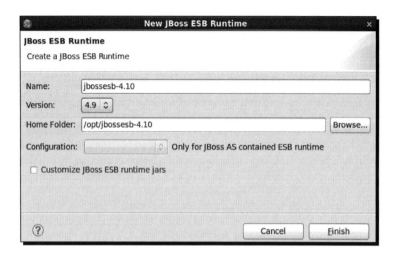

3. After you press **Finish**, you should see that the runtime you just defined is marked with a checkmark. This indicates that the runtime is active.

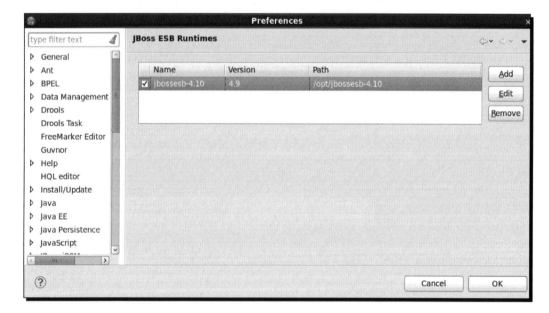

OK. After you have the runtime defined, it's time to start up the JBoss AS server. Note that if you still have a server running, such as the server that we started earlier in the book, you should stop it now.

Ordinarily, we would have to leave JBDS and open up a shell window to start a server. Remember how we said that the "I" in IDE stands for integrated? We'll run the server from inside JBDS. Follow these steps:

1. Select **Window | Show View | Other | Servers** and you'll see the following dialog displayed:

2. After you select **OK**, you'll see the following dialog. Where did the `jboss-5.1.0.GA` server come from? Remember how we defined this when we installed JBDS? That's where it came from.

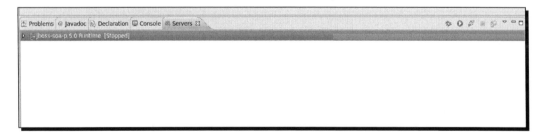

3. Now that we have a server defined, let's start it. Right-click on the server and you'll see the following dialog:

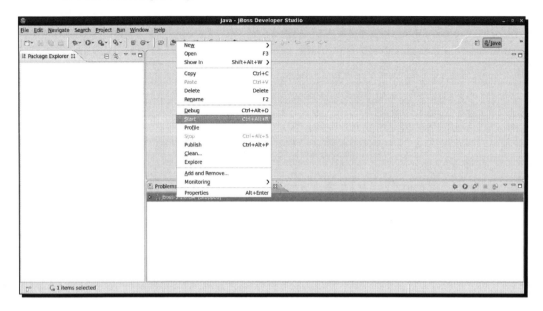

4. Click **Start**, and you'll see the **Console** view open automatically. This view displays the `server.log` file for the server. JBDS knows which server profile to start because we selected the all profile when we defined the ESB run-time.

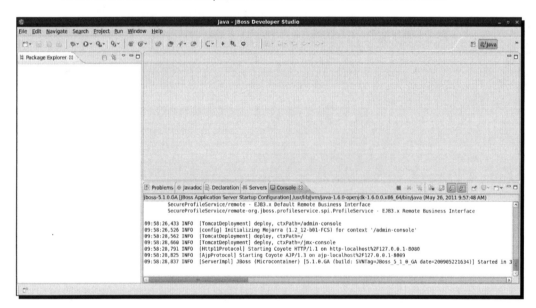

The server appears to be running, but let's make sure by going to its web console at `http://localhost:8080`. We'll use JBDS' internal browser:

1. Select **Window | Show View | General** and you'll see the following dialog. Select **Internal Web Browser**.

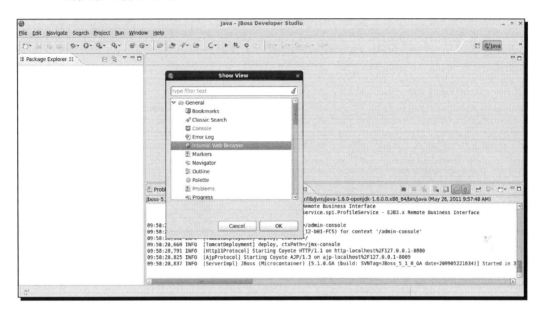

2. Enter `http://localhost:8080` and you'll see the following window:

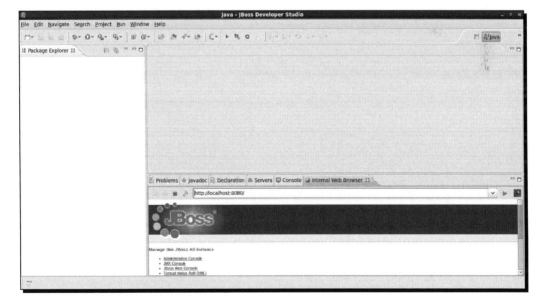

What just happened?

At this point, we have JBDS fully configured with the JBoss AS server and JBoss ESB. Also, we can control these without having to exit JBDS.

What's next? Let's run that quickstart from inside JBDS.

Time for action – using JBDS to run the quickstart

Follow these steps to install and run the quickstart:

1. Our first step is to install the quickstart into our JBDS workspace. Go to **Help** | **Project Examples** as shown in the following screenshot:

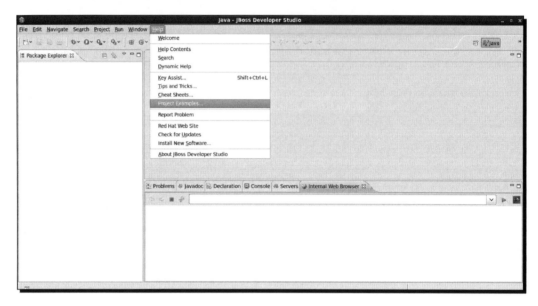

2. Then select **ESB for SOA-P 5.0** from the list of possible examples. "SOA-P 5.0" stands for the JBoss SOA Platform (`http://www.jboss.com/products/platforms/soa/`). This is a commercial product sold by JBoss that incorporates JBoss ESB. The same ESB-based examples can be run with JBoss ESB or the SOA Platform.

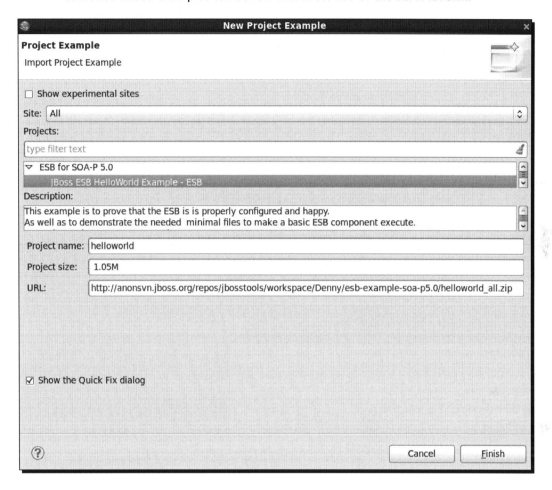

3. Next, the quickstart is downloaded and installed into the workspace:

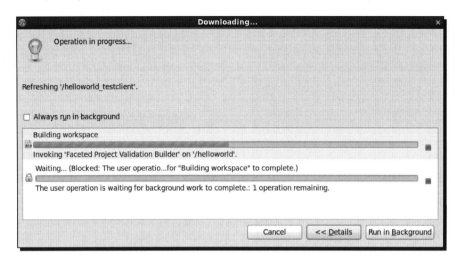

Deploying the quickstart in JBDS

When the download is completed, the quickstart is ready to be deployed. Note that unlike the previous quickstart configured to run with ant from a terminal window, the quickstart in JBDS includes a second "testclient" binary. We'll use this client to actually invoke the quickstart after it is deployed to the server.

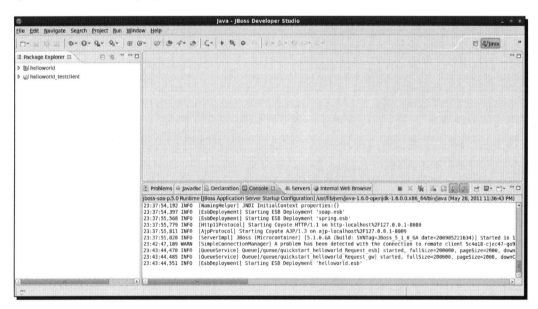

Time for action – deploying the quickstart

It's easy to deploy the quickstart to the server in JBDS. Follow these steps:

1. Right-click on the server and select **Add and Remove** to add (in other words, deploy) the quickstart to the server:

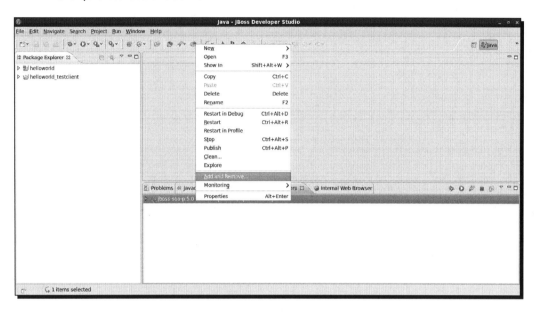

2. Select the quickstart from the list of available applications:

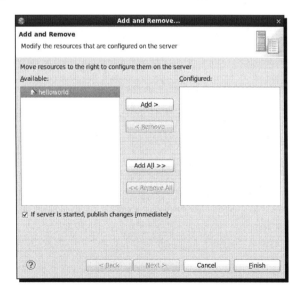

3. Click **Finish**:

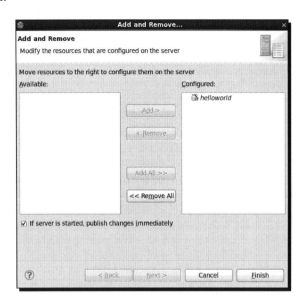

4. At this point, you'll see deployment messages in the Console (see the following screenshot). To run the quickstart, select either the `SendEsbMessage.java` client code (to send a message directly to the ESB listener) or the `SendJMSMessage.java` client code to send a message to the ESB listener through the JMS gateway listener. It's a good idea to make a mental note of these programs as they are also used in many other quickstarts. For this example, we'll select `SendJMSMessage.java` as our client.

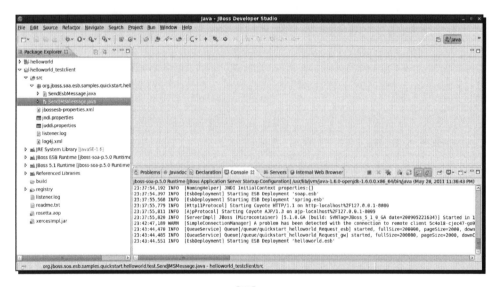

5. The mode in which `SendJMSMessage.java` will run will be as a Java application, so we'll choose that:

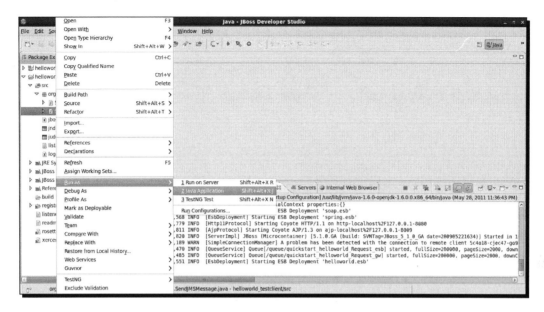

Finally, here's the output from the quickstart!

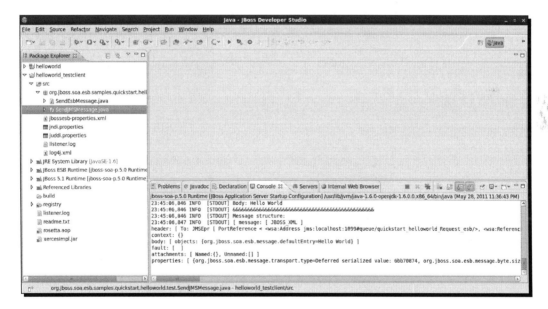

What just happened

Before we move on, let's think about what we just accomplished. We created and started a JBoss AS server, deployed a JBoss ESB quickstart to it, and then invoked a client to run the quickstart. We did all this without having to switch between windows and GUIs and we were able to do all of this from inside JBDS.

Have a go hero - there are other quickstarts to explore

Hang on there. The same approach that we followed for the smallest of the quickstarts can be used for the other, more elaborate quickstarts. Try downloading and running them in JBDS. Remember to look in the server console for the server log, as this is where you'll see most of the output from the quickstarts.

Pop quiz

Before we move on, it's time to see what you've learned. Pencils ready? Let's begin!

1. How do we set quickstart-specific properties, like the server home, FTP login information, or jBPM user information?

    a. In a very expensive database

    b. Through shell environment variables

    c. In the `quickstarts.properties` file

2. What file determines the order in which queues are deployed?

    a. `deployment.xml`

    b. `jboss-esb.xml`

    c. It's a trick question, the order is random

3. What's the easiest way to deploy and undeploy an ESB archive?

    a. To deploy, just copy the file to the server's deploy directory, to undeploy, just delete it

    b. E-mail it to yourself

    c. The **Add and Remove** feature in JBDS

4. How do I find the directions for a specific quickstart?

    a. In the `readme.txt` files

    b. In the `HELP_ME.txt` files

    c. Through a Google search

5. How can I deploy an archive if I don't have command-line access to a remote machine?

    a. Sorry, you're out of luck

    b. Buy the sysadmin lobster for lunch

    c. By using the JBoss AS admin console

Summary

You've now been introduced to the wonderful world of quickstarts! You should now know how to run the quickstarts from either a command line or through an IDE, and you can choose whichever is more comfortable for you. Go ahead and find one that interests you and try to run it—check the readme for any specific run instructions related to that quickstart. We'll be using the quickstarts later on in the book to demonstrate specific functionality around other JBoss ESB features.

In this chapter, we learned about the:

- JBoss ESB "quickstart" example programs
- Configuration elements of a service
- Deployment of services
- How to download and install JBDS
- How to run servers, deploy and run quickstarts, all from inside of JBDS

We saw a single service in action when we ran the quickstart in this chapter. In the next chapter, we'll examine designing and building JBoss ESB services, how to invoke services, how to have services inter-communicate with each other and with legacy applications.

3

Understanding Services

The core of any Enterprise Service Bus (ESB) revolves around the definition of services and the way in which these services communicate with each other. How you choose to break up your application into services, whether dealing with the integration of legacy components or designing new functionality, and how they communicate can have a large effect on the performance, flexibility and resilience of your application.

It is important to spend time thinking about these issues. Get it right and you will end up with a loosely coupled system that reuses functionality rather than reimplements it. In order to make effective architectural decisions it is first necessary to understand the concepts behind the JBoss ESB Service, including their communication "on the bus", so that these can best be applied to your application.

In this chapter we will cover JBoss ESB Services, explaining the structure of the ESB message, the mechanics behind the Action Pipeline and the choices you have for implementing actions.

You will learn about:

- ◆ The structure of ESB messages and how to validate them
- ◆ The configuration mechanism within JBoss ESB
- ◆ The service pipeline and service actions
- ◆ Service chaining and continuations
- ◆ Transactional behavior and its effect on the pipeline
- ◆ Security context and its propagation

So let's get on with it...

Preparing JBoss Developer Studio

The examples in this chapter are based on a standard ESB application template that can be found under the Chapter3 directory within the sample downloads. We will modify this template application as we proceed through this chapter.

Before we start, please make sure that you have set up JBoss Developer Studio and the **JBoss 5.1 Runtime** as described in *Chapter 2*.

Time for action – opening the Chapter3 app

Follow these steps:

1. Click on the **File** menu and select **Import**.

2. Now choose **Existing Projects into workspace** and select the folder where the book samples have been extracted:

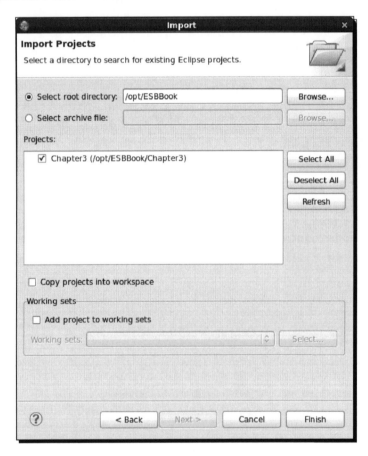

3. Then click on **Finish**. Now have a look at the `jboss-esb.xml` file. You can see that it has a single service and action as defined in the following snippet:

```xml
<jbossesb parameterReloadSecs="5"
 xmlns="http://anonsvn.labs.jboss.com/labs/jbossesb/trunk/
        product/etc/schemas/xml/jbossesb-1.3.0.xsd"
 xmlns:xsi="http://www.w3.org/2001/XMLSchema-instance"
 xsi:schemaLocation="http://anonsvn.labs.jboss.com/labs/
                     jbossesb/trunk/product/etc/schemas/xml/
                     jbossesb-1.3.0.xsd
                     http://anonsvn.jboss.org/repos/labs/
                     labs/jbossesb/trunk/product/etc/
                     schemas/xml/jbossesb-1.3.0.xsd">
  <providers>
    <jms-provider connection-factory="ConnectionFactory"
                  name="JBossMQ">
      <jms-bus busid="chapter3GwChannel">
        <jms-message-filter dest-name="queue/chapter3_Request_gw"
                            dest-type="QUEUE"/>
      </jms-bus>
      <jms-bus busid="chapter3EsbChannel">
        <jms-message-filter dest-name="queue/chapter3_Request_esb"
                            dest-type="QUEUE"/>
      </jms-bus>
    </jms-provider>
  </providers>
  <services>
    <service category="Chapter3Sample"
             description="A template for Chapter3"
             name="Chapter3Service">
      <listeners>
        <jms-listener busidref="chapter3GwChannel"
                      is-gateway="true"
                      name="Chapter3GwListener"/>
        <jms-listener busidref="chapter3EsbChannel"
                      name="Chapter3Listener"/>
      </listeners>
      <actions mep="OneWay">
        <action class="org.jboss.soa.esb.actions.SystemPrintln"
                name="PrintBefore">
          <property name="message"/>
          <property name="printfull" value="true"/>
        </action>
      </actions>
    </service>
  </services>
</jbossesb>
```

Examining the structure of ESB messages

A service is an implementation of a piece of business logic which exposes a well defined service contract to consumers. The service will provide an abstract service contract which describes the functionality exposed by the service and will exhibit the following characteristics:

◆ **Self contained**: The implementation of the service is independent from the context of the consumers; any implementation changes will have no impact.

◆ **Loosely coupled**: The consumer invokes the service indirectly, passing messages through the bus to the service endpoint. There is no direct connection between the service and its consumers.

◆ **Reusable**: The service can be invoked by any consumer requiring the functionality exposed by the service. The provider is tied to neither a particular application nor process.

Services which adhere to these criteria will be capable of evolving and scaling without affecting any consumers of that service. The consumer no longer cares which implementation of the service is being invoked, nor where it is located, provided that the exposed service contract remains compatible.

Examining the message

The structure of the message, and how it can be manipulated, plays an important part in any ESB application as a result of the message driven nature of the communication between service providers and consumers. The message is the envelope which contains all of the information relevant to a specific invocation of a service.

All messages within JBoss ESB are implementations of the `org.jboss.soa.esb.message.Message` interface, the major aspects of which are:

◆ **Header**: Information concerning the identity, routing addresses, and correlation of the message

◆ **Context**: Contextual information pertaining to the delivery of each message, such as the security context

◆ **Body**: The payload and additional details as required by the service contract

◆ **Attachment**: Additional information that may be referenced from within the payload

◆ **Properties**: Information relating to the specific delivery of a message, usually transport specific (for example the original JMS queue name)

Time for action – printing the message structure

Let us execute the Chapter3 sample application that was opened up at the beginning of this chapter. Follow these steps:

1. In JBoss Developer Studio, click **Run** and select **Run As** and **Run on Server**. Alternatively you can press *Alt + Shift + X*, followed by *R*.

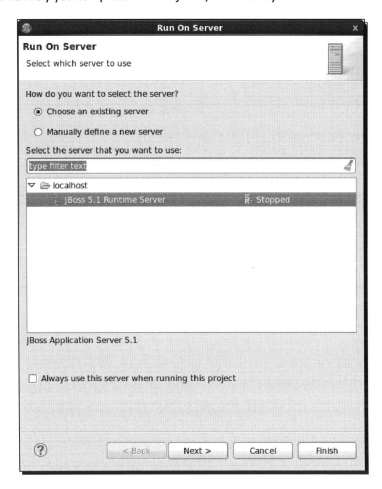

2. You can see the server runtime has been pre-selected. Choosing the **Always use this server when running this project** check box will always use this runtime and this dialog will not appear again.

3. Click **Next**. A window with the project pre-configured to run on this server is shown. Ensure that we have only our project `Chapter3` selected to the right hand side.

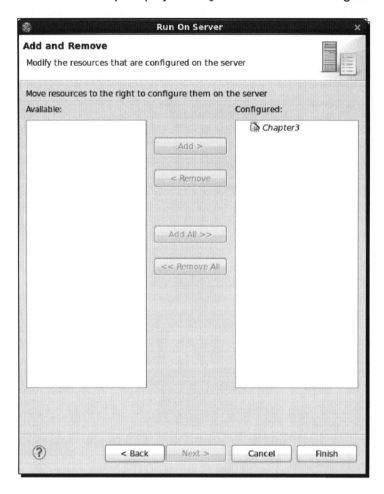

4. Click **Finish**.

5. The server runtime will be started up (if not already started) and the ESB file will be deployed to the server runtime.

6. Select the `src` folder, expand it till the `SendJMSMessage.java` file is displayed in the tree. Now click **Run**, select **Run As** and **Java Application**.

The entire ESB message contents will be printed in the console as follows:

```
INFO   [STDOUT] Message structure:

INFO   [STDOUT] [ message: [ JBOSS_XML ]

header: [ To: JMSEpr [ PortReference < <wsa:Address
jms:localhost:1099#queue/chapter3_Request_esb/>,
<wsa:ReferenceProperties jbossesb:java.naming.factory.
initial : org.jnp.interfaces.NamingContextFactory/>,
<wsa:ReferenceProperties jbossesb:java.naming.provider.url :
localhost:1099/>, <wsa:ReferenceProperties jbossesb:java.naming.
factory.url.pkgs : org.jnp.interfaces/>, <wsa:ReferenceProperties
jbossesb:destination-type : queue/>, <wsa:ReferenceProperties
jbossesb:destination-name : queue/chapter3_Request_esb/>,
<wsa:ReferenceProperties jbossesb:specification-version :
1.1/>, <wsa:ReferenceProperties jbossesb:connection-factory :
ConnectionFactory/>, <wsa:ReferenceProperties jbossesb:persistent :
true/>, <wsa:ReferenceProperties jbossesb:acknowledge-mode : AUTO_
ACKNOWLEDGE/>, <wsa:ReferenceProperties jbossesb:transacted : false/>,
<wsa:ReferenceProperties jbossesb:type : urn:jboss/esb/epr/type/
jms/> > ] MessageID: e694a6a5-6a30-45bf-8f6d-f48363219ccf RelatesTo:
jms:correlationID#e694a6a5-6a30-45bf-8f6d-f48363219ccf ]

context: {}

body: [ objects: {org.jboss.soa.esb.message.defaultEntry=Chapter 3
says Hello!} ]

fault: [  ]

attachments: [ Named:{}, Unnamed:[] ]

properties: [ {org.jboss.soa.esb.message.transport.type=Deferred
serialized value: 12d16a5, org.jboss.soa.esb.message.byte.size=2757,
javax.jms.message.redelivered=false, org.jboss.soa.esb.gateway.
original.queue.name=Deferred serialized value: 129bebb, org.jboss.soa.
esb.message.source=Deferred serialized value: 1a8e795} ] ]
```

What just happened?

You have just created a Chapter3.esb file and deployed it to the ESB Runtime on the JBoss Application Server 5.1. You executed a gateway client that posted a string to the Bus. The server converted this message to an ESB message and the complete structure was printed out. Take a moment to examine the output and understand the various parts of the ESB message.

Have a go hero – deploying applications

Step 1 through step 4 describe how to start the server and deploy our application from within JBoss Developer Studio. For the rest of this chapter, and throughout this book, you will be repeating these steps and will just be asked to deploy the application.

Message implementations

JBoss ESB provides two different implementations of the message interface, one which marshalls data into an XML format and a second which uses Java serialization to create a binary representation of the message. Both of these implementations will only handle Java serializable objects by default, however it is possible to extend the XML implementation to support additional object types.

Message implementations are created indirectly through the `org.jboss.soa.esb.message.format.MessageFactory` class.

In general any use of serializable objects can lead to a brittle application, one that is more tightly coupled between the message producer and consumer. The message implementations within JBoss ESB mitigate this by supporting a 'Just In Time' approach when accessing the data. Care must still be taken with what data is placed within the message, however serialization/marshalling of these objects will only occur as and when required.

Extending the ESB to provide alternative message implementations, and extending the current XML implementation to support additional types, is outside the scope of this book.

The body

This is the section of the message which contains the main payload information for the message, adhering to the contract exposed by the service. The payload should only consist of the data required by the service contract and should not rely on any service implementation details as this will prevent the evolution or replacement of the service implementation at a future date.

The types of data contained within the body are restricted only by the requirements imposed by the message implementation, in other words the implementation must be able to serialize or marshall the contents as part of service invocation.

The body consists of

- **Main payload**: accessed using the following methods:

```
public Object get() ;
public void add(final Object value) ;
```

- **Named objects**: accessed using the following methods:

```
public Object get(final String name) ;
public void add(final String name, final Object value) ;
```

Time for action – examining the main payload

Let us create another action class that simply prints the message body. We will add this action to the sample application that was opened up at the beginning of this chapter.

1. Right click on the `src` folder and choose **New** and select **Class**:

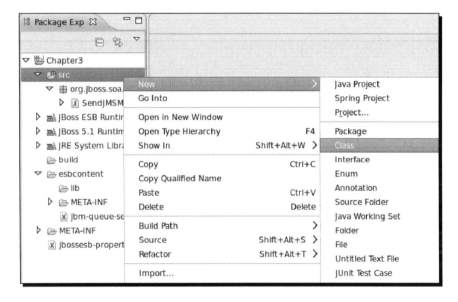

2. Enter the **Name** as "MyAction", enter the **Package** as "org.jboss.soa. samples.chapter3", and select the **Superclass** as "org.jboss.soa.esb. actions.AbstractActionLifecycle":

3. Click **Finish**.

4. Add the following imports and the following body contents to the code:

```java
import org.jboss.soa.esb.helpers.ConfigTree;
import org.jboss.soa.esb.message.Message;

protected ConfigTree  _config;
public MyAction(ConfigTree config) {
    _config = config;
}

public Message displayMessage(Message message) throws Exception {
    System.out.println(
        "&&&&&&&&&&&&&&&&&&&&&&&&&&&&&&&&&&&&&&&&&&&&&&&&&");
```

```
System.out.println("&&&&&&&&&&&&&&&&&&&&&&&&&&&&&&");
System.out.println("Body: " + message.getBody().get());
System.out.println("&&&&&&&&&&&&&&&&&&&&&&&&&&&&&&");
return message;
}
```

5. Click **Save**.

6. Open the `jboss-esb.xml` file in **Tree** mode, expand till **Actions** is displayed in the tree. Select **Actions**, click **Add | Custom Action**:

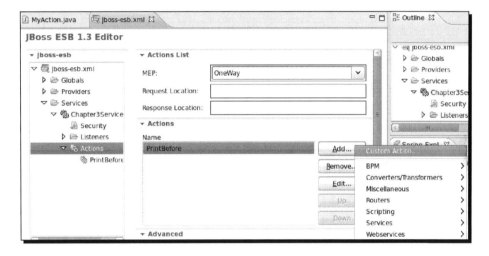

7. Enter the **Name** as "BodyPrinter" and choose the "MyAction" class and "displayMessage" process method:

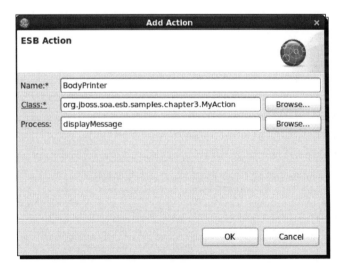

8. Click **Save** and the application will be deployed. If the server was stopped then deploy it using the **Run** menu and select **Run As | Run on Server**:

9. Once the application is deployed on the server, run `SendJMSMessage.java` by clicking **Run | Run As | Java Application**.

The following can be seen displayed in the console output:

```
12:19:32,562 INFO   [STDOUT] &&&&&&&&&&&&&&&&&&&&&&&&&&&&&&&&
12:19:32,562 INFO   [STDOUT] Body: Chapter 3 says Hello!
12:19:32,562 INFO   [STDOUT] &&&&&&&&&&&&&&&&&&&&&&&&&&&&&&&&
```

What just happened?

You have just created your own action class that used the Message API to get the main payload of the message and printed it to the console.

Have a go hero – additional body contents

Now add another miscellaneous `SystemPrintln` action after our `BodyPrinter`. Name it `PrintAfter` and make sure `printfull` is set to `true`. Modify the `MyAction` class and add additional named content using the `getBody().add(name, object)` method and see what gets printed on the console.

Here is the `actions` section of the `config` file

```xml
<actions mep="OneWay">
  <action class="org.jboss.soa.esb.actions.SystemPrintln"
        name="PrintBefore">
    <property name="message"/>
    <property name="printfull" value="true"/>
  </action>
  <action class="org.jboss.soa.esb.samples.chapter3.MyAction"
        name="BodyPrinter" process="displayMessage"/>
  <action class="org.jboss.soa.esb.actions.SystemPrintln"
        name="PrintAfter">
    <property name="message"/>
    <property name="printfull" value="true"/>
  </action>
</actions>
```

The following is the listing of the `MyAction` class's modified `displayMessage` method

```
public Message displayMessage(Message message) throws Exception {
    System.out.println("&&&&&&&&&&&&&&&&&&&&&&&&&&&&&&&&");
    System.out.println("Body: " + message.getBody().get());
    message.getBody().add("Something", "Unknown");
    System.out.println("&&&&&&&&&&&&&&&&&&&&&&&&&&&&&&&&");
    return message;
}
```

The header

The message header contains the information relating to the identity, routing, and the correlation of messages. This information is based on, and shares much in common with, the concepts defined in the **W3C WS-Addressing** specification.

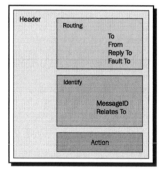

 It is important to point out that many of these aspects are normally initialized automatically by other parts of the codebase; a solid understanding of these concepts will allow the developer to create composite services using more advanced topologies.

Routing information

Every time a message is sent within the ESB it contains information which describes who sent the message, which service it should be routed to, and where any replies/faults should be sent once processing is complete. The creation of this information is the responsibility of the invoker and, once delivered, any changes made to this information, from within the target service, will be ignored by that service.

The information in the header takes the form of Endpoint References (EPRs) containing a representation of the service address, often transport specific, and extensions which can contain relevant contextual information for that endpoint. This information should be treated as opaque by all parties except the party which was responsible for creating it.

There are four EPRs included in the header, they are as follows:

- ◆ To: This is the only mandatory EPR, representing the address of the service to which the message is being sent. This will be initialized by ServiceInvoker with the details of the service chosen to receive the message.

- ◆ From: This EPR represents the originator of the message, if present, and may be used as the address for responses if there is neither an explicit ReplyTo nor FaultTo set on the message.

- ◆ ReplyTo: This EPR represents the endpoint to which all responses will be sent, if present, and may be used as the address for faults if there is no explicit FaultTo set on the message. This will normally be initialized by ServiceInvoker if a synchronous response is expected by the service consumer.

- ◆ FaultTo: This EPR represents the endpoint to which all faults will be sent, if present.

When thinking about the routing information it is important to view these details from the perspective of the service consumer, as the EPRs represent the wishes of the consumer and must be adhered to. If the service implementation involves more advanced topologies, like chaining and continuations, which we will discuss later in the chapter, then care must be taken to preserve these EPRs when messages are propagated to subsequent services.

Message identity and correlation

There are two parts of the header which are related to the identity of the message and its correlation with a preceding message. These are as follows:

- ◆ MessageID: A unique reference which can be used to identify the message as it progresses through the ESB. The reference is represented by a **Uniform Resource Name (URN)**, a specialized **Uniform Resource Identifier (URI)** which will represent the identity of the message within a specific namespace. The creator of the message may choose to associate it with an identity which is specific to the application context within which it is being used, in which case the URN should refer to a namespace which is also application context specific. If no MessageID has been associated with the message then the ESB will assign a unique identifier when it is first sent to a service.

- ◆ RelatesTo: When sending a reply, this represents the unique reference of the message representing the request. This may be used to correlate the response message with the original request.

Service action

The action header is an optional, service-specific URN that may be used to further refine the processing of the message by a service provider or service consumer. The URN should refer to an application-specific namespace.

There are no restrictions on how this header is to be used by the application including, if considered appropriate, ignoring its contents.

Time for action – examining the header

Let us go back and modify `MyAction` to display some of the header information that we need:

1. Open `MyAction` and edit the `displayMessage` method as follows:

    ```
    public Message displayMessage(Message message) throws Exception {
        System.out.println("&&&&&&&&&&&&&&&&&&&&&&&&&&&&&&&&");
        System.out.println("From: " +
                message.getHeader().getCall().getFrom());
        System.out.println("To: " +
                message.getHeader().getCall().getTo());
        System.out.println("MessageID: " +
                message.getHeader().getCall().getMessageID());
        System.out.println("&&&&&&&&&&&&&&&&&&&&&&&&&&&&&&&&");
        return message;
    }
    ```

2. Remove the `PrintBefore` and `PrintAfter` actions if they exist. Make sure that we have only the **BodyPrinter** action:

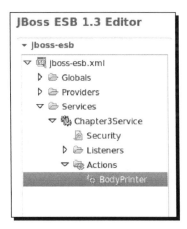

3. Click on **Save**.

4. If the server was still running (and a small red button appears in the console window), then you might notice the application gets redeployed by default.

5. If this did not happen then deploy the application using the **Run** menu and select **Run As | Run on Server.** The following output will be displayed in the console:

```
INFO   [EsbDeployment] Stopping 'Chapter3.esb'

INFO   [EsbDeployment] Destroying 'Chapter3.esb'

WARN   [ServiceMessageCounterLifecycleResource] Calling cleanup on
existing service message counters for identity ID-7

INFO   [QueueService] Queue[/queue/chapter3_Request_gw] stopped

INFO   [QueueService] Queue[/queue/chapter3_Request_esb] stopped

INFO   [QueueService] Queue[/queue/chapter3_Request_esb] started,
fullSize=200000, pageSize=2000, downCacheSize=2000

INFO   [QueueService] Queue[/queue/chapter3_Request_gw] started,
fullSize=200000, pageSize=2000, downCacheSize=2000

INFO   [EsbDeployment]  Starting ESB Deployment 'Chapter3.esb'
```

6. Run `SendJMSMessage.java` by clicking **Run | Run As | Java Application**. The following messages will be printed in the console

```
INFO   [STDOUT] &&&&&&&&&&&&&&&&&&&&&&&&&&&&&&&&

INFO   [STDOUT] From: null

INFO   [STDOUT] To: JMSEpr [ PortReference < <wsa:Address
jms:localhost:1099#queue/chapter3_Request_esb/>,
<wsa:ReferenceProperties jbossesb:java.naming.factory.
initial : org.jnp.interfaces.NamingContextFactory/>,
<wsa:ReferenceProperties jbossesb:java.naming.provider.url :
localhost:1099/>, <wsa:ReferenceProperties jbossesb:java.naming.
factory.url.pkgs : org.jnp.interfaces/>, <wsa:ReferenceProperties
jbossesb:destination-type : queue/>, <wsa:ReferenceProperties
jbossesb:destination-name : queue/chapter3_Request_esb/>,
<wsa:ReferenceProperties jbossesb:specification-version :
1.1/>, <wsa:ReferenceProperties jbossesb:connection-factory :
ConnectionFactory/>, <wsa:ReferenceProperties jbossesb:persistent
: true/>, <wsa:ReferenceProperties jbossesb:acknowledge-mode :
AUTO_ACKNOWLEDGE/>, <wsa:ReferenceProperties jbossesb:transacted :
false/>, <wsa:ReferenceProperties jbossesb:type : urn:jboss/esb/
epr/type/jms/> > ]

INFO   [STDOUT] MessageID: 46e57744-d0ac-4f01-ad78-b1f15a3335d1

INFO   [STDOUT] &&&&&&&&&&&&&&&&&&&&&&&&&&&&&&&&
```

What just happened?

We examined some of the header contents through the API. We printed the From, To, and the MessageID from within our MyAction class.

Have a go hero – additional header contents

Now modify the MyAction class to print the Action, ReplyTo, RelatesTo, and FaultTo contents of the header to the console.

Here is the listing of the modified MyAction class's method:

```
public Message displayMessage(Message message) throws Exception {
    System.out.println("&&&&&&&&&&&&&&&&&&&&&&&&&&&&&&&&");
    System.out.println("From: " +
            message.getHeader().getCall().getFrom());
    System.out.println("To: " +
            message.getHeader().getCall().getTo());
    System.out.println("MessageID: " +
            message.getHeader().getCall().getMessageID());
    System.out.println("Action: " +
            message.getHeader().getCall().getAction());
    System.out.println("FaultTo: " +
            message.getHeader().getCall().getFaultTo());
    System.out.println("RelatesTo: " +
            message.getHeader().getCall().getRelatesTo());
    System.out.println("ReplyTo: " +
            message.getHeader().getCall().getReplyTo());
    System.out.println("&&&&&&&&&&&&&&&&&&&&&&&&&&&&&&&&");
    return message;
}
```

The context

The message context is used to transport the active contextual information when the message is sent to the target service. This may include information such as the current security context, transactional information, or even context specific to the application. This contextual information is not considered to be part of the service contract and is assumed to change between successive message deliveries.

Where the message context really becomes important is when a service pipeline is invoked through an InVM transport, as this can allow the message to be passed by reference. We will learn more about InVM transport in *Chapter 5*. When the transport passes the message to the target service it will create a copy of the message header and message context, allowing each to be updated in subsequent actions without affecting the invoked service.

Have a go hero – printing message context

Modify the `MyAction` class to print the context of the ESB message; obtain the context through the `getContext()` method. You will notice that the context is empty for our sample application as we currently have no security or transactional context attached to the message.

Message validation

The message format within JBoss ESB allows the consumer and producer to use any payload that suits the purpose of the service contract. No constraints are placed on this payload other than the fact that it must be possible to marshall the payload contents so that the messages can be transported between the consumer and producer.

While this ability is useful for creating composite services, it can be a disadvantage when you need to design services that have an abstract contract, hide the details of the implementation, are loosely coupled, and can easily be reused. In order to encourage the loose coupling of services it is often advantageous to choose a payload that does not dictate implementation, for example XML.

JBoss ESB provides support for enforcing the structure of XML payloads for request and response messages, through the XML schema language as defined through the W3C. An **XML Schema Document (XSD)** is an abstract, structural definition which can be used to formally describe an XML message and guarantee that a specific payload matches that definition through a process called validation.

Enabling validation on a service is simply a matter of providing the schema associated with the request and/or response messages and specifying the `validate` attribute, as follows:

```
<actions inXsd="/request.xsd" outXsd="/response.xsd" validate="true">
   ...
</actions>
```

This will force the service pipeline to validate the request and response messages against the XSD files, if they are specified, with the request validation occurring before the first service action is executed and the response validation occurring immediately before the response message is sent to the consumer.

If validation of the request or response message does fail then a `MessageValidationException` fault will be raised and sent to the consumer using the normal fault processing as defined in the MEPs and responses section. This exception can also be seen by enabling DEBUG logging through the mechanism supported by the server.

Have a go hero – enabling validation

Add a `request.xsd` or a `response.xsd` or both to your actions in the sample application provided. Enable validation and test the output.

Configuring through the ConfigTree

JBoss ESB handles the majority of its configuration through a hierarchical structure similar to the W3C DOM, namely, `org.jboss.soa.esb.helpers.ConfigTree`. Each node within the structure contains a name, a reference to the parent node, a set of named attributes, and references to all child nodes.

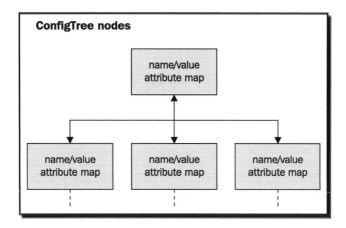

This structure is used, directly and indirectly, within the implementation of the service pipeline and action processors, and will be required if you are intending to create your own action processors. The only exception to this is when using an annotated action class when the configuring of the action will be handled by the framework instead of programmatically; see the section on *Annotated actions* in *Chapter 4* for more details.

Configuring properties in the jboss-esb.xml file

The `ConfigTree` instance passed to an action processor is a hierarchical representation of the properties as defined within the action definition of the `jboss-esb.xml` file. Each property defined within an action may be interpreted as a `name`/`value` pair or as hierarchical content to be parsed by the action. For example the following:

```
<action ....>
  <!-- name/value property -->
  <property name="propertyName" value="propertyValue"/>
  <!-- Hierarchical property -->
```

```
      <property name="propertyName">
        <hierarchicalProperty attr="value">
          <inner name="myName" random="randomValue"/>
        </hierarchicalProperty>
      </property>
    </action>
```

This will result in the following `ConfigTree` structure being passed to the action:

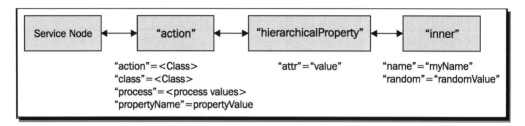

Traversing the ConfigTree hierarchy

Traversing the hierarchy is simply a matter of using the following methods to obtain access to the parent or child nodes:

```
public ConfigTree getParent() ;
public ConfigTree[] getAllChildren() ;
public ConfigTree[] getChildren(String name) ;
public ConfigTree getFirstChild(String name) ;
```

Accessing attributes

Attributes are usually accessed by querying the current `ConfigTree` instance for the value associated with the required name, using the following methods:

```
public String getAttribute(String name) ;
public String getAttribute(String name, String defaultValue) ;
public long getLongAttribute(String name, long defaultValue) ;
public float getFloatAttribute(String name, float defaultValue) ;
public boolean getBooleanAttribute(String name, boolean defaultValue)
;
public String getRequiredAttribute(String name)   throws
ConfigurationException ;
```

It is also possible to obtain the number of attributes, names of all the attributes, or the set of key/value pairs using the following methods:

```
public int attributeCount() ;
public Set<String> getAttributeNames() ;
public List<KeyValuePair> attributesAsList() ;
```

Time for action – examining configuration properties

Let us add some configuration properties to our `MyAction`. We will make the & and the number of times it needs to be printed as configurable properties. Follow these steps:

1. Add two members to the `MyAction` class:

```
public String SYMBOL = "&";
public int COUNT = 48;
```

2. Modify the constructor as follows:

```
_config = config;
String symbol = _config.getAttribute("symbol");
if (symbol != null) {
    SYMBOL = symbol;
}
String count = _config.getAttribute("count");
if (count != null) {
    COUNT = Integer.parseInt(count);
}
```

3. Add a `printLine()` method:

```
private void printLine() {
    StringBuffer line = new StringBuffer(COUNT);
    for (int i = 0; i < COUNT; i++) {
        line.append(SYMBOL);
    }
    System.out.println(line);
}
```

4. Modify the `printMessage()` method as shown in the following snippet:

```
printLine();
System.out.println("Body: " + message.getBody().get());
printLine();
return message;
```

5. Edit the `jboss-esb.xml` file and select the action, `BodyPrinter`. Add two properties `symbol` as `*` and `count` as `50`:

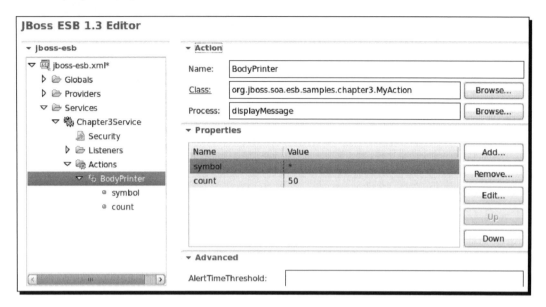

6. Click on **Save** or press *Ctrl + S*.

7. Deploy the application using the **Run** menu and select **Run As | Run on Server**.

8. Run `SendJMSMessage.java` by clicking **Run**, select **Run As** and **Java Application**. The following message will be printed in the console:

```
INFO   [STDOUT] **************************************************
INFO   [STDOUT] Body: Chapter 3 says Hello!
INFO   [STDOUT] **************************************************
```

What just happened?

You just added two properties to the `MyAction` class. You also retrieved these properties from the `ConfigTree` and used them.

Have a go hero – additional header contents

Experiment with the other API methods. Write `hierarchicalProperty` and see how that can be retrieved.

Service pipeline and service invocation

In JBoss ESB, the structure of a service consists of a simple action pipeline that is responsible for processing each request in a sequential manner. There are no restrictions placed on the content or structure of the requests or on the functionality that can be exposed through a service.

The service pipeline is the real workhorse of JBoss ESB, responsible for the following:

- Controlling the lifecycle of each action
- Validation and delivery of the message through the action processors
- Generating appropriate responses once the request is complete.

A service can consist of any number of actions, each processing the output from the preceding action in the pipeline.

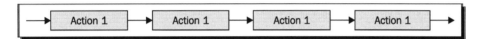

The pipeline treats each action as if it was an implementation of the `org.jboss.soa.esb.actions.ActionPipelineProcessor` interface, containing the lifecycle and processing methods supported by the pipeline. If the service action does not directly implement this interface then the pipeline will create an adapter which is responsible for invoking the methods using the overriding mechanism (see the *Dynamic Methods* section later in this chapter).

One instance of each action will be instantiated on initialization of the action pipeline, and created in the sequence defined by the configuration of the service pipeline. Each action must contain a public constructor with a single `ConfigTree` parameter, used to pass in the configuration of the action, unless it is an annotated action when annotated fields and methods can be used to configure the action.

Lifecycle methods

Action lifecycle methods are represented by the `org.jboss.soa.esb.actions.ActionLifecycle` interface, consisting of the following methods:

```
public void initialise() throws ActionLifecycleException ;
public void destroy() throws ActionLifecycleException ;
```

These are invoked during the initialization and destruction phases of the action pipeline. Actions should restrict their initialization and cleanup tasks to within the lifecycle methods, they should not occur within the creation of the action or within the processing methods.

The service pipeline will initialize each action in the order defined within the service definition and, once complete, will be able to process any messages delivered to the service. The following sequence diagram highlights the successful initialization of a pipeline:

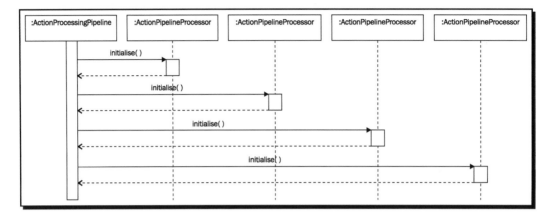

If an exception occurs during the initialization of an action then the pipeline will invoke the destroy method of each preceding action, in reverse order, before terminating the pipeline. The following sequence diagram highlights the processing of a failure during the initialization phase:

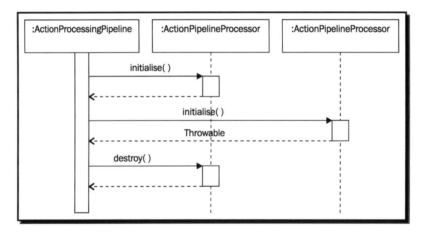

The service pipeline will continue to process messages until such time as it is asked to stop. Once current processing is complete the pipeline will invoke the destroy method of each action, in reverse order, before terminating the pipeline. The following sequence diagram highlights the termination phase of the pipeline:

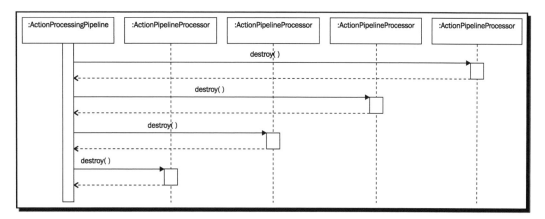

Have a go hero – understanding lifecycle methods

You have already seen our MyAction class in action. Override the initialise() and destroy() methods, from AbstractActionLifecycle, with some printlns and see how these methods are invoked.

Processing methods

Action processing methods are represented by the org.jboss.soa.esb.actions. ActionPipelineProcessor interface, which extends the ActionLifecycle interface to add the following methods:

```
public Message process(final Message message)
     throws ActionProcessingException ;
public void processException(final Message message,
                              final Throwable th) ;
public void processSuccess(final Message message) ;
```

The implementations of these methods must be thread-safe, as they may be invoked concurrently.

The service pipeline is responsible for obtaining the incoming message and controlling its progression through the actions in the pipeline. The process method of each action processor will be invoked, in the same order as the actions are defined within the service, using the response from the preceding action as the message input parameter. Each action processor can therefore choose whether to reuse the same message instance or create a new instance for subsequent processors.

If the message processing is successful then the service pipeline will invoke the `processSuccess` method of each action processor, in reverse order. The following sequence diagram highlights a successful invocation of a service pipeline:

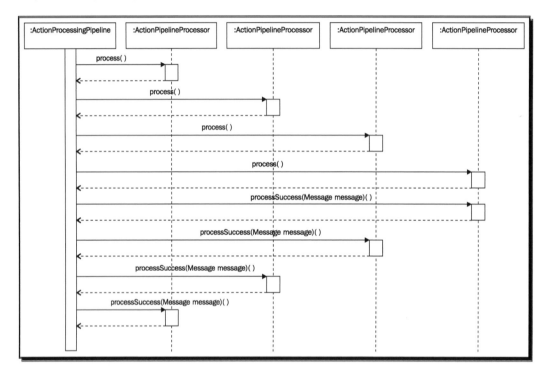

If the message processing causes an exception to be thrown from any of the process method invocations then the service pipeline will invoke the `processException` method of each processor, in reverse order starting from the processor which generated the exception. The following sequence diagram highlights an exception being thrown by one of the action processors within the pipeline:

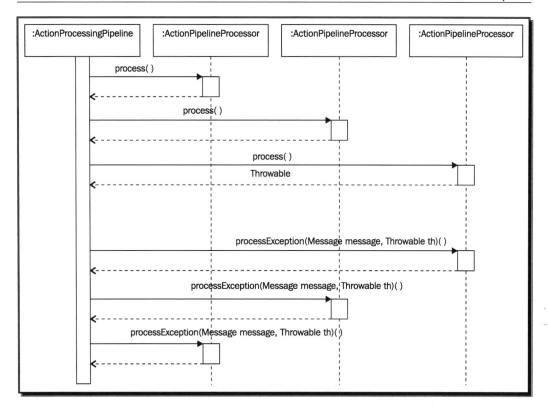

Time for action – examining exceptions

Let us now add an exception handler method to our `MyAction` class:

1. Add the following method to the `MyAction.java` file:

```
public void processException(final Message message,
    final Throwable th) {
    System.out.println("Something happened: " + th.getMessage());
}
```

2. Let us throw an exception deliberately from one of our process methods. Add a new method as follows:

```
public Message causesException(Message message)
    throws ActionProcessingException {
        System.out.println("About to cause an exception");
        throw new ActionProcessingException("BAD STUFF HAPPENED");
}
```

3. Add the following `import` statement:

```
import org.jboss.soa.esb.actions.ActionProcessingException;
```

4. Open the `jboss-esb.xml` file and add another action with **Name** specified as "BadAction" to the service **Class** as "org.jboss.soa.esb.samples.chapter3.MyAction" and "causesException" as the **Process** method:

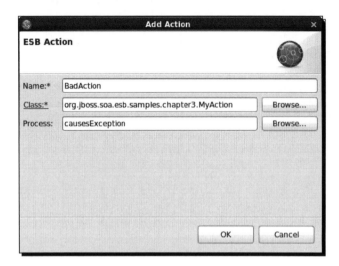

5. Add a new property to our `BodyPrinter` action. Enter **Name** as "exceptionMethod" and **Value** as "processException":

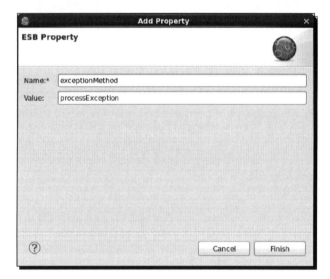

6. Click **Finish** and then **Save**.

7. Deploy the application using the **Run** menu and select **Run As | Run on Server**.

8. Run `SendJMSMessage.java` by clicking **Run**, select **Run As | Java Application**.

The following will be displayed in the console

```
INFO    [STDOUT]  ***************************************************
INFO    [STDOUT]  Body: Chapter 3 says Hello!
INFO    [STDOUT]  ***************************************************
INFO    [STDOUT]  About to cause an exception
INFO    [STDOUT]  Something happened: BAD STUFF HAPPENED
WARN    [ActionProcessingPipeline] No fault address defined for
fault message!
```

What just happened?

You just created an exception processing method and threw an exception from another new action. You can see the exception bubble up to the first action and its `processException` method is called.

Have a go hero – extending from AbstractActionPipelineProcessor

Write a new action class that extends `AbstractActionPipelineProcessor` and see what methods are provided by default. See how the default methods get executed when you use this action in our service.

Dynamic methods

JBoss ESB can allow the service definition to request the dynamic invocation of methods within the action class, allowing the action class to provide alternative processing methods which can be chosen through the configuration. The signature of the methods being invoked dynamically must match the signature of the original methods as they are defined in the `ActionPipelineProcessor` interface.

The following example shows how the alternative method implementations could be defined within the action class.

```java
public class DynamicAction extends AbstractActionLifecycle {
    public Message alternativeProcess(final Message message)
        throws ActionProcessingException  {
            ...
        }
    public void alternativeProcessSuccess(final Message message) {
```

```
        . . .
    }
    public void alternativeProcessException(final Message message,
                                            final Throwable th) {
        . . .
    }
}
```

These methods can then be used within the action configuration as follows:

```
<action class="DynamicAction" name="DynamicAction">
    <property name="process"
            value="alternativeProcess"/>
    <property name="okMethod"
            value="alternativeProcessSuccess"/>
    <property name="exceptionMethod"
            value="alternativeProcessException"/>
</action>
```

The configuration can specify multiple process methods, for example:

```
<property name="process"
        value="displayBody, displayHeader, displayContext"/>
```

This will result in each process method being invoked in sequence.

Have a go hero – multiple process methods

When we created the MyAction class we overrode the default process method with the displayMessage method. Now go ahead and add some more additional methods to displayBody, displayHeader, and so on, and see what appears in the console. Notice the order of execution as you defined in jboss-esb.xml.

MEP (Message Exchange Pattern) and responses

Any decision to send a response from a specific service pipeline is driven by three criteria:

♦ **The behavior of the actions within the service pipeline**: Each action is given an opportunity to process the message as it progresses through the pipeline. It can then decide whether the pipeline should continue to process the subsequent actions (or not) by returning the message to be passed to the next action. If an action decides to terminate the pipeline early then it must return null as its response. If the last action returns a message then this will be considered as the service pipeline response, subject to the following conditions also being met.

- **The value specified for the service MEP attribute**: The MEP (Message Exchange Pattern) attribute defines the intention of the current pipeline with regard to generating responses. The pipeline may represent one part of a composite service, in which case it does not determine how the composite service handles responses but rather the expectations of this individual section. The MEP can be defined as follows:

Service MEP	Service response behavior
Undefined	If the mep attribute is undefined then the response behavior is determined by whether the final action returns a message or not. If the final action returns a message then this will be considered as the response, otherwise the null response will terminate the pipeline without generating a response to the consumer.
OneWay	A OneWay MEP instructs the service pipeline to ignore the result of the final action and never process a response message, however a null response from an action can still cause the pipeline to terminate early.
RequestResponse	A RequestResponse MEP instructs the service pipeline to expect a response from the final action in the pipeline. Early termination of the pipeline, through one of the actions returning null, is considered exceptional behavior and will result in a warning message being emitted.

- **The routing information in the incoming message header**: If the preceding conditions have been met, and a response message has reached the end of the pipeline, then the final decision on whether to send a response will lie with the consumer of the service. When the consumer invokes the service it can specify its expectations by including a ReplyTo or From EPR within the header of the original message. These values will be cached at the beginning of the pipeline and, once the pipeline has completed, these will be used to determine the target endpoint for any response. If there is no ReplyTo nor From EPR specified within the header of the original message then the consumer is explicitly stating that it does not wish to receive a normal response from the execution of the pipeline.

The decision process for sending a fault message back to the consumer is a much simpler process, relying solely on the routing information specified by the consumer of the service. If the routing information includes a FaultTo, ReplyTo, or From EPR then this will identify the endpoint that must be used as the target endpoint for receiving any fault message. This endpoint need not be the same as the one which will receive a response message and, in fact, the consumer may declare that it does not wish to receive a response message but that it is still interested in receiving fault messages.

ServiceInvoker

Each service deployed within the ESB must be associated with one or more ESB Aware Listeners, physical endpoints through which the service can be invoked. An ESB Aware Listener is simply one which receives a message by means of a transport mechanism and will pass it through to a service pipeline for execution.

The current transport mechanisms supported by ESB Aware Listeners are as follows:

Transport	Description
Java Message Service (JMS)	A transactional, **Message Oriented Middleware** (**MOM**) transport which supports delivery and consumption of messages using point-to-point (Queue) and publish/subscribe (Topic) models.
InVM	A transactional transport which supports delivery and consumption of messages within the same Java virtual machine, using a point-to-point (Queue) model. The transport has no persistent storage, resulting in a loss of messages should the virtual machine terminate.
SQL	A transactional transport which uses a database as the persistent storage mechanism, supporting delivery and consumption of messages using a point-to-point (Queue) model.
File/FTP/FTPS/SFTP	A non-transactional transport which uses a local file system or remote File Transfer Protocol server as the persistent storage mechanism.

The ESB Aware Listener, as part of its initialization, will create an opaque EPR which represents the physical endpoint through which a service can be addressed. This EPR will be associated with the service through registration within the Service Registry and will be removed from the registry once the physical endpoint is no longer active. Service consumers can then discover the EPRs associated with every provider of a service by querying the Service Registry.

Although accessing a service seems complicated, all details associated with querying the registry and communicating with the physical endpoints are taken care of by the `org.jboss.soa.esb.client.ServiceInvoker` utility class. The service consumer only has to handle the creation of the message and decide whether the invocation should be synchronous (requiring a response) or asynchronous (deferred or no response).

The `ServiceInvoker` instance is intended to be cached by the consumer and reused for multiple invocations of the service. Creation of the `ServiceInvoker` will result in a query to the Service Registry, a relatively expensive operation, and this should be avoided when possible.

Synchronous delivery

Synchronous delivery is intended to be used by code requiring a response from a service before it can continue, such as the following:

```
final ServiceInvoker invoker = new ServiceInvoker(category, name) ;
final Message response = invoker.deliverSync(request, timeout) ;
```

The service consumer invokes the `deliverSync` method, specifying a timeout declaring how long it is prepared to wait for a response from the service invocation. An invocation may time out if the physical endpoint is no longer processing requests or if the load on the service is so great that it cannot process the request within the specified timeout period.

If the invocation does time out then the `ServiceInvoker` can choose to respond in one of two ways, depending on the current ESB configuration, they are as follows:

- **Throw a ResponseTimeoutException**: No further attempts will be made to deliver the request to the service, however, the request may still be processed by the service provider.

- **Obtain an EPR representing a different physical endpoint and attempt delivery**: The consumer will receive a response message if the next endpoint can process the request within the specified timeout period, however, the request may still be processed by the original endpoint. The application must be written to handle this scenario should it arise.

Asynchronous delivery

Asynchronous delivery can be used by code which does not expect a response or which is written to handle responses in an asynchronous manner, such as the following:

```
final ServiceInvoker invoker = new ServiceInvoker(category, name) ;
invoker.deliverAsync(request) ;
```

The service consumer does not wait for a response from the invocation, knowing that the message will be delivered and processed at some future point.

Using an asynchronous approach to invocations can result in an architecture that is more robust and performant than using synchronous delivery, after all a consumer which is not blocking while it waits for a response can be processing the next service request.

Time for action – examining exceptions

Let us now create a new way to invoke our service. Let us use the `ServiceInvoker`. Follow these steps:

1. Remove `BadAction` from our service list:

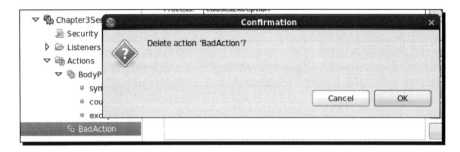

2. Click **OK**. Ensure that we have only one action, `BodyPrinter`.

3. Create a new class. Enter **Name** as "SendEsbMessage", **Package** as "org.jboss.soa.esb.samples.chapter3.test", check the box before **public static void main(String[] args)**:

4. Click **Finish**.

5. Add the following `imports` statements:

```
import org.jboss.soa.esb.message.Message;
import org.jboss.soa.esb.message.format.MessageFactory;
import org.jboss.soa.esb.client.ServiceInvoker;
```

6. Add `throws Exception` to the static `main` method:

```
public static void main(String args[]) throws Exception
```

7. Add the following to the `main` method:

```
System.setProperty("javax.xml.registry.ConnectionFactoryClass",
        "org.apache.ws.scout.registry.ConnectionFactoryImpl");
Message esbMessage = MessageFactory.getInstance().getMessage();

esbMessage.getBody().add(
                "Chapter 3 says Hello via ServiceInvoker!");
new ServiceInvoker("Chapter3Sample",
        "Chapter3Service").deliverAsync(esbMessage);
```

8. Select the `jboss-esb.xml` file, click **Save**.

9. Deploy the application using the **Run** menu and select **Run As | Run on Server**.

10. Select the `src` folder, expand it till the `SendEsbMessage.java` file is displayed in the tree. Now click **Run**, select **Run As | Java Application**.

The following message will be printed in the console

```
INFO   [STDOUT] ***********************************************
INFO   [STDOUT] Body: Chapter 3 says Hello via ServiceInvoker!
INFO   [STDOUT] ***********************************************
```

What just happened?

You created a new file (`SendEsbMessage.java`) and added a few lines of code and voila, we were able to send an ESB message to the bus targeting our service. How did this work? The underlying mechanism is hidden by the `ServiceInvoker`. The `ServiceInvoker` uses the `jbossesb-properties.xml` file found under the root of our application project. This file contains all needed configurations for the `ServiceInvoker` to read and query the registry. Have a brief look at this file in JBoss Developer Studio before proceeding further.

Have a go hero – experimenting with MEPs and sync delivery

Go ahead and modify the MEP for our service as `RequestResponse`. You will need the following modifications to `SendEsbMessage`:

```
Message response = new ServiceInvoker("Chapter3Sample",
        "Chapter3Service").deliverSync(esbMessage, 5000);
System.out.println(response.getBody().get());
```

You will also need to add a reply queue to the `jbm-queue-service.xml` file:

```
<mbean code="org.jboss.jms.server.destination.QueueService"
       name="jboss.esb.book.samples.destination:
             service=Queue,name=chapter3_Request_esb_reply"
       xmbean-dd="xmdesc/Queue-xmbean.xml">
  <depends optional-attribute- name="ServerPeer">
    jboss.messaging:service=ServerPeer
  </depends>
  <depends>jboss.messaging:service=PostOffice</depends>
</mbean>
```

Update the `MyAction` class to modify the payload on the return message. See how the application behaves.

Composite services

One of the major advantages of an ESB is the ability to define composite services, in other words taking existing services and combining them to create new services which can take advantage of existing functionality. This is possible because of the loose coupling and reusability encouraged in an SOA environment.

Service Chaining

Service Chaining is a topology whereby a service can be implemented through the execution of two or more service implementations, in sequence, with each service within the composite, providing specific, reusable functionality.

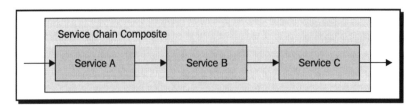

Each service in the chain, with the possible exception of the last in the sequence, will be declared with a service `mep` attribute value of `OneWay`. This will tell the framework that these service implementations will not provide a direct response to the service consumer, but rather this should be handled by the last service in the chain.

An example configuration for these services could be as follows:

```
<service category="composite" name="ChainedService"
        description="Chained Service Service A">
  ...
  <actions mep="OneWay">
    ...
    <action name="routeToNext"
            class="org.jboss.soa.esb.actions.StaticRouter">
      <property name="destinations">
        <route-to service-category="composite"
                service-name="ChainedServiceB"/>
      </property>
    </action>
  </actions>
</service>

<service category="composite" name="ChainedServiceB"
        description="Chained Service Service B">
  ...
  <actions mep="OneWay">
    ...
    <action name="routeToNext"
            class="org.jboss.soa.esb.actions.StaticRouter">
      <property name="destinations">
        <route-to service-category="composite"
                service-name="ChainedServiceC"/>
      </property>
    </action>
  </actions>
</service>

<service category="composite" name="ChainedServiceC"
        description="Chained Service Service C">
  ...
  <actions mep="RequestResponse">
    ...
  </actions>
</service>
```

The example uses a `StaticRouter` action to forward the message from one service within the chain to the next service in the sequence. The application may choose to route the message using other actions, for example `ContentBasedRouter`, in order to support topology defining multiple chains which react to the contents of the message.

Have a go hero – adding more services

Based on what you learned in this section, add more services to our `Chapter3` application. Experiment with some more additional `action` classes. Try using `ServiceInvoker` in your custom action instead of `StaticRouter`.

Service Continuations

Service Continuations is a topology whereby a service implementation can be split into multiple parts in order to allow the synchronous invocations of services to occur in an asynchronous manner. The main benefits of executing a synchronous invocation in this manner are:

◆ **Increased performance**: Service consumers are no longer waiting to receive a response from the service provider, allowing the consuming pipeline to process the next message in its queue.

◆ **Increased reliability**: Each part can be encompassed in a transactional unit of work, allowing the processing of the service to move from one consistent state to the next.

A typical example of a synchronous invocation may look as follows:

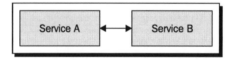

The disadvantages of this implementation are:

◆ The processing of **Service A** will be blocked while it awaits the response from **Service B**, preventing any resources it may hold from being reused.

◆ The processing of **Service A** cannot occur within a transactional context as the delivery of the request message to **Service B** will not occur until the transaction commits.

The processing involved in **Service A** can be split into two services, the first containing the functionality being executed up until the point where the synchronous invocation of **Service B** would be made, the second service (the continuation) containing the functionality which would be executed after the response is received.

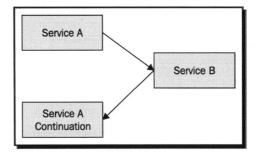

Service A would now send an asynchronous request to **Service B**, specifying the Continuation service as the ReplyTo endpoint within the request header. This will allow the execution of **Service A** to be encompassed by a transactional context, providing atomic and consistent execution, and will then allow it to release any resources being held in order to process any subsequent requests in its queue.

Service B would process the request as before, completely oblivious to the changes that have been made within **Service A**. Once complete, the pipeline for **Service B** would send the response to the continuation service, which can then resume processing of the original request within a second transactional context.

 While it is important to be aware of Service Continuations and their benefit to the architecture of an application, the specifics of implementing this topology is an advanced topic that goes beyond the scope of this book.

Transactions

One of the most important functional aspects supported by the service pipeline is that of the transactional execution of the pipeline, in other words the ability to execute all of the actions and message deliveries within a single, consistent context.

Transactional behavior is usually defined using the acronym ACID:

- **Atomicity**: A transactional context is atomic, which means that every transactional resource within the context will be updated if the transaction is successful. If the transaction is unsuccessful then the transactional resources will remain unchanged.

- **Consistency**: If the transaction is successful then each transactional resource will move from one consistent state to another.

◆ **Isolation**: Each transactional context is isolated from any other transactional context. Any modifications to a transactional resource will not be visible to other contexts until the transaction has successfully committed.

◆ **Durability**: A successful transaction will result in the transactional resources persisting their state in such a way that they can be recovered, should anything go wrong.

JBoss ESB supports three transactional transports, JMS, SQL, and InVM, with both the JMS and SQL transports supporting full ACID properties. The InVM transport relaxes the ACID properties and does not support durability, its message queue is maintained in volatile memory and will be lost should the ESB server terminate.

When a message is delivered to the service pipeline, using one of the transports that supports transactional delivery, it is possible to execute all of the actions in the pipeline within a transactional context. Each transactional resource accessed within the actions will be enlisted as part of the transaction, allowing the transaction manager to control the consistent outcome of the pipeline execution.

When using a transactional transport to deliver messages it is important to understand when the messages will be sent. Each message sent using a transactional transport will be associated with the encompassing transaction and will only be sent once the transaction commits. The consequence of this is that sending a message to a service, then waiting for the response within the same transaction, will not work.

If the framework detects an attempt to execute a synchronous invocation, while in a transactional context, then it will raise an `IncompatibleTransactionScopeException` exception.

One way to handle this requirement is to split the processing of the pipeline into two sections, each with their own transactional context. See Continuations for more information on this topology.

Have a go hero – transactional quickstart

Have a look at the `jms_transacted` quickstart. This demonstrates the usage of transacted JMS queues. Modify the quickstart and add `MyAction` to it so that the context information is printed. Do you see anything in the context?

Security context

The service pipeline supports security through the standard **Java Authentication and Authorization Service (JAAS)**. Using this mechanism a service can require that a consumer of the service must provide valid authentication credentials within the message context, and may also require that the authenticated principal be associated with specific roles.

The service security requirements are configured by including the security element within the service definition, as in the following:

```
<service category="SecuredCategory" name="SecuredService"
         description="Secured Service">
  <security moduleName="securedModule" rolesAllowed="worker">
    <property name="alias" value="certtest"/>
  </security>
  ...
</service>
```

Where `moduleName` specifies the name of the module within the JAAS configuration and `rolesAllowed` specifies any roles that are required to be associated with the authenticated principal.

When a message is sent to another service, using `ServiceInvoker`, the security context from the consumer will be automatically attached to the outgoing message as part of the message context and propagated to the service provider. This security context consists of two parts:

◆ **An encrypted, pre-authenticated, principal**: If this principal exists within the context of the message then it will be trusted as long as the service provider exists within the same ESB server (virtual machine) as the original signer, the principal has been authenticated by the same JAAS module and that the encrypted object has not yet expired. If any of these conditions are not satisfied then re-authentication will occur.

◆ **An encrypted authentication request**: The authentication request contains the information necessary to authenticate the consumer, by default this will be the name associated with a security principal and its password credential.

The authentication request will usually be created automatically, as the request comes onto the bus, however, it is also possible to create an authentication request through the following programmatic mechanism:

```
final AuthenticationRequest authRequest =
    new AuthenticationRequestImpl.Builder()
        .username(name)
        .password(password.toCharArray())
        .build();

message.getContext().setContext(SecurityService.AUTH_REQUEST,
PublicCryptoUtil.INSTANCE.encrypt((Serializable) authRequest));
```

The security mechanisms supported by JBoss ESB can be extended in a number of ways, supporting authentication using certificates, single sign-on, and so on.

Have a go hero – security quickstart

Have a look at the `security_basic` quickstart. Modify the quickstart action `MyListenerAction.java` so that the context information is printed. Do you see anything in the context?

Summary

In this chapter we have spent a significant amount of time covering the main aspects of the Action Pipeline and how these aspects can affect the design decisions which are made when implementing services.

You should now have a good understanding of:

♦ The structure of an ESB message, including the header and message context

♦ Enforcing payload contracts through XML and XSD

♦ How the configuration is represented within the service and associated actions, including how it can be traversed

♦ The lifecycle and processing behavior for the actions within the pipeline

♦ How processing methods can be overridden through configuration

♦ How response behavior is controlled through the pipeline actions, MEP service attributes, and consumer requirements

♦ More advanced service topologies such as Service Chaining and Service Continuations

♦ The transactional behavior of the pipeline

♦ The principles behind the security context and its propagation

In some of these areas we have only touched the surface, providing enough information to allow you to begin exploring what is possible within a service. There are many external resources which can provide a deeper understanding of the more advanced sections.

Now that we've learned about Services, we're ready to look deep into action classes and some built-in actions, which is the topic of the next chapter.

4

JBoss ESB Service Actions

Actions are the basic building blocks of ESB services. In the previous chapter, we discussed ESB services and their behavior, how to combine services, and touched on the use of actions within a service. In this chapter we'll go into a deeper discussion of actions, how and when to write your own action, and what actions are provided to you within JBoss ESB.

You'll learn about:

◆ What actions are and how you can combine actions into an "action chain" to have your services perform complex, multi-step tasks.

◆ How you can make use of JBoss ESB's extensive set of out-of-the-box (OOTB) actions to perform tasks without your having to write custom code.

◆ And finally, how you can write custom actions to perform tasks that are not already supported by OOTB actions.

Understanding actions

For JBoss ESB services, actions are literally where the action is. Sorry, pardon the pun, please!

But, seriously, actions are the means by which services perform their tasks. Actions are how you route messages between services, convert (or "transform") data from one form to another, execute scripts or exercise integrations between JBoss ESB and other packages.

There are two types of actions:

- ◆ **Out-of-the-box actions**: A wide array of out-of-the-box (OOTB) actions ship with JBoss ESB. When you are designing your services, the place to start is the out-of-the-box actions. These have all been tested with JBoss ESB and they've also been documented and used as examples by the quickstarts.

- ◆ **Custom actions**: These are actions that you design and build yourself. We'll discuss both types of actions, how you use them, and, for custom actions, how you build them, in this chapter.

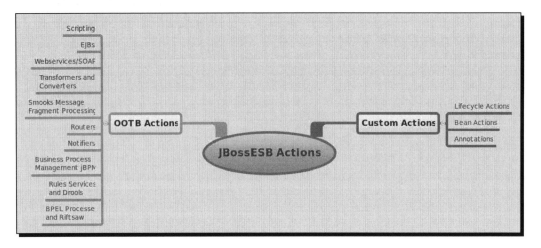

What is an action class?

An action class is simply a class which processes a message.

An action can be as simple as a class which prints some of the contents of the message or as complex as one that triggers process flows based upon the message. An action class is activated by the service receiving a message.

As part of a service, actions are generally combined in an action chain, where a single message will be processed by multiple actions. Actions classes usually perform a single atomic action upon a message, but the combination of action classes within an action chain allows services to perform complex tasks and processing of messages.

Action classes are externally configured by properties and settings within the jboss-esb.xml configuration file. The configuration appears within the action class as a ConfigTree object.

An action class usually has initialize and destroy methods, which set up and clean up resources. Additionally there is a process method that performs some sort of stateless action upon the message.

The action chain

In the course of explaining actions in this chapter, and illustrating actions in many of the quickstarts, we'll mostly concentrate on one action at a time. While this is a useful approach for learning how to use actions, it doesn't make use of the full power of what JBoss ESB can achieve with the "action chain". By chaining actions together, where the message that is the output from one action serves as the input (message) to another action, JBoss ESB enables your services to be constructed of building blocks of loosely coupled, reusable code.

The following code is a sample action chain, defined in the `jboss-esb.xml` configuration file. This action chain has three actions—a custom action (`action1`), an OOTB action which prints the message to the console (`action2`), and an OOTB action which stores the message's contents in a JMX MBean for integration testing (`action3`).

```
<actions mep="OneWay">
    <action name="action1"
            class="org.jboss.soa.esb.samples.quickstart.
                    helloworld.MySampleAction"
            process="displayMessage" />
    <action name="action2"
            class="org.jboss.soa.esb.actions.SystemPrintln">
        <property name="printfull" value="false"/>
    </action>
    <!-- The next action is for Continuous Integration testing -->
    <action name="testStore"
            class="org.jboss.soa.esb.actions.TestMessageStore"/>
</actions>
```

Each action has a `name`, a `class`, and an optional `process` attribute, which specifies the method in the class which will be executed when it receives a message. If no `process` attribute is specified, it assumes that there is a method within your class

Within the action chain, the service name must be unique—you cannot have two services with the same name or you will receive an error upon deploying your ESB archive.

Notice in the example that there is an `mep` property on the `actions` element. MEP stands for Message Exchange Pattern and the supported values of MEP for an action chain are:

◆ `OneWay`: A `OneWay` MEP means that pipeline will not send a response, that is, at the end of the action chain, it does not send a response.

◆ `RequestResponse`: This MEP means that the pipeline will send a message to the `ReplyTo` EPR or the `From` EPR if that isn't specified. We'll talk about what an EPR is in *Chapter 7*, but for now know that you'll want to use `RequestResponse` in certain instances, such as when you are using the `HttpGateway`, or if you are using the `ServiceInvoker` in synchronous mode.

Let's look at an example:

```
<actions mep="OneWay">
    <action name="action0"
            class="org.jboss.soa.esb.actions.SystemPrintln">
        <property name="printfull" value="false"/>
    </action>
    <action name="action1"
            class="org.jboss.soa.esb.samples.quickstart.
                    helloworld.SimpleAdditionAction"
            process="addMessageContent"/>
    <action name="action2"
            class="org.jboss.soa.esb.actions.SystemPrintln">
        <property name="printfull" value="false"/>
    </action>
    <action name="action3"
            class="org.jboss.soa.esb.samples.quickstart.
                    helloworld.SimpleAdditionAction"
            process="addMessageContent"/>
    <action name="action4"
            class="org.jboss.soa.esb.actions.SystemPrintln">
        <property name="printfull" value="false"/>
    </action>
</actions>
```

For example, if we send a message containing the number "1" to the chain, the custom action `SimpleAdditionAction` assumes that the message content is an integer, and adds 1 to it. In this case, we would see output like the following:

```
15:56:22,407 INFO   [STDOUT] Message structure:
15:56:22,407 INFO   [STDOUT] [1].
15:56:25,408 INFO   [STDOUT] Message structure:
15:56:25,409 INFO   [STDOUT] [2].
15:56:28,409 INFO   [STDOUT] Message structure:
15:56:28,409 INFO   [STDOUT] [3].
```

The message is printed three times (by action0, action2, and action4). As you notice, you can use the same action class multiple times in the same actionChain in order to repeat functionality. In this case, we print the initial message (1), then add 1 to it, print it (2), add 1 to it again, and then print it a final time (3).

Custom actions

We'll start with custom actions to give you an understanding of the structure of an action class. There are three different approaches you can take to have your code function as a custom action:

- Lifecycle actions
- JavaBean actions
- Custom actions using annotations

Lifecycle actions

The first approach is to create lifecycle actions.

These are used by many of the OOTB JBoss ESB actions. These actions implement the org. jboss.soa.esb.actions.ActionLifecycle interface, or its sub-interface org.jboss. soa.esb.actions.ActionPipelineProcessor.

You can see the list of these actions here:

http://docs.jboss.org/jbossesb/docs/4.10/javadoc/esb/org/jboss/soa/esb/actions/ActionLifecycle.html

The actions are listed in the javadoc as the classes implementing the interface. These actions implement the life-cycle model for an action through these methods:

- initialize
- destroy
- process (ActionPipelineProcessor only)
- processSuccess (ActionPipelineProcessor only)
- processException (ActionPipelineProcessor only)

In this context, "lifecycle" refers to the lifecycle of a stateless action pipeline.

The initialize and destroy methods can be overridden to enable you to create resources that will be used throughout the execution of the action pipeline.

Any methods that you implement in your custom actions beyond these methods are located and executed by Java reflection.

To make things easier, abstract base classes (org.jboss.soa.esb.actions. AbstractActionPipelineProcessor and org.jboss.soa.esb.actions. AbstractActionLifecycle) that implement these interfaces are included with JBoss ESB. You can simply extend either of these abstract classes in your custom actions. These classes include sub methods for everything except the process methods.

The lifecycle actions have to include a constructor which uses an org.jboss.soa. esb.helpers.ConfigTree instance as a parameter. The ConfigTree refers to the configuration of the action.

Now let's look at some examples of lifecycle actions.

The simplest lifecycle action that you're likely to ever see is included in the "helloworld" quickstart. The lifecycle action is referenced in the jboss-esb.xml file as shown:

```
<action name="action1"
        class="org.jboss.soa.esb.samples.quickstart.
            helloworld.MyJMSListenerAction"
        process="displayMessage" />
```

What are the properties defined for this action? They are as follows:

- name: A unique (again, unique within the given service) name for the action
- class: The full class name for the custom action. We'll look at the source code for this action in a moment.
- process: Remember how we talked about overriding the process method? This is an example.

Here's the source for the action (the file is under the quickstart helloworld directory: src/ org/jboss/soa/esb/samples/quickstart/helloworld/ MyJMSListenerAction.java):

```
package org.jboss.soa.esb.samples.quickstart.helloworld;
import org.jboss.soa.esb.actions.AbstractActionLifecycle;
import org.jboss.soa.esb.helpers.ConfigTree;
import org.jboss.soa.esb.message.Message;
public class MyJMSListenerAction extends AbstractActionLifecycle {
    protected ConfigTree _config;
    public MyJMSListenerAction(ConfigTree config) {
        _config = config; }
    public Message displayMessage(Message message) throws Exception{
        System.out.println(
            "&&&&&&&&&&&&&&&&&&&&&&&&&&&&&&&&&&&&&&&&&&&&&&&&&&&&&");
```

```
                System.out.println("Body: " + message.getBody().get()) ;
                System.out.println(
                    "&&&&&&&&&&&&&&&&&&&&&&&&&&&&&&&&&&&&&&&&&&&&&&&&");
                return message;
            }
        }
```

Let's take a closer look at this code:

- The `import` statements bring in the `AbstractActionLifecycle` and ESB's message. The `ConfigTree` is needed by ESB to access the action's set of attributes, parse its XML configuration, and so on. The action's constructor must initialize the `ConfigTree`.

- The class definition shows how the action class extends the `AbstractActionLifecycle` interface.

- The `displayMessage` method definition corresponds to the overridden `process` method defined in the listener's definition in `jboss-esb.xml`.

The `custom_action` quickstart demonstrates these other types of lifecycle actions:

- In the following lifecycle action, JBoss ESB looks for a method named `process` when the action fires:

```
<action class="org.jboss.soa.esb.samples.quickstart.
                customaction.MyBasicAction"
        exceptionMethod="exceptionHandler" />
```

- In the following lifecycle action, the three methods defined by the `process` property are executed in sequence, when the action fires:

```
<action class="org.jboss.soa.esb.samples.quickstart.
                customaction.StatefulAction"
        process="methodOne,methodTwo,displayCount"
        exceptionMethod="exceptionHandler" />
```

- The following lifecycle action shows you can create your own custom attributes for the action tag and even have child elements for that action. As the quickstart's documentation points out, this approach can be used to make the action more easily configurable, as follows:

```
<action class="org.jboss.soa.esb.samples.quickstart.
                customaction.CustomConfigAction"
        process="displayConfig" myStuff="rocks"
        moreStuff="rocks harder">
    <subElement1>Value of 1</subElement1>
    <subElement2>Value of 2</subElement2>
    <subElement3>Value of 3</subElement3>
</action>
```

JavaBean actions

The second approach for building custom actions is to create JavaBean actions. These actions implement the `org.jboss.soa.esb.actions.BeanConfiguredAction` interface. These actions are differentiated from the lifecycle actions in several ways, as follows:

- They set properties with "setter" methods. These methods map to the actions' property names.

- They do not support the lifecycle methods (`initialize`, `destroy`, `process`, `processSuccess`, and `processException`). Instead, these actions are instantiated when a message is processed by the action pipeline.

- Unlike lifecycle actions, JavaBean actions' `process` methods are always executed through Java reflection.

An example of this type of action is also illustrated in the `custom_action` quickstart:

```
<action name="seventh"
        class="org.jboss.soa.esb.samples.quickstart.
               customaction.CustomBeanConfigAction">
    <property name="information" value="Hola Mundo" />
    <property name="repeatCount" value="5"/>
</action>
```

In this action definition, the bean's setter methods will be invoked with the properties defined in the `jboss-esb.xml` file.

And here's a fragment from the `org.jboss.soa.esb.samples.quickstart.customaction.CustomBeanConfigAction` class. Note that the setter methods correspond to the property names:

```
public void setInformation(String information) {
    this.information = information;
}
public void setRepeatCount(Integer repeatCount) {
    this.repeatCount = repeatCount;
}

    public Message process(Message message) throws
            ActionProcessingException {
    System.out.println("[" + serviceCategory + ":" +
            serviceName + "] Repeat message: " + information +
            " " + repeatCount + " times:");
    for (int i=0; i < repeatCount; i++) {
        System.out.println(information);
    }
    return message;
}
```

Custom actions using annotations

One common trend in Java programing is that of simplifying complex structures and technologies with annotations. For example, EJB3 removed several of the complex and annoying requirements of EJB2 through the use of annotations. The third approach to creating custom actions that JBoss ESB provides is an annotation mechanism through which an action class can be created and configured. In order for the class to be identified as an annotated action, one or more of its public methods must be annotated with the `org.jboss.soa.esb.actions.annotation.Process` annotation.

When using an annotated action class it is no longer necessary to handle the `ConfigTree`, the configuration being handled through annotating fields or setter methods from within the class. There are some restrictions in the configuration types which can be used through this mechanism.

Fields and setter methods should be annotated with the `org.jboss.soa.esb.configure.ConfigProperty` annotation, for example:

```
@ConfigProperty
private int intConfig;

@ConfigProperty(use=Use.OPTIONAL)
private String stringConfig;

@ConfigProperty(name="AlternativeName")
public void setEnumConfig(final MyEnum value) {
   ...
}
```

The `ConfigProperty` annotation can be configured through the following annotation elements:

- `name`: An optional element which defines the `ConfigTree` attribute name. If this element is not specified then the attribute name will match the name of the field or will be derived from the setter method using the JavaBean conventions.

- `use`: An optional element which defines whether the property is `REQUIRED` or `OPTIONAL`, defaulting to `REQUIRED`. It is an error if a `REQUIRED` property cannot be assigned a value.

- `DefaultVal`: An optional element which defines the default value to use for the property if a value has not been specified within the action configuration.

- `Choice`: An optional element which restricts the property values to a specified set. It is an error if a property is configured to a value not present within the choice set.

Note that annotations using the `ConfigTree` annotation can only be configured using simple `name`/`value` properties, it is not possible to use hierarchical configurations nor to traverse the `ConfigTree` hierarchy. The property types must be primitive or must define a constructor taking a single String parameter.

Lifecycle annotations

An annotated action can define any number of public initialization methods, each of which must be annotated with the `org.jboss.soa.esb.lifecycle.annotation.Initialize` annotation. For example:

```
@Initialize
public void firstInit() {
    ...
}

@Initialize
public void secondInit(final ConfigTree configTree)
        throws ActionLifecycleException {
    ...
}
```

The `Initialize` methods may take an optional `ConfigTree` parameter and may throw an `ActionLifecycleException`.

An annotated action can also define any number of public destroy methods, each being annotated with the `org.jboss.soa.esb.lifecycle.annotation.Destroy` annotation. For example:

```
@Destroy
public void firstDestroy() {
    ...
}

@Destroy
public void secondDestroy(final ConfigTree configTree)
        throws ActionLifecycleException {
    ...
}
```

The `Destroy` methods may take an optional `ConfigTree` parameter and may throw an `ActionLifecycleException`.

Processing annotations

An annotated action can define any number of public `process` methods, each being annotated with the `org.jboss.soa.esb.actions.annotation.Process` annotation, however only one method may be executed and this must be chosen through the action configuration.

```
@Process
public Message process(final Message message)
        throws    ActionProcessingException {
    ...
}
```

`Process` methods may be defined with any number of parameters and may choose not to return a value, for example:

```
// method expecting the default message payload to be of type MyType,
// returning a String value for the response payload.
@Process
public String processMyType(final MyType payload) {
    ...
}

// method accessing the full message without updating
// the response payload
@Process
public void processMessage(final Message message) {
    ...
}

// method ignoring message contents and updating response payload
@Process
public MyType process() {
    ...
}
```

The parameter values passed to a `process` method may be configured using a number of annotations; if none are present then the values are resolved as follows:

- **Message type**: Pass the current message as the parameter.
- **Type matches default payload type**: Pass the default payload as the parameter.
- **Other type**: Locate an entry in the message body, property, or attachment which can be assigned to the parameter type.

- **org.jboss.soa.esb.actions.annotation.BodyParam**: This annotation takes an optional value which identifies which part of the message body to pass to the method. If not specified then the parameter is resolved by searching through all entries in the message body for the first value which can be assigned to the parameter type.

- **org.jboss.soa.esb.actions.annotation.PropertyParam**: This annotation takes an optional value which identifies which part of the message properties to pass to the method. If not specified then the parameter is resolved by searching through all entries in the message properties for the first value which can be assigned to the parameter type.

- **org.jboss.soa.esb.actions.annotation.AttachmentParam**: This annotation takes an optional value which identifies which part of the message attachments to pass to the method. If not specified then the parameter is resolved by searching through all entries in the message attachments for the first value which can be assigned to the parameter type.

Examples of these annotations are as follows:

```
public String processAnnotations(
        @BodyParam("MyBody") MyBodyType body,
        @PropertyParam("MyProperty") Integer property,
        @AttachmentParam("MyAttachment") byte[] attachment) {
    . . .
}
```

 Note that relying on any of the cascading searches through body, property, and attachments sections of the message could result in a non-deterministic resolution of the parameter if more than one entry may be assigned to the property type.

An annotated action can define any number of public `processSuccess` methods, each of which must be annotated using the `org.jboss.soa.esb.actions.annotation.OnSuccess` annotation. Each `processSuccess` method will be invoked when a successful invocation of the pipeline has occurred and may be defined with no parameters or with a single `Message` parameter, for example:

```
@OnSuccess
public void firstSuccess() {
    . . .
}

@OnSuccess
public void secondSuccess(final Message message) {
    . . .
}
```

An annotated action may also define any number of public `processException` methods, each of which must be annotated using the `org.jboss.soa.esb.actions.annotation.OnException` annotation. Each `processException` method will be invoked when an exception is raised during an invocation of the pipeline and may be defined with no parameters, a single `Message` parameter or a `Message` and `Throwable` parameters, for example:

```
@OnException
public void firstException() {
    ...
}

@OnException
public void secondException(final Message message) {
    ...
}

@OnException
public void thirdException(final Message message, final Throwable th)
{
    ...
}
```

Out-of-the-box (OOTB) actions—how and when to use them

The out-of-the-box actions implemented in JBoss ESB are divided into the following functional groups:

- **Scripting**: Automating tasks in scripting languages
- **EJBs**: Invoking EJBs
- **Web services/SOAP**: Support for web services
- **Transformers/Converters**: How your services can change data from one form to another
- **Smooks message fragment processing:** How your services can split, enrich, or validate data with Smooks
- **Routers**: How your services can move messages between services
- **Notifiers**: How your services can send messages to destinations outside ESB
- **Business Process Management**: Integrating with JBoss jBPM
- **Rules Services**: Integrating with Drools

- ◆ **BPEL Processes**: Integrating with Riftsaw
- ◆ **Miscellaneous**: There's also a miscellaneous group that includes only one very simple action—`org.jboss.soa.esb.actions.SystemPrintln`. This action prints off a message.

We'll examine each of these groups of out-of-the-box actions in the sections that follow.

Scripting

Scripting actions make it possible for you to actually create custom actions, from within an OOTB action, by writing the custom code using a scripting language. This approach mirrors the way in which scripting languages are being used instead of compiled code to greater and greater degrees every year. As of release 4.10 of JBoss ESB, the following scripting actions are supported:

- ◆ **GroovyActionProcessor**:
  `org.jboss.soa.esb.actions.scripting.GroovyActionProcessor`
  The name is a dead give-away; as this action enables you to use Groovy scripts. Here's an example of an action that invokes the OOTB `GroovyActionProcessor` action:

  ```
  <action name="groovyHelloWorld"
          class="org.jboss.soa.esb.actions.scripting.
                 GroovyActionProcessor">
      <property name="script" value="/scripts/helloWorld.groovy" />
  </action>
  ```

- ◆ **ScriptingAction**:
  `org.jboss.soa.esb.actions.scripting.ScriptingAction`
  This action enables you to use the **Bean Scripting Framework (BSF**—`http://jakarta.apache.org/bsf/`). This framework supports BeanShell, Jython, and JRuby scripts. Here's an example of an action that invokes the OOTB ScriptingAction action:

  ```
  <action name="add_beanshell_link" class="org.jboss.soa.esb.
  actions.scripting.ScriptingAction">
      <!-- use a .beanshell extension vs. bsh or the
  BeanShellDeployer will pick it up inadvertently -->
      <property name="script" value="/scripts/link.beanshell" />
  </action>
  ```

Pay attention to the comment. If you use a `.bsh` file extension, the BeanShellDeployer (this is a tool that enables you to deploy scripts or services for one-time use—see `http://community.jboss.org/wiki/BSHDeployer`) will deploy the script.

Services—invoking EJBs

As we've mentioned more than once already, one of the great strengths of JBoss ESB is how it makes it possible for you to integrate different types of services and systems together, and have them communicate through a loosely coupled architecture, by sending messages over the ESB. One way in which JBoss ESB makes this integration possible is by enabling you to interact with EJBs.

The **EJBProcessor** (`org.jboss.soa.esb.actions.EJBProcessor`) action accepts a message and uses it to locate and invoke an EJB. You can send parameters to an EJB and retrieve values from EJBs. Let's look at an example of an action that invokes an EJB, and sends it parameters.

```
<action name="EJBTestVoid"
        class="org.jboss.soa.esb.actions.EJBProcessor">
    <property name="ejb3" value="true" />
    <property name="method" value="printMessage" />
    <property name="jndi-name" value="SimpleSLSB/remote" />
    <property name="initial-context-factory"
            value="org.jnp.interfaces.NamingContextFactory" />
    <property name="provider-url" value="localhost:1099" />
    <property name="ejb-params">
        <arg0 type="java.lang.String">
            org.jboss.soa.esb.message.defaultEntry
        </arg0>
    </property>
</action>
```

What's interesting to note here is that in order for the `EJBProcessor` action to be able to locate the EJB and find the right method to invoke, the parameter list includes as message properties the EJB's `jndi-name`, its `initial-context-factory` and the other parameters needed by the EJB.

 Note that JBoss ESB supports both EJB2 and EJB3 through this action.

Web services/SOAP

There are three web service-related out-of-the-box actions in JBoss ESB. Each serves a different function and they are detailed in the following:

♦ SOAPProcessor: This action is used to expose web service endpoints. Write a service wrapper web service (JSR181) that calls your target web service and exposes it through JBoss ESB listeners. These three types of JBoss WS web service endpoints can be exposed through JBoss ESB listeners using this action:

   ❑ **Web service bundled into a JBoss ESB .esb archive**: When the web service .war is bundled into a deployed .esb archive

   ❑ **Web service bundled into a .ear**: When the .war is bundled into a deployed .ear

   ❑ **Standalone web service**: When the web service .war is deployed

♦ WISE SOAPClient: This action uses the WISE client service to create a JAX-WS client class and then call the target service. The message is then routed to that service.

♦ SOAPClient: This action uses the soapUI client service to create a SOAP message and then route that message to the target service.

Time for action – running the quickstart

We will see the web services quickstart in the following steps:

1. Change your current directory to the quickstart's directory samples/quickstarts/webservice_consumer1. Deploy the quickstart using the ant deploy command.

2. Before running the quickstart, review the jboss-esb.xml file and see how the message is directed towards a SOAP endpoint which this quickstart also installs.

3. Run the quickstart using the ant runtest command.

4. Review the quickstart's output in the server.log file.

What just happened?

In this quickstart, the ESB deploys both a WAR and an ESB archive. The WAR archive contains a web service, HelloWorldWS. When we invoked the runtest target, we sent a JMS message to the service, which then invoked HelloWorldWS using the request we provided from the JMS message. The SOAP response is then displayed on the console by the custom MyResponseAction action.

Transformers/converters

These OOTB actions are used by services that expect data in different forms to communicate with each other, without you having to create glue code to convert that data from one form to another. The specific data that transformers and converters process is a message's "payload" (the message body and the message's attachments and defined properties). The default way for an action to get/set a message's payload is through the `MessagePayloadProxy` class.

The specific actions in the transformers and converters actions group are:

- **ByteArrayToString**:
  `org.jboss.soa.esb.actions.converters.ByteArrayToString`
  This action converts a `byte[]` message payload into a Java String.

- **LongToDateConverter**:
  `org.jboss.soa.esb.actions.converters.LongToDateConverter`
  This action converts a Java Long type in the message payload into a `java.util.Date`.

- **ObjectInvoke**:
  `org.jboss.soa.esb.actions.converters.ObjectInvoke`
  This action takes a serialized object, which consists of full message payload, and passes it to a configured processor class. The processed results then become the new message payload.

- **ObjectToCSVString**:
  `org.jboss.soa.esb.actions.converters.ObjectToCSVString`
  This action converts a message into a comma separated string based on a list of property names that you supply.

- **ObjectToXStream**:
  `org.jboss.soa.esb.actions.converters.ObjectToXStream`
  This action is similar to the `ObjectInvoke` action, except that it converts the object to XML using Xstream.

- **XStreamGToObject**:
  `org.jboss.soa.esb.actions.converters.ObjectToXStream`
  This action converts XML to an object using XStream.

- **PersistAction**:
  `org.jboss.soa.esb.actions.MessagePersister`
  This action doesn't really transform or convert a message, it writes it to the persistent message store. The most common use of the action is that it is how JBoss ESB itself writes messages to the dead letter queue (DLQ), but it can be used in any situation when you want to store a message.

◆ **SmooksAction**:

`org.jboss.soa.esb.smooks.SmooksAction`

This action enables you to use a powerful set of Smooks operations with JBoss ESB. We'll examine this action in detail in the next section.

Smooks message fragment processing

Let's look at transformations and the `SmooksAction` OOTB action.

But first, let's take a minute to introduce JBoss Smooks (`http://www.smooks.org`).

Smooks is best known as a transformation engine, that is, a utility to perform data transformations from one form to another (for example from XML to POJO's). However, that's a misconception (not to mention a disservice to Smooks) as Smooks has many more capabilities. A more accurate way to view Smooks is as a framework to enable you to perform different types of processing on message fragments, where a message fragment is a selected subset of the information in a message.

Smooks is able to handle different types of message fragments, and is able to perform different types of processing due to its modular design. Smooks' design is based on "visitor logic". A Smooks "visitor" is Java code that is designed to perform a specific type of operation on a specific type of message fragment. The message transformation types that Smooks performs include:

◆ **Templating**: Smooks enables you to define templates with XSLT or FreeMarker (`http://freemarker.sourceforge.net/`) to govern the message transformation.

◆ **Java Binding**: A very common, and very annoying task, is binding data to Java objects. Smooks provides dedicated visitor logic to perform this binding so you don't have to design the logic yourself.

◆ **Message Splitting**: We reviewed different types of message routing OOTB actions earlier in this chapter. One characteristic that all these have in common is that they treat the messages being routed as atomic units. In contrast, Smooks supports splitting messages into fragments and then routing the fragments to different destinations. In addition, you can even route these message fragments over different transports.

◆ **Enrichment**: Another common message processing task is to use information in a message as a "seed" to be used to add additional information to the message. Smooks enables you to "enrich" a message fragment with data extracted from a database.

◆ **Persistence**: As a counter point to enrichment, Smooks supports persisting message fragments into databases.

- **Validation**: Smooks provides visitor logic to perform validation, of data in message fragments.

However, when should you use Smooks for content-based routing? The types of situations in which you should consider using Smooks for content-based routing include:

- **When you have to split messages**: As we described earlier, one of Smooks' most powerful features is the ability to perform message splitting. If you use Smooks for content-based routing, you can split messages into fragments, route the fragments to different destinations in different formats (for example, routing XML to one service, Java to another, CSV data to another, and so on), and enrich or otherwise process the message fragments as they are routed. In addition, you can process the fragments into data in different formats.

- **When performance and scalability are required**: Another advantage of using Smooks for message splitting and routing is Smooks' high throughput rate and ability to handle very large messages (over 50 MB in size) efficiently.

Let's take a look an example of transformations and the `SmooksAction` out-of-the-box action.

The example is the aptly named `transform_XML2XML_simple` quickstart. This quickstart performs a message transformation by applying an XSLT (EXtensible Stylesheet Language Transformations) to an XML message. The message is then transformed into XML in a different form. The interesting parts of the quickstart's jboss-esb.xml file are:

- The following is an example of a `mep` that we described earlier in this chapter. The pattern used by this quickstart is `OneWay` in that the requester invokes a service (by sending it a message) and then does not wait for a response:

```
<actions mep="OneWay">
```

- The following action results in the message being written to the server log before it undergoes XSLT transformation. A similar action is also invoked after the transformation.

```
<action name="print-before"
        class="org.jboss.soa.esb.actions.SystemPrintln">
    <property name="message"
            value="[transform_XML2XML_simple]
                    Message before transformation"/>
</action>
```

- And here is the `SmooksAction`:

```
<action name="simple-transform"
        class="org.jboss.soa.esb.smooks.SmooksAction">
    <propertyname="smooksConfig" value="/smooks-res.xml"/>
</action>
```

◆ The set of Smooks commands to be executed is defined in the `smooks-res.xml` file. This file contains:

```xml
<?xmlversion='1.0'encoding='UTF-8'?>
  <smooks-resource-listxmlns=http://www.milyn.org/xsd/
                              smooks-1.0.xsd>


    <resource-configselector="OrderLine">
      <resourcetype="xsl">
        <![CDATA[<line-item>
          <product>
            <xsl:value-of select="./Product/@productId"/>
          </product>
          <price>
            <xsl:value-of select="./Product/@price"/>
          </price>
          <quantity>
            <xsl:value-of select="@quantity"/>
          </quantity>
        </line-item>]]>
      </resource>
      <paramname="is-xslt-templatelet">true</param>
    </resource-config>
</smooks-resource-list>
```

If this file looks a bit confusing, don't worry. The XPath commands that will be used by the `SmooksAction` and XSLT to transform the message into a different form are highlighted.

Time for action – running the quickstart

Follow these steps to run the `transform_XML2XML_simple` quickstart:

1. Change your current directory to the quickstart's directory `samples/quickstarts/transform_XML2XML_simple`.

2. Deploy the quickstart using the `ant deploy` command.

3. Before running the quickstart, review the original message that is used by the quickstart. Note the `ProductID`, `price`, and `quantity` elements. These are the elements that were defined in the `smooks-res.xml` file:

```xml
<Order orderId="1" orderDate="Wed Nov 15 13:45:28 EST 2006"
       statusCode="0" netAmount="59.97" totalAmount="64.92"
       tax="4.95">
    <Customer userName="user1" firstName="Harry"
```

```
                    lastName="Fletcher" state="SD"/>
        <OrderLines>
            <OrderLine position="1" quantity="1">
                <Product productId="364"
                         title="The 40-Year-Old Virgin "
                         price="29.98"/>
            </OrderLine>
            <OrderLine position="2" quantity="1">
                <Product productId="299" title="Pulp Fiction"
                         price="29.99"/>
            </OrderLine>
        </OrderLines>
    </Order>
```

4. Run the quickstart using the `ant runtest` command.

5. Review the quickstart's output in the `server.log` file. Make note of how the data from the message has been transformed into a new format:

```
2011-07-17 18:16:59,258 INFO [STDOUT] (pool-33-thread-1)
[transform_XML2XML_simple] Message after transformation:
2011-07-17 18:16:59,258 INFO   [STDOUT] (pool-33-thread-1)
[<Order netAmount="59.97" orderDate="Wed Nov 15 13:45:28 EST 2006"
orderId="1" statusCode="0" tax="4.95" totalAmount="64.92">
    <Customer firstName="Harry" lastName="Fletcher" state="SD"
              userName="user1"></Customer>
    <OrderLines>
        <line-item>
            <product>364</product>
            <price>29.98</price>
            <quantity>1</quantity>
        </line-item>
        <line-item>
            <product>299</product>
            <price>29.99</price>
            <quantity>1</quantity>
        </line-item>
    </OrderLines>
</Order>].
```

What just happened?

As you can see from the server output, the original message is printed out, the message is transformed and then it is printed out again. The smooks resource file specifies a transform which changes `<OrderLine/>` elements into `<line-item/>` elements and a number of subsequent attributes into child elements.

Routers

JBoss ESB supports static routing of messages to services, where messages are always routed to the same service based on the configuration. However, JBoss ESB also supports multiple approaches for content-based routing, where a message's route is determined dynamically at run-time, based on the content of the message.

You've probably noticed by now that in our examining the features provided by JBoss ESB, one recurring theme is that, on the ESB, "everything is either a service or a message". In order to make sure that our services can communicate via messages, JBoss ESB has to have a way to get messages to the right service. The ESB does this through message routing.

JBoss ESB supports multiple routing-related actions, these are as follows:

♦ **Aggregator**:
`org.jboss.soa.esb.actions.Aggregator`
This action aggregates information from multiple messages. For example, if you want to collect information from a message that contains a customer's mailing address with information about that customer's country's import/export laws. The `Aggregator` action is an implementation of the Aggregator Enterprise Integration Pattern (`http://www.enterpriseintegrationpatterns.com/Aggregator.html`)

♦ **EchoRouter**:
`org.jboss.soa.esb.actions.routing.EchoRouter`
This router is much simpler. As its name implies, it simply echos the incoming message to the server log and then returns the message.

♦ **HttpRouter**:
`org.jboss.soa.esb.actions.routing.HttpRouter`
This router sends the incoming message to an HTTP URL that you define in the action.

♦ **JMSRouter**:
`org.jboss.soa.esb.actions.routing.JMSRouter`
One of the ways in which you can achieve the loose coupling that we want in a service-oriented architecture is by using asynchronous messaging. In this approach, the sending service inserts messages into a JMS queue or topic for a receiving service to retrieve. What makes this asynchronous is that the sending service does not have to wait for the receiving service to "pick up" the message. The sending service is able to continue to perform tasks without blocking or waiting for the receiving service.

- **StaticRouter**:
  `org.jboss.soa.esb.actions.StaticRouter`
  In some cases, messages will always follow the same route. For example, messages from the sales service will always be directed to the credit check service. For static routes such as these, `StaticRouter` can be used.

- **StaticWiretap**:
  `org.jboss.soa.esb.actions.StaticWiretap`
  This action implements the Enterprise Integration Pattern for a wiretap (`http://www.enterpriseintegrationpatterns.com/WireTap.html`).

  The action enables you to inspect each processed message, without otherwise changing the actions performed. It lets you "listen in" on the messages, without actually changing them.

- **ContentBasedRouter**:
  `org.jboss.soa.esb.actions.ContentBasedRouter`
  The most interesting set of OOTB router actions deals with content-based routing. For these actions, the content in the messages determines the route that a message will follow.

  JBoss ESB supports multiple ways to perform content-based routing. You can define XPath semantics or regular expression pattern matching in the action definition. For example:

```
<action class="org.jboss.soa.esb.actions.ContentBasedRouter"
        name="ContentBasedRouter">
    <property name="cbrAlias" value="XPath"/>
    <property name="destinations">
        <namespace prefix="ord"
                   uri="http://org.jboss.soa.esb/Order" />
        <route-to service-category="BlueTeam"
                  service-name="GoBlue"
                  expression="/ord:Order[@statusCode='0']" />
        <route-to service-category="RedTeam"
                  service-name="GoRed"
                  expression="/ord:Order[@statusCode='1']" />
        <route-to service-category="GreenTeam"
                  service-name="GoGreen"
                  expression="/ord:Order[@statusCode='2']" />
    </property>
</action>
```

The `expression` defines the XPath pattern that must be matched to route messages to the desired service.

JBoss ESB also supports using JBoss Drools to define the content-based routing. We'll look at the JBoss ESB-Drools integration later in this chapter. Drools provides a declarative, "rules based" programming model for routing patterns too complicated to be easily handled by XPath semantics or a regular expression pattern. Finally, JBoss ESB also supports using JBoss Smooks for content-based routing. Smooks is the best choice if you also want to perform tasks such as message splitting as part of the content-based routing. We will also look at the JBoss ESB-Smooks integration later in this chapter.

Let's look at an example.

Time for action – implementing content-based routing

The `fun_cbr` quickstart performs content based routing, where the contents of a message dynamically "fire" procedural rules defined in JBoss Drools to determine the message's route. The quickstart action chain, including message routing, is initiated when a JMS message is inserted into a queue on which a JMS gateway listener is monitoring. When the gateway detects the message, it passes it to an ESB-aware listener, which in turn passes the message to the routing action. Based on the contents of the message, the message is delivered to one of three destination JMS queues.

Follow these steps to run the quickstart:

1. Like most of the other quickstarts, `fun_cbr` is deployed using the `ant deploy` command.

2. Running this quickstart, however, is a little different. As we mentioned earlier, messages, based on their content, are routed to one of three output queues. Each of these queues is monitored by a client. Each client represents one of three teams of order processors named for colors; red, blue, and green. When a client detects that a message has been received, it displays the message. So, before you run the quickstart, you have to open up three terminal windows, and start a client in each of them with one of these commands:

    ```
    ant receiveBlue
    ant receiveRed
    ant receiveGreen
    ```

3. The clients have been started, now let's run the quickstart:

    ```
    ant runtest
    ```

What just happened

In its out of the box configuration, the quickstart sends a message to the blue team. The message routing depends on the `statusCode` attribute in the `SampleOrder.xml` file from which the input message is generated. The message starts in the form of a SOAP request as is seen in `SampleOrder.xml`. The output shown by the `receiveBlue` client looks like this:

```
receiveBlue: [echo] Runs Test JMS Receiver

[java] Receiving on: queue/quickstart_Fun_CBR_Blue_Alert

[java] 11:18:09,506 DEBUG [main][TimedSocketFactory] createSocket,
hostAddr:
                localhost/127.0.0.1, port: 1099, localAddr: null,
localPort: 0, timeout: 0

[java] Initialised

[java] ************************************************************

[java] <Order xmlns="http://org.jboss.soa.esb/Order" orderId="1"
orderDate="Wed
                Nov 15 13:45:28 EST 2006" statusCode="0"

[java] netAmount="59.97" totalAmount="64.92" tax="4.95">

[java] <Customer userName="user1" firstName="Harry" lastName="Fletcher"
                state="SD"/>

[java] <OrderLines>

[java] <OrderLine position="1" quantity="1">

[java] <Product productId="364" title="The 40-Year-Old Virgin "
price="29.98"/>

[java] </OrderLine>

[java] <OrderLine position="2" quantity="1">

[java] <Product productId="299" title="Pulp Fiction" price="29.99"/>

[java] </OrderLine>

[java] </OrderLines>

[java] </Order>
```

Have a go hero

To get a better idea of how content-based routing works, change the status code in the quickstart's `SampleOrder.xml` to a value of 1 or 2 and watch the message be routed to the green and red clients. But, don't stop there! Try your hand at modifying the rules that govern the quickstart's message routing.

Notifiers

How do you move an ESB message out of your service into ESB-unaware services like a JMS queue, a file, or a SQL table? Notifiers convert ESB-aware messages into data in a format these services can understand.

Notifiers are specified within a `NotificationList`, which allows you to specify more than one notifier at the same time. This allows you to notify multiple targets, like a JMS queue and the console.

Note that notifiers are to be used only to communicate with ESB-unaware services. Do not try to notify JMS queues that contain ESB-aware messages.

Another thing to note is that while the action pipeline generally works sequentially, it has two stages—normal processing and outcome processing. Notifiers do not perform any processing of messages during that first stage of "normal processing". They send notifications during the second stage. The notification occurs after the processing of the action pipeline, in the outcome processing phase. This means that you should be careful when designing your action chain that you understand that if you place actions in a chain subsequent to a notifier, those actions might be performed before the notifier.

The following notification targets (the names are very self-explanatory) are supported by the JBoss ESB:

- **NotifyConsole**: Prints the contents of the ESB message to the server log
- **NotifyFiles**: Prints the message contents to a file or files
- **NotifySQLTable**: Inserts the message contents into an existing database table
- **NotifyFTP**: Prints the message contents to a file and then sends the file to a server via FTP
- **NotifyQueues** and **NotifyTopics**: Writes the message contents into a JMS message and adds the JMS message to a specified JMS queue or topic
- **NotifyEmail**: Sends the message contents in a mail message

Time for action – let's see how notifiers work

Let's see how notifiers work. Follow these steps:

1. Change your current directory to the quickstart's directory `samples/quickstarts/helloworld_file_notifier`.

2. Deploy the quickstart using the `ant deploy` command.

3. Before you run the quickstart, review the `jboss-esb.xml` file and see how the message is routed to two different services—one which displays the message and the other which notifies the console and a file.

4. You might notice that this quickstart has a `jboss-esb-unfiltered.xml` file. This is because it contains a bit of `ant build` formatting to allow the ant script to insert the absolute location of the quickstart directory in the `jboss-esb.xml`.

5. Run the quickstart using the `ant runtest` command.

6. Review the quickstart's output in the `server.log` file. Check the `results.log` file for the contents of the message.

What just happened?

In this quickstart, the `runtest` target sends a message to a service which routes the message to two different services. One of the services displays the message to `System.out`, and the other one calls a notifier—which writes the message to the console and a `results.log` file.

Business Process Management

This action group contains only one out-of-the-box action (`org.jboss.soa.esb.services.jbpm.actions.BpmProcessor`), but that one action supports the JBoss ESB-jBPM integration within JBoss ESB. This integration enables your services to make calls to a jBPM process through the jBPM Command API. Of the commands in the command API, the following (three) are available for use from ESB:

- **NewProcessInstanceCommand**: This creates a new `ProcessInstance` using a process definition that has already been deployed to jBPM. The process instance is left in the start state so that tasks referenced by start node are executed.

- **StartProcessInstanceCommand**: This is the same as `NewProcessInstanceCommand`, except that the process instance that is created is moved from the start position to the first node in the process graph.

- **CancelProcessInstanceCommand**: As its name implies, this cancels a process instance.

However, this is only part of the JBoss ESB-jBPM integration. The integration also supports the orchestration of services from jBPM processes. The appendix to this book includes more details on JBoss ESB-jBPM integration, including the orchestration of services from jBPM processes.

Drools

JBoss ESB can use Drools as its rules processing engine through the
`BusinessRulesProcessor` action. The following is an example of the use of the
`BusinessRulesProcessor` in the `business_rules_processor` quickstart:

```
<action class="org.jboss.soa.esb.actions.BusinessRulesProcessor"
        name="BRP">
    <property name="ruleSet" value="MyBusinessRules.drl"/>
    <property name="ruleReload" value="true"/>
    <property name="object-paths">
        <object-path esb="body.orderHeader"/>
        <object-path esb="body.customer"/>
    </property>
</action>
```

The rules are contained in a `.drl` file, in this instance, `MyBusinessRules.drl`. The
object-paths listed here are MVEL (`http://mvel.codehaus.org`) expressions that
are used to extract objects from those locations in the message, in this instance, the
`OrderHeader` object from the body, and the `Customer` object from the `body`. Those
objects then can be used within your rules file.

The appendix to this book includes more details on JBoss ESB-Drools integration.

BPEL processes

JBoss ESB also supports integration with JBoss Riftsaw (`http://www.jboss.org/
riftsaw`). Riftsaw is an open source WS-BPEL 2.0 engine that is based on Apache ODE
(`http://ode.apache.org/`). With its Riftsaw integration, JBoss ESB services can directly
invoke a RiftSaw BPEL process by using the OOTB `BPELInvoke` action (`org.jboss.soa.
esb.actions.bpel.BPELInvoke`).

The JBoss ESB-Riftsaw integration uses web services to support a two-way integration:

- ◆ Riftsaw works by exposing BPEL processes as web services. JBoss ESB actions can
  invoke those Riftsaw BPEL processes by invoking the web service that Riftsaw
  exposes, through its WSDL interface, and in the other direction.

- ◆ A BPEL process can invoke a JBoss ESB service that is accessible as a web service. For
  example, a service that is exposed by a proxied web service. In this case, the BPEL
  process invokes the JBoss ESB service just as if it was any other web service.

Note that Riftsaw and its JBoss ESB quickstarts and user documentation is not installed by default with JBoss ESB. To make use of the JBoss ESB-Riftsaw integration, you have to download and install Riftsaw from `http://www.jboss.org/riftsaw/downloads` and install it into a JBoss AS installation.

The appendix to this book includes more details on the JBossESB - Riftsaw integration.

Pop quiz

1. When writing a custom action, what method handles a message?

    a. That's really up to you. Hey, it's a "custom" action, isn't it?

    b. The `process` method.

    c. It's a trick question; custom actions can't handle messages.

2. How can you have messages routed to the correct services based on the information in the messages?

    a. You have to write custom actions to "break open" the messages.

    b. The routes are all based on unique message ID properties.

    c. With content-based routing.

3. What would you use to send an ESB-aware message outside the ESB?

    a. Why would you want to do that? It's scary outside there!

    b. With a notifier OOTB action.

    c. This is the type of task that requires a custom action.

4. How do you convert content in a message from one form to another?

    a. Dust off your old Perl books.

    b. With a converter/transformer OOTB action.

    c. With a notifier OOTB action.

5. Which OOTB action allows you to expose a web service?

    a. The `SOAPProcessor` action—you write a web service that calls your web service and exposes it through JBoss ESB listeners.

    b. The `WebserviceExpose-Amatic`—it's an OOTB action and a kitchen appliance.

    c. You're on your own—you have to create a custom action for this task.

Chapter bibliography

Also refer to JBoss in Action by Jamae, Javid, and Johnson, Peter (Manning, 2009).

```
http://docs.jboss.org/jbossesb/docs/4.9/javadoc
```

```
http://docs.jboss.org/jbossesb/docs/4.10/manuals/html/Programmers_
Guide/
```

```
http://www.enterpriseintegrationpatterns.com
```

```
http://www.dzone.com/links/outofthebox_soa_without_the_twinturbine_
engine.html
```

Summary

You've now been introduced to the JBoss ESB actions, the building blocks of services. You should now know how to create your own custom actions, and how to make use of the extensive set of OOTB actions that JBoss provides. When you start designing your services and need to perform a specific action, the place to start is with the OOTB actions. You can save yourself a lot of time, and a lot of trouble too, as the OOTB actions have been tested and are fully documented.

5

Message Delivery on the Service Bus

In previous chapters we introduced you to the important aspects of JBoss ESB Services, such as:

- *The structure of ESB messages*
- *How the configuration mechanism works*
- *An explanation of the service pipeline*
- *Service composition*
- *Writing actions*

In this chapter we will introduce the final part of the service puzzle, how services connect into the ESB and consume messages. We will cover the following topics:

- InVM transport and its interactions with transactional contexts
- The difference between pass-by-value and pass-by-reference semantics and its pitfalls
- Lock-step delivery with InVM transports
- JMS transports
- SQL transports
- Remote file system transports
- Local file system transport

So let's get on with it...

The bus

At the core of JBoss ESB is the concept of a bus, an abstract representation of the transports through which request messages will be delivered to the target services and their response messages, if appropriate, returned to the service invoker. Each service 'plugs into the bus' by defining the configuration for its associated transports within the `jboss-esb.xml` file, the details of which will then be used to create and register **Endpoint References (EPRs)** within the Service Registry.

The `ServiceInvoker`, used by clients to invoke ESB services, will query the service registry to locate the EPRs associated with the service, choose one based on the current policy in force, and send the message through the transport associated with the chosen EPR.

The Endpoint References are opaque structures which contain the information necessary for the transport to identify a service endpoint and, potentially, a specific conversation handled by that endpoint. No assumptions should be made about these contents as they relate to the specific transport and may change with different releases of JBoss ESB.

A graphical representation of the bus is as follows:

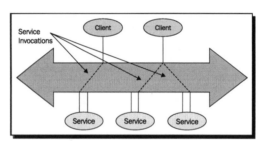

In the diagram we can see three services deployed into the bus, each of which is registering two distinct endpoints. Each service endpoint represents a specific transport configuration through which the services can be contacted.

The diagram also highlights three service invocations from two distinct clients. Each client is isolated from the specifics of the transport configuration, through the registry and endpoint references, allowing the invocations to be made using various transports and targeted at multiple service destinations.

In keeping the client isolated from the details of the service and its invocation, the ESB is encouraging a loosely coupled architecture through which the service and client can evolve without having a direct impact on the other end of the invocation. Clients and services may be located on disparate systems with these invocations occurring over multiple transport types in a synchronous or asynchronous manner.

With all this in mind, let's now take a look at how this appears in practice. We will walk you through the configuration of JBoss Developer Studio and follow up with some examples covering the service invocations.

Preparing JBoss Developer Studio

The examples in this chapter are based on a standard ESB application template that can be found under the `Chapter5` directory within the sample downloads. We will modify this template application as we proceed through this chapter. Before we start, please make sure that you have set up JBoss Developer Studio and the **JBoss 5.1 Runtime** as described in *Chapter 2*.

Time for action – creating File Filters

In this section we will demonstrate the necessary steps for creating a File Filter within the Server Runtime environment. This File Filter will allow us to discover those temporary files which are created as part of the execution of the following examples, matching on the pattern used for their naming. Follow these steps to create a File Filter:

1. Expand the **JBoss 5.1 Runtime Servers** and locate **Filesets**, right click on it and select **Create File Filter**:

2. In the **New File Filter** dialog, enter **Name** as "FileProvider", **Root Directory** as "server/${jboss_config}/tmp" and **Includes** as "*.sentToEsb":

3. Click **OK** and there should be an entry for **FileProvider**, as follows:

4. Right click on the **FileProvider** filter and click **Edit File Filter**:

5. This should open up the **New File Filter** dialog again. Click **OK** and the files should get refreshed.

What just happened?

We have now created a File Filter that will allow us to discover the temporary files which are created during execution of the examples. By repeating step 4 and step 5, after having executed the examples, we will be able to refresh the list of files that are detected.

Time for action – opening the Chapter5 app

We will now take a look at the Chapter5 application and examine the configuration as it currently stands:

1. Click on **File** menu and select **Import**.

2. Choose **Existing Projects into workspace** and select the folder where the book samples have been extracted.

3. Choose the **Chapter5** project and click on **Finish**.

4. Examine the jboss-esb.xml file and you will notice that the application defines two services but only one provider configuration. The second service makes use of the InVM transport, referenced through the use of the invmScope attribute on the service. The file will have the following content:

```
<providers>
  <fs-provider name="Chapter5FSprovider">
    <fs-bus busid="Chapter5FileChannel">
      <fs-message-filter directory="${jboss.server.temp.dir}"
                error-delete="false"
                error-directory="${jboss.server.temp.dir}"
                error-suffix=".IN_ERROR"
                input-suffix=".dat" post-delete="false"
                post-directory="${jboss.server.temp.dir}"
                post-suffix=".sentToEsb"
                work-suffix=".esbWorking"/>
    </fs-bus>
  </fs-provider>
</providers>
```

The list of services is as follows:

```
<services>
  <service category="Chapter5Sample"
          description="A template for Chapter5"
          name="Chapter5Service">
    <listeners>
      <fs-listener busidref="Chapter5FileChannel"
                name="Chapter5FSprovider"/>
    </listeners>
    <actions mep="OneWay">
      <action class="org.jboss.soa.esb.actions.SystemPrintln"
              name="printMessage">
        <property name="message" value="Incoming"/>
      </action>
      <action class="org.jboss.soa.esb.actions.StaticRouter"
              name="RouteToB">
        <property name="destinations">
          <route-to service-category="Chapter5Sample"
                service-name="Chapter5BService"/>
        </property>
      </action>
    </actions>
  </service>
  <service category="Chapter5Sample"
          description="Chapter5 B Service"
          name="Chapter5BService"
          invmScope="GLOBAL">
    <actions mep="OneWay">
```

```
                  <action class="org.jboss.soa.esb.actions.SystemPrintln"
                          name="printMessage">
                    <property name="message" value="Incoming to B"/>
                  </action>
                </actions>
              </service>
            </services>
```

The following is a screenshot of this configuration loaded in the JBoss ESB editor:

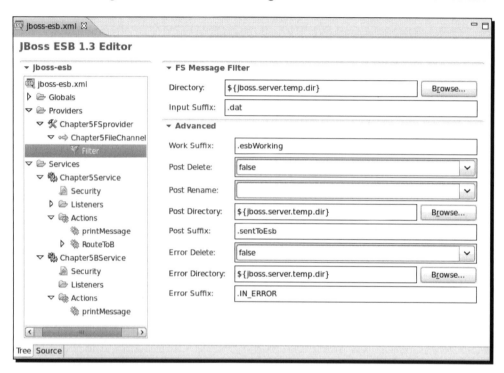

Transport providers

JBoss ESB provides a set of transport providers which can be used to communicate with ESB services, otherwise known as ESB-aware endpoints. We have already seen some of these transports in action, while working through the examples in *Chapter 3*; it is now time to examine them in more detail.

Some of the ESB-aware transport providers can handle execution within a transactional context, which means that any messages sent or received over these transports will be managed by the encompassing transaction. These are the JMS, InVM, and SQL transports. An additional transactional provider is the schedule provider, useful for triggering periodic execution of a pipeline.

It is important to be aware that sending a message over a transactional provider, if done within the context of a transaction, has an effect on the delivery of messages; the message will only be delivered on the transport once the transaction commits.

The File, FTP, FTPS, and SFTP transports are not transactionally aware, any message sent on these transports will be sent immediately.

Let us now include a File and InVM transport in the Chapter5 application.

Time for action – using a File provider

First, let's execute the Chapter5 sample application that was opened at the beginning of this chapter:

> ***1.*** In JBoss Developer Studio, select the **Chapter5** project and click **Run | Run As | Run on Server**.

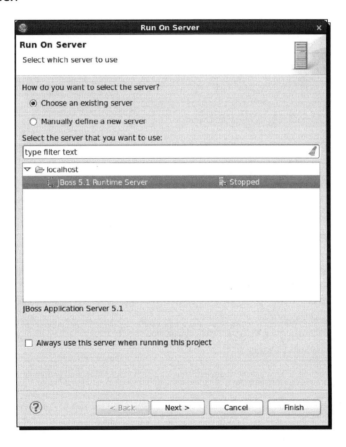

2. Click **Next**. A window with the project pre-configured to run on this server is shown. Ensure that we have only our project **Chapter5** selected on the right-hand side.

3. Click **Finish**.

4. Select the `src` folder, expand it till the `SendEsbMessage.java` file is displayed in the tree. Now click **Run | Run As | Java Application**.

   A log will be printed in the server console showing the following output:

```
INFO   [STDOUT] Incoming:
INFO   [STDOUT] [Chapter 5 says Hello!].
INFO   [STDOUT] Incoming to B:
INFO   [STDOUT] [Chapter 5 says Hello!].
```

5. Now refresh the **FileProvider** Filter created at the beginning of this chapter by selecting **Edit File Filter** and then clicking **OK**. You should now see the temporary file which was created, as shown. The name of the file will be different but it will have the extension **.dat.sentToEsb**.

What just happened?

You created a File based bus provider that was used by `ServiceInvoker` to invoke the `Chapter5Service` and also an InVM bus that was used by this service to invoke a second `Chapter5BService` service. The temporary file was the result of the message being serialized into the file system.

Have a go hero – examine the contents of a temp file

Go ahead and open the temporary file in a standard text editor to see the message contents. Experiment with more messages and see how the temp files are created when you edit the **FileProvider** filter.

InVM transport

The InVM transport allows messages to be sent within the same JVM instance but without any I/O overhead, such as networking or writing to the disk, and can either be enabled for every service deployed into the ESB or specified explicitly as part of the service declaration. An example configuration would be:

```
<service category="Chapter5Sample" name="Chapter5Service"
        invmScope="GLOBAL">
  <actions mep="OneWay">
    <action name="action"
            class="org.jboss.soa.esb.actions.SystemPrintln"/>
  </actions>
</service>
```

The specification of the InVM transport can be in addition to the configuration of other listeners, allowing communication with the service to occur over the InVM transport, if within the same JVM, or over a remote transport.

Explicit declaration of the InVM transport for a service is handled through the `invmScope` attribute on the `<service>` element. The attribute currently supports two scopes:

- **NONE**: The service is not invokable over the InVM transport
- **GLOBAL**: The service is invokable over the InVM transport from within the same JVM.

The default InVM scope for any JBoss ESB service can also be set in the `jbossesb-properties.xml` file through the `core:jboss.esb.invm.scope.default` config property. If not defined, the default scope is NONE.

A service can choose to explicitly exclude the use of the InVM transport through the `invmScope` attribute on the `<service>` element of their services configuration, such as in the following example:

```
<service category="Chapter5Sample" name="Chapter5Service"
         invmScope="NONE">
</service>
```

> The decision to enable the InVM transport for every service is specific to the context of those services being deployed. It is usually recommended to have the default scope set to NONE and explicitly declare support for the InVM transport, when necessary, in the service level configuration as this is more likely to avoid any confusion when the services are not intended to be invoked over the InVM transport.

Transactions with InVM transport

The InVM transport can participate in transactions in a similar way to the other transactional transports. The decision whether to enable the use of transactions can be an explicit configuration or, if not specified, can be derived implicitly using the information in the other configured listeners.

The transactional behavior will be implicitly enabled if there are any other transactional transports configured on the service, either JMS, SQL, or scheduled, and one of those transports has support for transactions.

Explicit configuration of the transactional behavior is handled by specifying the `invmTransacted` attribute on the `<service>` element. This configuration will always take precedence, irrespective of the existence of any other transactional listener configured for the service.

> One caveat to be aware of is that, although transactional, the InVM transport does not support full ACID semantics, specifically due to the lack of a durable store. Any message sent using an InVM transport would be lost, should the JVM crash or halt through normal operation, and may lead to inconsistency should the transaction involve multiple transactional resources such as accessing databases.
>
> If full ACID semantics are desired then it is recommended to use an alternative transport such as JMS (Java Message Service) or SQL transports.

Time for action – testing InVM transactions

Let us now see the real effect of the `invmTransacted` attribute on a service. Follow these steps:

1. In JBoss Developer Studio, select **Chapter5** and expand the `esbcontent` folder. You will see there is another file called `jboss-esb-transacted.xml`:

2. Before we rename it, we need to remove the deployed application from the server. Click on the **Servers** tab, right click on the **Chapter5** application and click **Remove**.

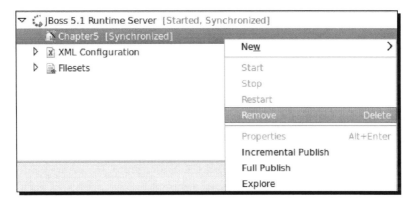

3. Rename `jboss-esb.xml` to `jboss-esb-first.xml`.

4. Open `jboss-esb-transacted.xml`.

5. Select **File** | **Save As**, choose `Chapter5/esbcontent/META-INF` and enter the **File name** as "jboss-esb.xml".

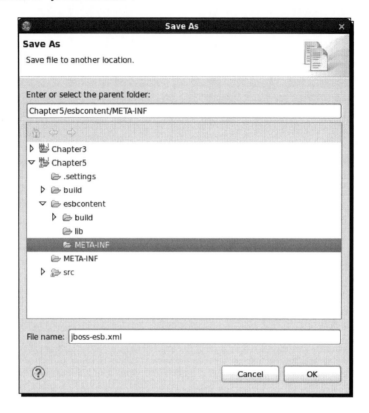

6. Click **OK**.

7. Now the `esbcontent` folder should look like this:

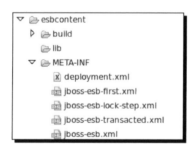

8. Select the **Chapter5** project and click **Run** | **Run As** | **Run on Server**.

9. Select the `src` folder, expand it till the `SendEsbMessage.java` file is displayed in the tree. Now click **Run | Run As | Java Application**.

You will notice that the following message is printed six times on the server console:

```
INFO    [STDOUT] Body: Chapter 5 says Hello!
INFO    [STDOUT] About to cause an exception
```

What just happened?

You created a transacted InVM listener and, when a runtime exception was thrown, the transaction was rolled back resulting in the message being placed back in the InVM message queue. This happened five times before the rollback discarded the message, sending it to the DLQ.

Here is the configuration. Examine the highlighted section very carefully:

```xml
<providers>
  <jms-provider connection-factory="ConnectionFactory"
                name="JBossMQ">
    <jms-bus busid="Chapter5EsbChannel1">
      <jms-message-filter dest-name="queue/chapter5_Request_esb1"
                          dest-type="QUEUE" transacted="false"/>
    </jms-bus>
    <jms-bus busid="Chapter5EsbChannel2">
      <jms-message-filter dest-name="queue/chapter5_Request_esb2"
                          dest-type="QUEUE" transacted="true"/>
    </jms-bus>
  </jms-provider>
</providers>
<services>
  <service category="Chapter5Sample"
           description="A template for Chapter5"
           name="Chapter5Service">
    <listeners>
      <jms-listener busidref="Chapter5EsbChannel1"
                    name="Chapter5provider"/>
    </listeners>
    <actions mep="OneWay">
      <action class="org.jboss.soa.esb.actions.SystemPrintln"
              name="printMessage">
        <property name="message" value="Incoming"/>
      </action>
      <action class="org.jboss.soa.esb.actions.StaticRouter"
              name="RouteToB">
        <property name="destinations">
```

```
                <route-to service-category="Chapter5Sample"
                          service-name="Chapter5BService"/>
            </property>
        </action>
    </actions>
</service>
<service category="Chapter5Sample" description="Chapter5 B Service"
        invmScope="GLOBAL" name="Chapter5BService"
        invmTransacted="true">
    <actions mep="OneWay">
        <action class="org.jboss.soa.esb.samples.chapter5.MyAction"
                name="processTransaction"/>
        <!--  Will throw an Exception. This should trigger the
              transaction to be rolledback and the message placed
              back onto the InVM queue.   -->
        <action class="org.jboss.soa.esb.samples.chapter5.MyAction"
                name="throwException" process="causesException"/>
        <action class="org.jboss.soa.esb.actions.SystemPrintln"
                name="printMessage">
          <property name="message" value="Outgoing"/>
        </action>
    </actions>
</service>
</services>
```

Have a go hero – non transacted InVM listener

Go ahead and remove the `invmTransacted` attribute and see how the application behaves.

InVM message optimization

One additional optimization available to the InVM transport is the ability to pass messages using pass-by-reference semantics. This removes the necessity to serialize the message in one service scope and deserialize it in the target service scope.

While this does increase the performance of communication over the InVM transport there are caveats which must be understood:

The message parts accessed in the target service must share a `ClassLoader` scope with the invoking context

   ◆   Care must be taken not to modify the message within multiple services at the same time

The first issue usually arises when a message part is defined using different definitions of a common class or interface, leading to `ClassCastExceptions` being raised when the message part is accessed. This will normally occur when the two service scopes are each deployed with a JAR containing the common class or interface. If this cannot be rectified then the pass-by-reference semantics can be explicitly disabled, forcing the message to be serialized in the originating context and deserialized in the target context.

The second issue occurs when the message reference has been passed by reference to the target service yet the originating context continues to modify the contents of the message. These modifications will be visible to the target service although, as a result of the concurrent nature of the execution, it will always be uncertain as to when this will occur. This leads to undesirable race conditions within the application, often hard to track down. If it is not possible to modify the behavior of the services then disabling the pass-by-reference semantics will cause a separate instance of the message to be delivered to the target service as a consequence of the serialization/deserialization.

The pass-by-reference semantics are disabled by explicitly enabling pass-by-value on the service, done by setting the `inVMPassByValue` property on the `<service>` element to `true`. An example configuration would look like this:

```
<service category="Chapter5Sample" name="Chapter5Service"
         invmScope="GLOBAL">
  <property name="inVMPassByValue" value="true"/>
</service>
```

Have a go hero – examine the body address

Modify the custom action to print the body object's address using `Integer.toHexString(System.identityHashCode(message.getBody()))` and see what gets printed when it is printed both from `Chapter5Service` and `Chapter5BService`. You will have to add `MyAction` to your service like this:

```
<service category="Chapter5Sample"
         description="A template for Chapter5"
         name="Chapter5Service">
  <listeners>
    <jms-listener busidref="Chapter5EsbChannel1"
                  name="Chapter5provider"/>
  </listeners>
  <actions mep="OneWay">
    <action class="org.jboss.soa.esb.actions.SystemPrintln"
            name="printMessage">
      <property name="message" value="Incoming"/>
    </action>
```

```
        <action class="org.jboss.soa.esb.samples.chapter5.MyAction"
                name="printAddress"/>
        <action class="org.jboss.soa.esb.actions.StaticRouter"
                name="RouteToB">
          <property name="destinations">
            <route-to service-category="Chapter5Sample"
                      service-name="Chapter5BService"/>
          </property>
        </action>
      </actions>
    </service>
    <service category="Chapter5Sample" description="Chapter5 B Service"
            invmScope="GLOBAL" name="Chapter5BService">
      <actions mep="OneWay">
        <action class="org.jboss.soa.esb.samples.chapter5.MyAction"
                name="printAddress"/>
      </actions>
    </service>
```

Your `MyAction.java` file would look like this:

```
public Message process(Message message) throws Exception {
    System.out.println("Body: " + Integer.toHexString(
                        System.identityHashCode(message.getBody())));
    return message;
}
```

Does it change when `inVMPassByValue` is set to true?

Controlling InVM message delivery

One of the problems which may surface when using the InVM transport is that the target service may become swamped by the incoming messages, with the message originators being able to send messages to the service faster than the service can process them.

JBoss ESB includes a mechanism which enables the automatic throttling of the message originator in order to prevent this scenario, known as **lock-step** delivery.

The "lock-step" delivery mechanism blocks the originator until the service is in a position to consume the message or until a specified timeout has occurred, preventing the originator from producing messages at a significantly faster rate than the consumer can process.

It should be noted that this is not a synchronous delivery mechanism, it is the delivery of the message which releases the originator and not a response from the service.

Lock-step delivery is disabled by default but can be explicitly enabled on a service using the `inVMLockStep` and `inVMLockStepTimeout` properties.

- ◆ `inVMLockStep`: Set this to true to enable lock-step delivery.
- ◆ `inVMLockStepTimeout`: The maximum number of milliseconds that the originator will be blocked while awaiting the consumption of the message by the target service. If not specified then it will default to 10 seconds.

An example configuration with lock-step delivery enabled would look like this:

```
<service category="Chapter5Sample" name="Chapter5Service"
        invmScope="GLOBAL">
  <property name="inVMLockStep" value="true"/>
  <property name="inVMLockStepTimeout" value="4000"/>
</service>
```

 When using InVM within the scope of a transaction, lock-step delivery will be disabled. The reason for this is that the transactional delivery of the message will not occur until the enclosing transaction successfully commits.

Time for action – using lock-step delivery

Let us see the real effect of the `invmLockStep` attribute on a service. The following steps will demonstrate how to use lock-step delivery:

1. In JBoss Developer Studio, select **Chapter5** and expand the `esbcontent` folder. You will see there is one more file called `jboss-esb-lock-step.xml`.

2. Have a look at this file. The relevant section for lock-step delivery has been highlighted here:

```
<service category="Chapter5Sample"
        description="Chapter5 B Service"
        invmScope="GLOBAL" name="Chapter5BService">
  <property name="inVMLockStep" value="true"/>
  <property name="inVMLockStepTimeout" value="4000"/>
  <actions mep="OneWay">
    <action class="org.jboss.soa.esb.samples.chapter5.MyAction"
            name="lockStepAction" process="lockStepAction"/>
    <action class="org.jboss.soa.esb.actions.SystemPrintln"
            name="printMessage">
      <property name="message" value="Incoming to B"/>
    </action>
  </actions>
</service>
```

3. Before we rename the file, we need to remove the deployed application from the server. Click on the **Servers** tab and right click on the **Chapter5** application and click **Remove**.

4. Now right click on the file `jboss-esb.xml` and click **Delete**.

5. Click **OK** on the **Confirm Delete** dialog.

6. Open `jboss-esb-lock-step.xml`. Select **File | Save As**, choose `Chapter5/esbcontent/META-INF` and enter the **File name** as "jboss-esb.xml".

7. Click **OK**.

8. Select the **Chapter5** project and click **Run | Run As | Run on Server**.

9. Select the `src` folder, expand it till the `SendLockStepMessage.java` file is displayed in the tree.

10. Examine the `SendLockStepMessage.java` file. You can see that it invokes the `Chapter5Service` ten times:

```java
public static void main(String[] args) throws Exception {
    System.setProperty(
            "javax.xml.registry.ConnectionFactoryClass",
            "org.apache.ws.scout.registry.ConnectionFactoryImpl");
    Message esbMessage =
            MessageFactory.getInstance().getMessage();
    esbMessage.getBody().add("Chapter 5 says Hello!");
    ServiceInvoker invoker = new ServiceInvoker(
            "Chapter5Sample", "Chapter5Service");
    for (int i = 0; i < 10; i++) {
        invoker.deliverAsync(esbMessage);
    }
}
```

Here is the listing of `MyAction.java` that highlights the code where the message processing is delayed:

```java
public class MyAction extends AbstractActionLifecycle {

    protected ConfigTree _config;

    public MyAction(ConfigTree config) {
        _config = config;
    }

    public Message process(Message message) throws Exception {
        System.out.println("Body: " + message.getBody().get());
```

```
            return message;
    }

    public Message lockStepAction(Message message)
            throws Exception {
        Thread.sleep(2000);
        return message;
    }

    public Message printMessage(Message message)
            throws Exception {
        System.out.println("Routing to B");
        return message;
    }
}
```

11. With the `SendLockStepMessage.java` file selected, click **Run | Run As | Java Application**.

The following is a sample output from the server console:

```
15:15:20,078 INFO   [STDOUT] Routing to B
15:15:20,093 INFO   [STDOUT] Routing to B
15:15:22,093 INFO   [STDOUT] Incoming to B:
15:15:22,093 INFO   [STDOUT] [Chapter 5 says Hello!].
15:15:22,093 INFO   [STDOUT] Routing to B
15:15:24,093 INFO   [STDOUT] Incoming to B:
15:15:24,093 INFO   [STDOUT] [Chapter 5 says Hello!].
15:15:24,093 INFO   [STDOUT] Routing to B
15:15:26,093 INFO   [STDOUT] Incoming to B:
15:15:26,093 INFO   [STDOUT] [Chapter 5 says Hello!].
15:15:26,093 INFO   [STDOUT] Routing to B
15:15:28,093 INFO   [STDOUT] Incoming to B:
15:15:28,093 INFO   [STDOUT] [Chapter 5 says Hello!].
15:15:28,109 INFO   [STDOUT] Routing to B
15:15:30,093 INFO   [STDOUT] Incoming to B:
15:15:30,093 INFO   [STDOUT] [Chapter 5 says Hello!].
15:15:30,109 INFO   [STDOUT] Routing to B
15:15:32,093 INFO   [STDOUT] Incoming to B:
15:15:32,093 INFO   [STDOUT] [Chapter 5 says Hello!].
15:15:32,109 INFO   [STDOUT] Routing to B
```

```
15:15:34,109 INFO   [STDOUT] Incoming to B:
15:15:34,109 INFO   [STDOUT] [Chapter 5 says Hello!].
15:15:34,109 INFO   [STDOUT] Routing to B
15:15:36,109 INFO   [STDOUT] Incoming to B:
15:15:36,109 INFO   [STDOUT] [Chapter 5 says Hello!].
15:15:36,109 INFO   [STDOUT] Routing to B
15:15:38,109 INFO   [STDOUT] Incoming to B:
15:15:38,109 INFO   [STDOUT] [Chapter 5 says Hello!].
15:15:40,109 INFO   [STDOUT] Incoming to B:
15:15:40,109 INFO   [STDOUT] [Chapter 5 says Hello!].
```

What just happened?

You executed an application that uses the InVM lock-step delivery mechanism in its configuration. Notice that the **Routing to B** message is displayed almost every two seconds, the time our `MyAction lockStepAction` method sleeps. The delivery of the message from `Chapter5Service` to `Chapter5Bservice` has been blocked until `ChapterBService` is able to retrieve it.

InVM threads

In the previous section you noticed that the message was printed after every two seconds. That is because the number of InVM threads that were available for processing was just one. The number of listener threads associated with the InVM transport can be controlled by the `maxThreads` property.

Time for action – increasing listener threads

Now let us add the `maxThreads` property to our InVM service and see how that affects our output:

1. Modify the `jboss-esb.xml` file and add the `maxThreads` property with a value of 5:

```xml
<service category="Chapter5Sample"
        description="Chapter5 B Service"
        invmScope="GLOBAL" name="Chapter5BService">
  <property name="maxThreads" value="5"/>
  <property name="inVMLockStep" value="true"/>
  <property name="inVMLockStepTimeout" value="4000"/>
  <actions mep="OneWay">
    <action class="org.jboss.soa.esb.samples.chapter5.MyAction"
```

```
            name="lockStepAction" process="lockStepAction"/>
    <action class="org.jboss.soa.esb.actions.SystemPrintln"
            name="printMessage">
      <property name="message" value="Incoming to B"/>
    </action>
  </actions>
</service>
```

2. Click on **Save** or press *Ctrl + S*.

3. If the server was still running then you might notice the application gets redeployed once again by default. If this did not happen then deploy the application using **Run | Run As | Run on Server**.

4. Select the `src` folder and expand it till the `SendLockStepMessage.java` file is displayed in the tree. Now click **Run | Run As | Java Application**.

The following is the server console output from a sample run:

```
15:30:49,687 INFO   [STDOUT] Routing to B
15:30:49,718 INFO   [STDOUT] Routing to B
15:30:49,718 INFO   [STDOUT] Routing to B
15:30:49,718 INFO   [STDOUT] Routing to B
15:30:49,718 INFO   [STDOUT] Routing to B
15:30:49,718 INFO   [STDOUT] Routing to B
15:30:51,703 INFO   [STDOUT] Incoming to B:
15:30:51,703 INFO   [STDOUT] [Chapter 5 says Hello!].
15:30:51,718 INFO   [STDOUT] Incoming to B:
15:30:51,718 INFO   [STDOUT] [Chapter 5 says Hello!].
15:30:51,718 INFO   [STDOUT] Routing to B
15:30:51,718 INFO   [STDOUT] Incoming to B:
15:30:51,718 INFO   [STDOUT] [Chapter 5 says Hello!].
15:30:51,718 INFO   [STDOUT] Routing to B
15:30:51,718 INFO   [STDOUT] Incoming to B:
15:30:51,718 INFO   [STDOUT] [Chapter 5 says Hello!].
15:30:51,718 INFO   [STDOUT] Routing to B
15:30:51,718 INFO   [STDOUT] Incoming to B:
15:30:51,718 INFO   [STDOUT] [Chapter 5 says Hello!].
15:30:51,718 INFO   [STDOUT] Routing to B
15:30:53,718 INFO   [STDOUT] Incoming to B:
15:30:53,718 INFO   [STDOUT] [Chapter 5 says Hello!].
```

```
15:30:53,718 INFO   [STDOUT]  Incoming to B:
15:30:53,718 INFO   [STDOUT]  [Chapter 5 says Hello!].
15:30:53,718 INFO   [STDOUT]  Incoming to B:
15:30:53,718 INFO   [STDOUT]  [Chapter 5 says Hello!].
15:30:53,718 INFO   [STDOUT]  Incoming to B:
15:30:53,718 INFO   [STDOUT]  [Chapter 5 says Hello!].
15:30:53,718 INFO   [STDOUT]  Incoming to B:
15:30:53,718 INFO   [STDOUT]  [Chapter 5 says Hello!].
```

What just happened?

You increased the InVM listener threads for our `Chapter5Bservice` from 1 to 5. Notice that the **Routing to B** message is displayed five times initially and the sixth is blocked until another listener thread becomes available. Although `Chapter5Service` picked up its sixth message to route it to `Chapter5Bservice` it has been blocked and hence the seventh message is picked up only after two seconds.

Have a go hero – threads and lock-step

Play around with different numbers of messages and `maxThreads` values and examine how the output behaves. Go ahead and remove the `invmLockStep` and `inVMLockStepTimeout` attributes and see what difference it produces in the output of the server console.

Provider configurations

We have concentrated on the InVM transport in this chapter, the most interesting and challenging provider to use, however JBoss ESB supports other transports for delivery of messages to a service.

Each of the following sub-sections will briefly cover the specialized tags of some of those providers, used when configuring the provider within the `jboss-esb.xml` file, and show snippets of the relevant quickstarts to provide an idea of their configuration and use.

You are encouraged to try out each provider, using the JBoss ESB Editor from Eclipse, and compare their behavior and capabilities with those of the InVM transport.

JMS provider

A JMS provider can be used to define providers that are based on JMS queues and topics. The transport-specific implementations are `<jms-provider>`, `<jms-bus>`, `<jms-listener>`, and `<jms-message-filter>` with the specification of the `<jms-message-filter>` being supported by both the `<jms-bus>` or `<jms-listener>` elements. The `<jms-provider>` and `<jms-bus>` elements are used to specify the JMS connection properties whereas the `<jms-message-filter>` element is used to specify the JMS queue or topic and also the details of any JMS selector which is necessary to filter the incoming messages.

A typical JMS provider configuration would look like this:

```
<jms-provider name="JBossMQ" connection-factory="ConnectionFactory">
  <jms-bus busid="quickstartGwChannel">
    <jms-message-filter dest-type="QUEUE"
        dest-name="queue/quickstart_helloworld_action_Request"/>
  </jms-bus>
  <jms-bus busid="quickstartEsbChannel">
    <jms-message-filter dest-type="QUEUE"
        dest-name="queue/quickstart_helloworld_action_esb"/>
  </jms-bus>
</jms-provider>
```

 For more information on the Java Message Service API you can check out the specification available at `http://jcp.org/en/jsr/detail?id=914`.

Have a go hero – JMS action quickstart

Have a look at the `helloworld_action` quickstart. This demonstrates the usage of the JMS provider and QUEUE selection from HornetQ, JBoss Messaging, and JBoss MQ.

FTP provider

An FTP provider can be used to define providers that are based on remote file system locations using a secure or unsecure connection. These transport specific implementations are `<ftp-provider>`, `<ftp-bus>`, `<ftp-listener>`, and `<ftp-message-filter>`. The `<ftp-message-filter>` can be added to either the `<ftp-bus>` or `<ftp-listener>` elements. Where `<ftp-provider>` and `<ftp-bus>` specify the FTP access properties, `<ftp-message-filter>` specifies the message/file selection and processing properties.

A typical FTP provider configuration would look like this:

```
<ftp-provider name="FTPprovider" hostname="@FTP_HOSTNAME@" >
  <ftp-bus busid="helloFTPChannel" >
    <ftp-message-filter username="@FTP_USERNAME@"
                        password="@FTP_PASSWORD@"
                        passive="false"
                        directory="@FTP_DIRECTORY@"
                        input-suffix=".dat"
                        work-suffix=".esbWorking"
                        post-delete="false"
                        post-rename="true"
                        post-suffix=".COMPLETE"
                        error-delete="false"
                        error-suffix=".HAS_ERROR"/>
  </ftp-bus>
</ftp-provider>
```

Have a go hero – the FTP action quickstart

Have a look at the `helloworld_ftp_action` quickstart. This demonstrates the usage of FTP provider and FTP message queues.

 JBoss ESB also supports the FTPS and SFTP protocols, however, discussion of these configurations is beyond the scope of this book.

SQL provider

A SQL provider can be used to define providers that are based on database systems using a secure or unsecure connection. These transport-specific implementations are `<sql-provider>`, `<sql-bus>`, `<sql-listener>`, and `<sql-message-filter>`. The `<sql-message-filter>` can be added to either the `<sql-bus>` or `<sql-listener>` elements. Where the `<sql-provider>` and `<sql-bus>` specify the JDBC connection properties, the `<sql-message-filter>` specifies the message/row selection and processing properties.

A typical SQL provider configuration would look like this:

```
<sql-provider name="SQLprovider"
              url="jdbc:hsqldb:hsql://localhost:1704"
              driver="org.hsqldb.jdbcDriver"
              username="sa" password="">
  <sql-bus busid="helloSQLChannel" >
    <sql-message-filter tablename="GATEWAY_TABLE"
```

```
                                status-column="STATUS_COL"
                                order-by="DATA_COLUMN"
                                where-condition="DATA_COLUMN like 'data%'"
                                message-column="message"
                                message-id-column="UNIQUE_ID"
                                insert-timestamp-column="TIMESTAMP_COL"/>
      </sql-bus>
    </sql-provider>
```

Have a go hero – the SQL action quickstart

Have a look at the `helloworld_sql_action` quickstart. This demonstrates the usage of
the SQL provider and row selection from `hsqldb` tables.

File provider

A file provider can be used to define providers that are based on file systems. These
transport-specific implementations are `<fs-provider>`, `<fs-bus>`, `<fs-listener>`,
and `<fs-message-filter>`. The `<fs-message-filter>` can be added to either the
`<fs-bus>` or `<fs-listener>` elements. Where the `<fs-provider>` and `<fs-bus>`
specify the file system properties, the `<fs-message-filter>` specifies the message/file
selection and processing properties.

A typical file system provider configuration would look like this:

```
    <fs-provider name="FSprovider1">
      <fs-bus busid="helloFileChannel" >
        <fs-message-filter directory="@INPUTDIR@"
                            input-suffix=".dat"
                            work-suffix=".esbWorking"
                            post-delete="false"
                            post-directory="@OUTPUTDIR@"
                            post-suffix=".sentToEsb"
                            error-delete="false"
                            error-directory="@ERRORDIR@"
                            error-suffix=".IN_ERROR"/>
      </fs-bus>
    </fs-provider>
```

Have a go hero – file providers

Modify the sample at the beginning of this chapter to include file prefixes as needed for
processing. Examine how those files are processed and experiment with the various
settings depicted here.

Summary

In this chapter we have looked at most of the bus providers available for delivering ESB messages to target services, focusing primarily on the InVM transport and its capabilities.

Having followed through this chapter you should now have a good understanding of:

- How to use a file system provider
- The InVM provider
- The difference between pass-by-value and pass-by-reference
- When to use the lock-step delivery mechanism
- How threading affects the InVM transport
- How the InVM transport works within a transactional context
- Which provider to choose based on transactional needs

We also revisited the JMS provider, used in many examples throughout this book, and introduced the configuration for the SQL and FTP providers.

Now that we've learned how to deliver messages to ESB services, let us look at how external systems and transports can be integrated with JBoss ESB through the use of gateways—the topic of the next chapter.

6
Gateways and Integrating with External Clients

In previous chapters we have discussed the main concepts of the JBoss Enterprise Service Bus, showing how services can be developed to expose functionality in a loosely coupled manner.

We began the journey by defining the desirable characteristics of a service and explaining why they are advantageous, covered the structure of the messages that pass between the service consumers and service providers, explained how services are addressed through the opaque endpoint references and how service actions, combined with the action pipeline, its lifecycle and its events, are used to construct these services.

By combining these services we are then able to create composite ESB applications that can perform a multitude of tasks and solve many of our problems. Even with these capabilities there still remains one area that we are yet to cover, an area which can be argued is more important than the rest. This is the ability to support the invocation of services from external clients.

Recall from our description of services at the beginning of Chapter 3 that one of their key benefits is the ability to reuse functionality that is exposed by those services. This capability is desirable for both internal clients (those which are aware of the ESB and how to invoke services) and external clients (those which communicate with service endpoints using different, often standards-based, protocols).

By supporting the invocation of ESB services from an external client we are also enabling another silo of applications, namely those that involve the integration of services which may already exist within the organization. This capability will allow the ESB to act as a mediator between external services, augmenting their invocations as and when necessary, with everything driven by the specific business requirements which have been implemented within the ESB services.

This chapter will cover the facilities within JBoss ESB which enable the support and integration of external clients and will cover the following topics:

- The purpose of a gateway and a notifier
- The difference between synchronous and asynchronous invocations
- How message composition works
- The JMS gateway
- The File gateway
- The HTTP gateway
- The Camel gateway
- The FTP gateway
- The UDP gateway
- The JBoss Remoting gateway
- The Groovy gateway
- The SQL gateway
- The JCA gateway

So let's get on with it...

What is a gateway and a notifier?

A **gateway** is a service endpoint through which an external client can talk to an ESB-aware service using a protocol that is supported by the external client. It may be that this protocol is based on a standard format, for example web service invocations over HTTP, or that the format is specific to existing applications within an organization, perhaps sent over a transport such as JMS. The gateway acts as a proxy between the two participants, adapting requests from the external client into a message that can be sent over the ESB to the target service.

Some of the gateways provided by JBoss ESB are based on a synchronous protocol, such as HTTP, and are required to handle processing of both requests and responses using the same connection. Other gateways support asynchronous protocols, such as sending messages over JMS or through a file system, and are only required to adapt the incoming request.

In order to handle the responses for the asynchronous gateway it is necessary to make use of another facility offered by JBoss ESB, the notifier. A **notifier** enables the sending of messages from an ESB-aware service to an external service endpoint and can be considered the inverse of the asynchronous gateway. A notifier not only handles responses, it can also be used to send asynchronous notifications to any external service which can receive them.

The behavior of the gateways and notifiers can be visualized as follows:

```
                    ┌──────────────┐              ┌──────────────┐
                    │  HTTP Client │              │  JMS Client  │
                    └──────────────┘              └──────────────┘
   Synchronous ____                               ____ Asynchronous
   Communication                                       Communication

              ┌──────────────┐   ┌──────────────┐   ┌──────────────┐
              │ HTTP Gateway │   │ JMS Gateway  │   │ JMS Notifier │
              └──────────────┘   └──────────────┘   └──────────────┘

                         Enterprise Service Bus

                    ┌─────────┐ ┌─────────┐ ┌─────────┐
                    │Service A│ │Service B│ │Service C│
                    └─────────┘ └─────────┘ └─────────┘
```

In the above diagram we are showing two different types of external invocations, a synchronous invocation using the HTTP transport, and an asynchronous invocation using the JMS transport. In both instances it is the gateways which are responsible for processing the incoming request, constructing an ESB message and passing it into the ESB to be handled by the target service(s). Where they differ is in the handling of the responses.

The JMS transport, by its nature, allows invocations to be made asynchronously. This allows the gateway to complete its part in the processing of the current request and move on to the next one arriving at the gateway. Any response to the client will come through a notifier, at a later point in time.

The HTTP transport, being a synchronous transport by default, requires any response to be sent back to the client using the same connection through which the request was received. The HTTP gateway must block in these circumstances, waiting for the reply from the ESB service before responding to the external client.

There is no requirement to use the same transport for receiving and responding to asynchronous requests, it is possible to mix the transports should it make sense to the application being developed.

How do we compose messages?

Every gateway must take an incoming request, in the native format, and convert it into a message that can be sent over the ESB to the target service, but how is this done?

Each gateway has a message composer associated with it, responsible for performing the conversion from a native request to an ESB message and, if necessary, vice-versa. By default it will use a composer appropriate for the supported transport, each composer implementing the `org.jboss.soa.esb.listeners.message.MessageComposer` interface.

The important methods within the interface are:

```
public Message compose(T messagePayload)
    throws MessageDeliverException;

public Object decompose(Message message,
                        T originalInputMessagePayload)
    throws MessageDeliverException;
```

The `compose` method is responsible for taking the incoming request and creating an ESB message representing the payload, returning this to the gateway so that it can be sent to the target ESB service.

The `decompose` method is responsible for taking the response, if it is necessary, and returning a payload that can then be sent to the external client as a native response. The `decompose` method also has access to the original request in case it contains information that may be relevant when creating the response.

Simple composer example

The following code snippet shows a simplistic composer for the File gateway:

```
public class ExampleMessageComposer<T extends File>
  implements MessageComposer<T> {

    public void setConfiguration(final ConfigTree config)
      throws ConfigurationException {
    }

    public Message compose(final T inputFile)
      throws MessageDeliverException {
        final Message message =
          MessageFactory.getInstance().getMessage();
        final byte[] contents ;
        try {
            contents = FileUtil.readFile(inputFile) ;
        } catch (final IOException ioe) {
            throw new MessageDeliverException(
              "Failed to obtain contents", ioe) ;
        }
        message.getBody().add(contents) ;
```

```
            return message;
    }

    public Object decompose(Message message, T inputFile)
      throws MessageDeliverException {
        return message.getBody().get() ;
    }
}
```

The gateway will invoke the compose method, passing in the File instance which identifies the incoming request. The MessageComposer is then responsible for retrieving the contents of this File and creating the message, initializing the content and properties of the message as required.

When the gateway receives a response from the ESB service it will invoke the decompose method in order to obtain the externalized response, passing in the response message from the ESB service, and the File instance which identifies the original request. The MessageComposer is then responsible for retrieving the necessary content from the ESB response message and returning this to the gateway.

This MessageComposer can be applied to the gateway by specifying the composer-class property on the listener, along with any other properties that may be required by the composer. An example configuration for the MessageComposer could be:

```
<listeners>
  <fs-listener name="example" busidref="examplebus" is-gateway="true"
               schedule-frequency="2">
    <property name="composer-class" value="ExampleMessageComposer"/>
    ...
  </fs-listener>
</listeners>
```

It is beyond the scope of this book to cover message composition in any further detail, as the default composers are sufficient for most needs, however it is important that their existence is understood.

Now that we have an understanding of the gateway functionalities, let's get started with the fun stuff.

Preparing JBoss Developer Studio

We will be using a standard ESB application template that can be found under the Chapter6 directory within the sample downloads. This consists of the bare-bone files necessary for us to work through this chapter. Fire up JBoss Developer Studio and make sure **JBoss 5.1 Runtime** is setup. Refer to *Chapter 2* on how to install JBoss Developer Studio.

The JMS gateway

In many of the examples in previous chapters we have used the JMS gateway without calling attention to it. This gateway, as the name suggests, handles the processing of messages which are carried over implementations of the Java Messaging Service, and is an asynchronous gateway.

Since the configuration of the JMS provider and listeners have been covered in the previous chapter, let us get into the action straight away.

Time for action – using the JMS gateway

We will now run the `Chapter6` sample application that demonstrates the usage of the JMS gateway. Follow these steps:

1. In JBoss Developer Studio, select the **Chapter6** project and click **Run | Run As | Run on Server**.

2. Click **Next**. A window with the project pre-configured to run on this server is shown. Ensure that we have only our project **Chapter6** selected on the right-hand side:

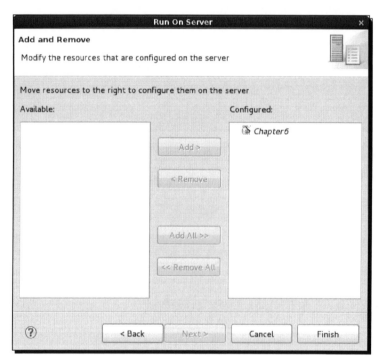

3. Click **Finish**.

4. Select the `src` folder, expand it till the `SendJMSMessage.java` file is displayed in the tree. Now click **Run | Run As | Java Application**.

The console will display the output as shown:

```
JMS Gateway says Hello!
```

What just happened?

We sent a message via the JMS gateway listener and our response was received, asynchronously, through a separate JMS queue. Configuring the gateway was as simple as declaring the type of the listener to be a gateway:

```
<listeners>
  <jms-listener busidref="chapter6ESBChannel"
                name="Chapter6ESBListener"/>
  <jms-listener busidref="chapter6GwChannel" is-gateway="true"
                name="Chapter6GwListener"/>
</listeners>
```

Since we intended to send a response to the external client, we have also included a notifier action, responsible for sending the asynchronous response to a separate JMS queue:

```
<action name="notificationAction"
        class="org.jboss.soa.esb.actions.Notifier">
  <property name="okMethod" value="notifyOK"/>
  <property name="notification-details">
    <NotificationList type="ok">
      <target class="NotifyQueues" >
        <queue jndiName="queue/chapter6_Request_gw_reply"/>
      </target>
    </NotificationList>
  </property>
</action>
```

Also notice how the client code reads the reply queue as shown:

```
...
replyQueue = (Queue) iniCtx.lookup("queue/chapter6_Request_gw_reply");
...
public void readReply() throws JMSException {
    QueueReceiver receiver = session.createReceiver(replyQueue);
    Message msg = receiver.receive();
    if (msg instanceof TextMessage) {
        System.out.println(((TextMessage) msg).getText());
    }
}
```

The File gateway

The File gateway uses a provider that we have used in previous chapters, although we have never seen it being used as a gateway. The processing of the requests is asynchronous with any response being sent through the notifiers.

Most of the configuration parameters have already been set up for you in the sample, so let us jump in and show you how it works.

Time for action – using the File gateway

We will now run the `Chapter6` sample application that demonstrates the usage of the File gateway:

1. In JBoss Developer Studio, open the `jboss-esb.xml` file in **Source** mode.

2. Append the following `listener` definition to the `<listeners>` tag:

```
<listeners>
  <jms-listener busidref="chapter6ESBChannel"
                name="Chapter6ESBListener"/>
  <jms-listener busidref="chapter6GwChannel" is-gateway="true"
                name="Chapter6GwListener"/>
  <fs-listener busidref="chapter6FileChannel" is-gateway="true"
               name="Chapter6FileGwListener"/>
</listeners>
```

3. Replace the following action:

```
<action name="notificationAction"
        class="org.jboss.soa.esb.actions.Notifier">
  <property name="okMethod" value="notifyOK"/>
  <property name="notification-details">
    <NotificationList type="ok">
      <target class="NotifyQueues" >
        <queue jndiName="queue/chapter6_Request_gw_reply"/>
      </target>
    </NotificationList>
  </property>
</action>
```

With this action:

```
<action name="notificationAction"
        class="org.jboss.soa.esb.actions.Notifier">
  <property name="okMethod" value="notifyOK"/>
  <property name="notification-details">
    <NotificationList type="ok">
      <target class="NotifyFiles">
        <file append="false" URI="${java.io.tmpdir}/results.log"/>
      </target>
    </NotificationList>
  </property>
</action>
```

4. Click the **Save** button and the modified application should now be deployed in the server.

5. Select the `src` folder and expand it till the `SendFileMessage.java` file is displayed in the tree. Now click **Run | Run As | Java Application**.

The console will display the output as follows:

```
File Gateway says Hello!
```

What just happened?

The File gateway picked up an incoming message through a file on the filesystem, sent it through the ESB and created a response in a separate file with the help of a notifier.

Let's now take a look at the client code, concentrating on the sections which are responsible for creating the original request:

```
public static void main(String[] args) throws Exception {
    String tmpDir = System.getProperty("java.io.tmpdir");
    File file = new File(tmpDir, "file.msg");
    BufferedWriter writer = new BufferedWriter(
                        new OutputStreamWriter(
                        new FileOutputStream(file)));
    writer.write("Hello File Gateway!");
    writer.close();
    Thread.sleep(300);
    File result = new File(tmpDir, "results.log");
    BufferedReader reader = new BufferedReader(
                        new InputStreamReader(
                        new FileInputStream(result)));
    String line = null;
    while((line = reader.readLine()) != null) {
        System.out.println(line);
    }
    reader.close();
}
```

The HTTP gateway

The HTTP gateway is an example of a gateway that processes both the request and response in a synchronous manner, waiting for a reply from the target ESB service before sending back the response, to the external client, using the same connection as the incoming request. The `MessageComposer` is responsible for handling the transformation of the messages in both directions.

A minimal configuration is as follows:

```
<service category="Chapter6Sample"
        description="A template for Chapter6"
        name="Chapter6Service">
  <listeners>
    <http-gateway name="Http"/>
  </listeners>
```

This code will expose an HTTP endpoint at `http://<host>:<port>/<deployment.esb>/http/Chapter6Sample/Chapter6Service` where `host` and `port` are the default values of the web server, typically `localhost` and `8080`.

Here is a complete list of configuration options that can be used with this listener:

```
<http-gateway name="Http" urlPattern="/*">
  <property name="allowedPorts" value="8080,8081"/>
  <property name="payloadAs" value="STRING"/>
  <property name="synchronousTimeout" value="30000"/>
</http-gateway>
```

The `urlPattern` attribute will override the default URL value used by the ESB, for example the previous attribute will result in the gateway being mapped to `http://<host>:<port>/<deployment.esb>/http/*`, in other words, any location which starts with the above URL ('*' not included).

If the web server has been configured to expose web deployments on multiple ports then the `allowedPorts` attribute can be used to specify which ports are allowed to expose the gateway. For example with the previous `urlPattern` and `allowedPorts` our HTTP endpoint will now be exposed through the following endpoints, assuming that the web server is configured to handle requests on each:

```
http://<host>:8080/<.esbname>/http
http://<host>:8081/<.esbname>/http
```

The behavior of the gateway is synchronous by default, causing the client to block until a response is received. The gateway will wait for a response from the target ESB service, until one has been received or until a specified timeout has been exceeded. This timeout value can be configured through the `synchronousTimeout` property, which by default is 30,000 milliseconds or 30 seconds.

If asynchronous behavior is required then it can be configured as follows:

```
<http-gateway name="Http">
  <asyncResponse statusCode="202">
    <payload classpathResource="/202-static-response.xml"
             content-type="text/xml"
             characterEncoding="UTF-8" />
  </asyncResponse>
</http-gateway>
```

The `statusCode` attribute and `payload` configuration are optional, by default the gateway will respond to an asynchronous request with a status code of 200 (OK) and a zero length payload, in which case all that is required is to specify an empty `asyncResponse` element as follows.

```
<http-gateway name="Http">
  <asyncResponse/>
</http-gateway>
```

Time for action – using the HTTP gateway

We will now run the `Chapter6` sample application that demonstrates the use of the HTTP gateway:

1. In JBoss Developer Studio, open the `jboss-esb.xml` file in **Source** mode.

2. Append the following `listener` definition to the `<listeners>` tag.
    ```
    <listeners>
      <jms-listener busidref="chapter6ESBChannel"
                    name="Chapter6ESBListener"/>
      <jms-listener busidref="chapter6GwChannel" is-gateway="true"
                    name="Chapter6GwListener"/>
      <http-gateway busidref="chapter6HttpGateway"
                    name="Chapter6HttpGwListener"/>
    </listeners>
    ```

3. Remove the following action:
    ```
    <action name="notificationAction"
            class="org.jboss.soa.esb.actions.Notifier">
      <property name="okMethod" value="notifyOK"/>
      <property name="notification-details">
        <NotificationList type="ok">
          <target class="NotifyFiles">
            <file append="false" URI="${java.io.tmpdir}/results.log"/>
    ```

```
        </target>
      </NotificationList>
    </property>
  </action>
```

4. Click the **Save** button and the modified application should now be deployed in the server.

5. Select the `src` folder and expand it till the `SendHttpMessage.java` file is displayed in the tree. Now click **Run | Run As | Java Application**.

The console will display the following:

`Http Gateway says Hello!`

What just happened?

We sent a message via the HTTP gateway listener and received a synchronous response, on the same connection which transferred the request.

Here is the listing of the client code for reference:

```java
public static void main(String[] args) throws Exception {
    String serverURL = "http://localhost:8080/Chapter6/http/
                        Chapter6Sample/Chapter6Service";
    HttpURLConnection connection =
        (HttpURLConnection)new URL(serverURL).openConnection();
    connection.setRequestMethod("POST");
    connection.setDoOutput(true);
    connection.setDoInput(true);
    connection.connect();
    PrintWriter out = new PrintWriter(
                    new OutputStreamWriter(
                    connection.getOutputStream()));
    out.println("Hello Http Gateway!");
    out.close();
    BufferedReader in = new BufferedReader(
                    new InputStreamReader(
                    connection.getInputStream()));
    String inputLine;
    while ((inputLine = in.readLine()) != null) {
        System.out.println(inputLine);
    }
    in.close();
}
```

Have a go hero – using asynchronous behavior

Go ahead and modify the listener to add asynchronous behavior. Are you able to send a GET request now? What status code does it return by default?

The HTTP bus and HTTP provider

Aspects of the HTTP configuration can be shared between multiple gateways, specified through the `<http-provider>` or `<http-bus>` elements.

The `<http-provider>` element exposes the shared configuration of the HTTP exception mappings. Using the `<exception>` element specifies the translations from exceptions into the appropriate HTTP response.

The `<http-bus>` element exposes the shared configuration of the HTTP methods that are supported using the `<protected-methods>` element, the security roles required to access the endpoint using the `<allowed-roles>` element, and any requirement to secure the HTTP transport using the `transportGuarantee` attribute.

A typical HTTP provider configuration would look like this:

```
<http-provider name="http">
  <http-bus busid="chapter6HttpGateway"
            transportGuarantee="CONFIDENTIAL">
    <allowed-roles>
      <role name="friend">
    </allowed-roles>
    <protected-methods>
      <method name="GET">
      <method name="PUT">
      <method name="POST">
      <method name="DELETE">
    </protected-methods>
  </http-bus>
  <exception mappingsFile="/http-exception-mappings.properties"/>
</http-provider>
```

Note that the configuration stipulates a requirement to use a CONFIDENTIAL transport, in other words SSL, and requires the user to authenticate using credentials that include the friend role.

The exception element can also be configured directly as shown in the following:

```
<exception>
  <mapping class="com.acme.AcmeException" status="503"/>
</exception>
```

Details from the original request are stored within the ESB message, represented by the `HttpRequest` class, and can be retrieved using the convenience method `org.jboss.soa.esb.http.HttpRequest.getRequest()`. This class provides access to the properties which describe the incoming HTTP request.

Have a go hero – configuring the HTTP provider

Go ahead and secure the `http-provider` in our sample. Try using exception mapping with HTTP status codes both globally in the `http-provider` and also in `http-gateway`.

The Camel gateway

The Camel gateway is, by default, a synchronous gateway which allows the ESB to take advantage of the transports provided by the Apache Camel project (`http://camel.apache.org/`). This transport exposes its configuration by using the `<camel-provider>`, `<camel-bus>`, and `<camel-gateway>` elements.

The gateway allows one or more transports to be defined using the Camel URI notification, either as a `from-uri` attribute or a set of nested `<from>` elements. It is also possible to override the timeout for synchronous invocations, using the `timeout` attribute, or declare the gateway to be asynchronous by specifying the `async` attribute.

These configurations can be specified on both the `<camel-bus>` and `<camel-gateway>` elements, allowing a deployment to share a configuration where appropriate.

A typical Camel provider configuration would look like this:

```
<camel-provider name="CamelProvider">
  <camel-bus busid="chapter6CamelChannel">
    <from uri="file://@INPUTDIR1@?delete=true"/>
    <from uri="http://localhost:9889"/>
    <from uri="jms://MyQueue?connectionFactory=ConnectionFactory"/>
  </camel-bus>
</camel-provider>
```

With the Camel gateway the configuration looks as follows:

```
<camel-gateway busidref="chapter6CamelChannel"
               name="Chapter6CamelGwListener"/>
```

It is also possible to configure the gateway without a reference to the bus, specifying the attributes or elements directly on the `<camel-gateway>` element as shown:

```
<camel-gateway name="Chapter6CamelGwListener"
               from-uri="file://@INPUTDIR1@?delete=true"/>
```

Have a go hero – run the Camel gateway quickstart

Have a look at the `camel_helloworld` quickstart. This demonstrates how to use the Camel gateway using the `file://` protocol.

The FTP gateway

The FTP gateway is an asynchronous provider that has been covered in a number of the previous exercises, albeit as an ESB-aware listener rather than as a gateway. In order to use this provider as a gateway it is simply a matter of setting the `is-gateway` attribute on the listener tag to `true`, as shown:

```
<ftp-listener busidref="ftpChannel" name="ftpGateway"
              is-gateway="true"/>
```

In addition to supporting the FTP protocol, this gateway can also target FTPS, the FTP protocol over a connection secured using SSL, and SFTP, a secure file transfer protocol which runs over SSH.

Due to the requirement for running against an external server, whether FTP, FTPS, or SFTP, and the multitude of configuration options available to each protocol, we are leaving the exploration of this gateway as an exercise for the reader.

The ESB Programmers Guide goes into detail about the options available for each protocol supported by this gateway.

Have a go hero – running the FTP gateway quickstart

Have a look at the `helloworld_ftp_action` quickstart. This demonstrates the usage of the FTP gateway. You will have to change the configuration so that it refers to an FTP server which is present within your organization. Please see the `readme.txt` file under this quickstart folder for more information.

The UDP gateway

The UDP gateway is an asynchronous gateway which can process messages received over the UDP protocol, a connectionless protocol based on top of IP, and is based on the Apache MINA project.

The gateway is configured through the `<udp-listener>` element and supports the following attributes:

- `Host`: for specifying the name of the local network interface
- `Port`: the port number through which the communication will occur
- `handlerClass`: the name of an optional handler class used to adapt the incoming MINA events onto the bus

The default behavior of the gateway is to consume the incoming UDP packet and create an ESB message with its payload being a byte array containing the bytes which represent the incoming packet.

A typical configuration for this gateway is shown:

```
<udp-listener name="Chapter6UDPListener" host="localhost"
              port="9999"/>
```

Time for action – using the UDP gateway

Let us now run the sample application that demonstrates the usage of the UDP gateway:

1. In JBoss Developer Studio, open the `jboss-esb.xml` file in **Source** mode.

2. Add the following `listener` to the `listeners` list:
```
<listeners>
  <jms-listener busidref="chapter6ESBChannel"
                name="Chapter6ESBListener"/>
  <jms-listener busidref="chapter6GwChannel" is-gateway="true"
                name="Chapter6GwListener"/>
  <udp-listener name="Chapter6UDPListener" host="localhost"
                port="9999" is-gateway="true"/>
</listeners>
```

3. Append the highlighted `action` definition to the `<actions>` tag:
```
<actions mep="RequestResponse">
  <action class="org.jboss.soa.esb.samples.chapter6.MyAction"
          name="MyAction"/>
  <action name="notificationAction"
          class="org.jboss.soa.esb.actions.Notifier">
    <property name="okMethod" value="notifyOK"/>
    <property name="notification-details">
      <NotificationList type="ok">
        <target class="NotifyTcp" >
          <destination URI="tcp://localhost:8899" />
```

```
        </target>
      </NotificationList>
    </property>
  </action>
</actions>
```

4. Click the **Save** button and the modified application should now be deployed in the server.

5. Select the `src` folder and expand it till the `SendUDPMessage.java` file is displayed in the tree. Now click **Run | Run As | Java Application**.

The console will display the output as:

`UDP Gateway says Hello!`

What just happened?

We sent a message via the UDP gateway listener and we received the response via a TCP socket. Here is the listing of the client code for reference:

```java
public static void main(String[] args) throws Exception {
    ResponseReceiver receiver = new ResponseReceiver();
    new Thread(receiver).start();

    DatagramSocket socket = new DatagramSocket();
    socket.setSoTimeout(3000);
    String msg = "Hello UDP Gateway!";
    DatagramPacket packet = new DatagramPacket(msg.getBytes(),
                                 msg.getBytes().length);
    InetAddress address = InetAddress.getByName("localhost");
    packet.setAddress(address);
    packet.setPort(9999);
    socket.send(packet);
    socket.close();
}

private static class ResponseReceiver implements Runnable {

    public void run() {
        try {
            ServerSocket receiveSocket = new ServerSocket(8899);
            Socket clientSocket = receiveSocket.accept();
            BufferedReader reader = new BufferedReader(
                            new InputStreamReader(
                            clientSocket.getInputStream()));
            System.out.println(reader.readLine());
            reader.close();
            clientSocket.close();
            receiveSocket.close();
```

```
        } catch (IOException e) {
            e.printStackTrace();
        }
    }
}
```

The JBoss Remoting gateway

The JBoss Remoting gateway is, by default, a synchronous gateway based on the JBoss Remoting project (http://www.jboss.org/jbossremoting). The gateway processes messages which are delivered over a number of the JBoss Remoting protocols, specifically HTTP, HTTPS, socket, and socketssl. This transport exposes its configuration using the <jbr-provider>, <jbr-bus>, and <jbr-listener> elements.

The <jbr-provider> element supports the configuration of two attributes, the host attribute specifying the name of the local network interface through which the messages will arrive and the protocol attribute which declares the remoting protocol for the endpoint.

The <jbr-bus> element supports the configuration of the port attribute, declaring the port number associated with the endpoint.

In addition to the standard configuration options it is possible to include other properties on any of the previous jbr elements, by specifying nested property elements. These properties include:

- serviceInvokerTimeout: used to specify the maximum time before which a response is expected
- synchronous: used to define the endpoint as asynchronous when false
- asyncResponse: used to define a resource containing the contents used as the asynchronous response
- composer-class: used to override the default composer

Sometimes JBoss Remoting requires an additional configuration which is not covered by these properties, something specific to the connector. If additional properties are required then they can be added into the service configuration by declaring the property using a name prefixed by jbr-.

A typical JBR provider configuration would look like this:

```
<jbr-provider name="JBRprovider"
              protocol="socket" host="localhost">
  <property name="serviceInvokerTimeout" value="20000"/>
  <jbr-bus busid="chapter6JBRChannel" port="8081"/>
</jbr-provider>
```

Time for action – using the JBR gateway

Let us now run the `Chapter6` sample application that demonstrates the usage of the JBR gateway:

1. In JBoss Developer Studio, open the `jboss-esb.xml` file in **Source** mode.

2. Add the following `provider` to the `providers` list:

```
<jbr-provider name="JBRprovider"
                protocol="htp" host="localhost">
  <property name="serviceInvokerTimeout" value="20000"/>
  <jbr-bus busid="chapter6JBRChannel" port="9888"/>
</jbr-provider>
```

3. Append the following `listener` definition to the `<listeners>` tag.

```
<listeners>
  <jms-listener busidref="chapter6ESBChannel"
              name="Chapter6ESBListener"/>
  <jms-listener busidref="chapter6GwChannel" is-gateway="true"
              name="Chapter6GwListener"/>
  <jbr-listener busidref="chapter6JBRChannel"
              name="Chapter6JBRGwListener" is-gateway="true"/>
</listeners>
```

4. Click the **Save** button and the modified application should now be deployed in the server.

5. Select the `src` folder and expand it till the `SendJBRMessage.java` file is displayed in the tree. Now click **Run | Run As | Java Application**.

6. The console will display the output as shown:

```
JBoss Remoting Gateway says Hello!
```

What just happened?

We sent a message via the JBR gateway listener and we received the response synchronously. Here is the listing of the client code for reference:

```
public static void main(String[] args) throws Exception {
    String serverURL = "http://localhost:9888";
    HttpURLConnection connection =
        (HttpURLConnection)new URL(serverURL).openConnection();
    connection.setRequestMethod("POST");
    connection.setDoOutput(true);
```

```
connection.setDoInput(true);
connection.connect();
PrintWriter out = new PrintWriter(
                new OutputStreamWriter(
                connection.getOutputStream()));
out.println("Hello JBoss Remoting Gateway!");
out.close();
BufferedReader in = new BufferedReader(
                new InputStreamReader(
                connection.getInputStream()));
String inputLine;
while ((inputLine = in.readLine()) != null) {
    System.out.println(inputLine);
}
in.close();
}
```

Have a go hero – using asynchronous JBR

Go ahead and modify the listener to add asynchronous behavior. Are you able to send a GET request now? What status code and response does it return by default?

The Groovy gateway

This gateway allows JBoss ESB services to integrate a Groovy script (http://groovy.codehaus.org/) and use it to drive messages into the bus. This powerful dynamic nature of the script allows you to integrate any supported type of external client.

The only configuration supported by this gateway is through the <groovy-listener> element which has a single attribute, script, containing the location of the script to execute.

The gateway creates three variables which can be accessed from within the script. The variables are:

◆ config: references the configuration passed to the gateway

◆ gateway and listener: both reference the gateway instance

A typical configuration for this gateway is shown below:

```
<groovy-listener name="Chapter6GroovyListener" script="mygroovyscript"
is-gateway="true"/>
```

Have a go hero – using Groovy scripts

The `groovy_gateway` quickstart demonstrates the usage of a Groovy script where a Swing form is displayed to collect the message that is passed on to the ESB. Have a look at the usage of `ServiceInvoker` inside `MessageInjectionConsole.groovy`.

The SQL gateway

This is another example of an asynchronous gateway that has been covered in previous chapters. Here we will see it being used as a gateway.

Time for action – using the SQL gateway

We will now run the `Chapter6` sample application that demonstrates the usage of the SQL gateway:

1. In JBoss Developer Studio, stop the runtime if it is already running.

2. Open the `deployment.xml` file and uncomment the following highlighted section:

```
<jbossesb-deployment>
  <depends>
    jboss.esb.book.samples.destination:service=Queue,
    name=chapter6_Request_esb
  </depends>
  <depends>
    jboss.esb.book.samples.destination:service=Queue,
    name=chapter6_Request_esb_reply
  </depends>
  <depends>
    jboss.esb.book.samples.destination:service=Queue,
    name=chapter6_Request_gw
  </depends>
  <depends>
    jboss.esb.book.samples.destination:service=Queue,
    name=chapter6_Request_gw_reply
  </depends>
  <depends>
    jboss.esb.book.samples.database:
    service=Chapter6SqlDatabaseInitializer
  </depends>
</jbossesb-deployment>
```

3. Rename the `chapter6-ds.xml.bak` file to `chapter6-ds.xml`. Also, rename the `jbossesb-service.xml.bak` file to `jbossesb-service.xml`.

4. Start the server runtime.

5. Open the `jboss-esb.xml` file in **Source** mode.

6. Append the following `listener` definition to the `<listeners>` tag:

```
<listeners>
  <jms-listener busidref="chapter6ESBChannel"
                name="Chapter6ESBListener"/>
  <jms-listener busidref="chapter6GwChannel" is-gateway="true"
                name="Chapter6GwListener"/>
  <sql-listener busidref="chapter6SQLChannel" is-gateway="true"
                name="Chapter6SQLGwListener"/>
</listeners>
```

7. Add the following `provider` to the `providers` list:

```
<sql-provider name="SQLprovider"
                url="jdbc:hsqldb:hsql://localhost:1704"
                driver="org.hsqldb.jdbcDriver"
                username="sa" password="">
  <sql-bus busid="chapter6SQLChannel">
    <sql-message-filter tablename="GATEWAY_TABLE"
                        order-by="GWDATA"
                        message-column="message"
                        message-id-column="UNIQUE_ID"
                        status-column="GWSTATUS"/>
  </sql-bus>
</sql-provider>
```

8. Add the following `notifier` action:

```
<action name="notificationAction"
        class="org.jboss.soa.esb.actions.Notifier">
  <property name="okMethod" value="notifyOK"/>
  <property name="notification-details">
    <NotificationList type="ok">
      <target class="NotifySqlTable"
              driver-class="org.hsqldb.jdbcDriver"
              connection-url="jdbc:hsqldb:hsql://localhost:1704"
              user-name="sa"
              password=""
              table="gateway_table"
              dataColumn="gwdata">
```

```
            <column name="gwstatus" value="R"/>
        </target>
     </NotificationList>
  </property>
</action>
```

9. Click the **Save** button and the modified application should now be deployed in the server.

10. Select the `src` folder and expand it till the `SendSQLMessage.java` file is displayed in the tree. Now click **Run | Run As | Java Application**.

11. The console will display the output as shown:

```
SQL Gateway says Hello!
```

What just happened?

We sent a message via a database table using the SQL gateway listener and our response was received to the same table with the help of a notifier. Have a look at the client code. Here is part of the listing for your understanding:

```java
public static void main(String[] args) throws Exception {
    Class.forName("org.hsqldb.jdbcDriver");
    Connection connection = DriverManager.getConnection(
                        "jdbc:hsqldb:hsql://localhost:1704",
                        "sa", "");
    Statement stmt = connection.createStatement();
    stmt.executeUpdate(
        "insert into gateway_table(gwdata, gwstatus) values(
                'Hello SQL Gateway!','P')");
    stmt.close();
    connection.commit();
    connection.close();
    Thread.sleep(3000);
    connection = DriverManager.getConnection(
                "jdbc:hsqldb:hsql://localhost:1704", "sa", "");
    stmt = connection.createStatement();
    ResultSet results = stmt.executeQuery(
      "select gwdata from gateway_table where gwstatus like 'R%'");
    while (results.next()) {
        System.out.println(results.getString("gwdata"));
    }
    stmt.executeUpdate(
        "delete from gateway_table where gwstatus like 'R%'");
    connection.commit();
    connection.close();
}
```

There are a few more files that were used in this example, such as `jbossesb-service.xml`, `create.sql`, and `chapter6-ds.xml`. The service in `jbossesb-service.xml` creates the SQL table during deployment while the `chapter6-ds.xml` creates the datasource used to reference the database where the table will reside.

The JCA gateway

J2EE application servers incorporate a standard framework for integrating Enterprise Information Servers with applications, called the J2EE Connection Architecture (JCA). JBoss ESB provides two gateways which integrate with this technology, the JMS/JCA gateway, and the generic JCA gateway.

The JCA framework supports a mechanism which allows a resource adapter to push messages concurrently to a registered listener, a process called **message inflow** in JCA terminology, with the type of message being specific to the Resource Adapter and its purpose.

The most common message type is JMS and, for that reason, JBoss ESB provides a specialized gateway to handle this use case. This gateway supports the configuration of the standard JMS gateway while allowing the JCA resource adapter specific configuration to be included.

Enabling the JMS/JCA gateway is simply a matter of modifying the configuration of the JMS gateway and changing the provider name from `<jms-provider>` to `<jms-jca-provider>`. The JMS/JCA gateway will then, by default, create an activation specification for the `jms-ra` JCA provider, although alternative JCA providers can also be used by specifying the name of their Resource Adapter deployment in the `adapter` attribute.

Have a go hero – using the JMS/JCA gateway

The `jms_transacted` quickstart demonstrates how to use the JMS/JCA provider as both a gateway and a listener for an ESB service. Run through the example and compare the configuration with that of the JMS provider, paying particular attention to the `<activation-config>` element which allows the ESB to specify properties to be applied directly to the activation specification of the JCA provider.

JBoss ESB also provides a gateway for processing message inflow from generic JCA resource adapters, allowing the ESB to handle any message types supported by the associated adapter. One example of this capability would be the processing of e-mails, where an Email Resource Adapter would push the message contents into the ESB through the JCA gateway.

Any discussion of this adapter is beyond the scope of this book as its configuration is tied very closely to the JCA Resource Adapter being used to inflow the messages. It is, however, important that its existence be known so that it can be explored should such a requirement arise.

Summary

In this chapter we have spent a lot of time covering gateways and their role in integrating external clients with the ESB. Specifically, we covered:

- Gateways and notifiers and their purpose in integrating external clients
- The difference between synchronous and asynchronous gateways
- The mechanism used to support composition when handling external messages
- Configuration and use of the JMS gateway
- Reintroducing the File gateway
- Briefly covered the FTP gateway and its associated protocols, FTPS and SFTP
- Configuration and use of the HTTP gateway
- Configuration and use of the UDP gateway
- Configuration and use of the JBoss Remoting gateway
- Configuration and use of the Camel gateway
- Configuration and use of the Groovy gateway
- Configuration and use of the SQL gateway

In many of these sections we have only touched the surface of what is possible, giving a flavor of the gateway capabilities with the hope that this will encourage further exploration.

Gateways play an important part in extending the reach of the Enterprise Service Bus, allowing the ESB to provide services which are reachable from external clients and, as a consequence, allowing it to intercept and augment communication between existing services.

Now that we've given a broad introduction to gateways we are ready to move on to our next topic and learn what part the registry plays within the JBoss ESB—the topic of the next chapter.

7

How ESB Uses the Registry to Keep Track of Services

When you work in software engineering, you spend a lot of your time looking for new ways to solve problems. It's often the case, however, that we use similar approaches to solve different problems. One type of problem that you frequently face is locating "stuff".

When the scale of human population reached the level where it was impossible to keep track of where individuals lived, the notion of an "address" was invented. When computer networking was invented, a similar problem was solved through IP (Internet Protocol) addresses. But, since human beings have a hard time remembering numeric addresses, DNS was invented to give us a way to "map" these numeric addresses to a hierarchical system of mnemonic names.

OK. That's all very interesting, but what does all this have to do with JBoss ESB?

Remember how we described services as being "plugged into" the ESB at the service endpoints? In order for the ESB to be able to deploy, undeploy, manage, and route messages to services over the ESB, the ESB needs a way to find the services' endpoints at runtime. How does JBoss ESB do this? By keeping track of service communication channels, or "Endpoint References" (EPRs) in a registry.

In this chapter, you'll learn about how:

- ◆ JBoss ESB makes use of a registry to keep track of services
- ◆ Services can be published to and queried in the registry
- ◆ Your client code can search for services in the registry
- ◆ You can design a federated registry usage model to give you more control over who can access your services
- ◆ To maintain and troubleshoot your registry

Let's begin by looking at just what a service registry is, how it works, and why it's a good thing.

The registry—what, how, and why?

The classic method of illustrating the operation of a registry is with a triangle-shaped diagram of a client (or "service requester"), a server (or a "service provider"), and a service registry. If you Google this set of words: "uddi register discovery" you'll find many variations of this simple diagram:

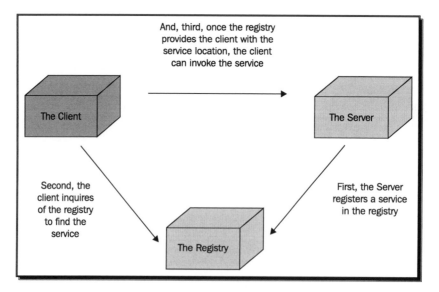

In this triangle, there are three players and three actions. The actions are:

1. The server registers (publishes) its services in the registry.
2. The client looks for (inquires) the service in the registry.
3. The client, once it has retrieved the service location from the registry, invokes the service.

Another classic way of describing a registry is to compare it to a telephone directory. However, instead of enabling people to find each other over the telephone network, a registry enables services to find each other.

UDDI—the registry's specification

In order to understand how the registry works, and how you can better exploit its capabilities, it's important to understand the underlying specification on which the registry is built. That specification is UDDI. For JBoss ESB, UDDI defines an XML-based registry within the bus.

In a nutshell, the UDDI specification is a standard that defines an XML-based registry, that supports means to define (register) and find (discover) services.

UDDI (Universal Description, Discovery, and Integration) was developed under the sponsorship of **OASIS** (the **Organization for the Advancement of Structured Information Standards**, more information can be found at `http://www.oasis-open.org`) with the goal of providing universal public web service registries that anyone in the world could access to locate specific businesses and services. This goal was never really reached, and in 2008, the UDDI public registry was taken down (`http://www.webservicessummit.com/News/UDDI2006.htm`).

But still, UDDI registries are widely used privately or at an organizational level.

The UDDI specification (you can find it at `http://www.oasis-open.org/standards#uddiv3.0.2`) provides for the definition (`http://www.uddi.org/pubs/uddi-tech-wp.pdf`) of the three building blocks of a UDDI registry, they are:

- Services
- Servers
- APIs

 Note that these are abstract definitions. The actual implementations are provided by the specific UDDI providers and APIs that we'll review later in this chapter.

Services are based on the following:

- **Business entities**: These are the groups, companies, or organizations that publish the services. Each business entity can include one or more business services.

- **Business services**: These are the services. Each service definition includes the service name and a description. Each business service can include one or more binding templates.

- ◆ **Binding templates**: A binding template defines the service's access points (typically URLs) and includes references to the service's technical data.
- ◆ **Technical data models**: Called as `tModels`, these define the specific interfaces to the service, and include information such as the transports through which the service can be invoked.

Servers are based on the following:

- ◆ **Nodes**: This is a single UDDI server. What qualifies a "server" to be a "UDDI server"? It has to be running at least a subset of the features defined in the UDDI standard.
- ◆ **Registries**: A registry is a grouping of one or more than one node that supports the full set of features defined in the UDDI standard. A registry can function on its own or it can also operate in a hierarchical group of "affiliated" registries.
- ◆ **Affiliated registries**: One type of grouping of registries is the "federation". In this context the federation refers to the division of service definition and access. For example, services can be divided into registries such that all groups in a company can access the company's employee benefits services, while a subset of those groups can access a company's payroll services.

Additionally, there are definitions of sets of APIs that enable the use and administration of the registry. There are Node API sets, as follows:

- ◆ **Inquiry API set**: The name says it all. This API supports performing inquiries of a registry, in order to find a service.
- ◆ **Publication API set**: A service cannot be found until it's first published. This API supports the publication of services.
- ◆ **Replication API set**: This API enables the copying of information about services between UDDI nodes.
- ◆ **Security Policy API set**: This API governs the use of authentication tokens for accessing services.
- ◆ **Custody and Ownership Transfer API set**: This API supports transferring custody of `businessEntities` or `tModels` between registry nodes.
- ◆ **Subscription API set**: This API enables subscribers (in other words, clients) to "subscribe" to a UDDI registry, so that they will receive information on changes made to the registry.
- ◆ **Value Set Validation API set**: This API enables the validation of a `tModel` service's `keyedReference` which is the relationship between two publishers. The validation ensures that both publishers actually have the authorization to publish the service.

And Client API sets:

- ◆ **UDDI Subscription Listener API set**: This is the counterpart to the Subscription API set. It enables the sending of the changes in a UDDI registry to subscribers.
- ◆ **UDDI Value Set Caching API set**: This API supports caching a set of values to be returned to clients performing a `keyedReference` validation.

That was a quick, and somewhat abstract view of UDDI. Next, we'll switch to a more concrete mode and look at a real implementation. We'll review how JBoss ESB operates with the registry that it is configured with, by default, Apache jUDDI (`http://juddi.apache.org/`).

jUDDI—JBoss ESB's default registry

jUDDI is the Apache open source reference implementation (written in Java) for the UDDI specification. Some of the defining characteristics of jUDDI are:

- ◆ **Standards based**: jUDDI supports the UDDI version 3.0 specification. Scout implements the Java API for XML Registries (JAXR). We'll review using Scout to inquire and publish services later on in this chapter.
- ◆ **Platform independent**: jUDDI is written in Java, so any place that you can run a JVM, you can run jUDDI.
- ◆ **Support for multiple databases for persistence**: The service definitions that you use are stored in a persistent database by jUDDI. jUDDI supports most major databases such as MySQL, PostgreSQL, Oracle, and others.
- ◆ **Configurable**: jUDDI can be configured in clusters for added reliability and performance, and can be integrated with authentication systems such as LDAP, or JAAS compliant systems. jUDDI also supports multiple transport protocols.

Configuring jUDDI for different protocols

As packaged with JBoss ESB, jUDDI is configured to use the "local" transport. Briefly, this configuration assumes (well, requires, actually) that the jUDDI server and JBoss ESB server share the same virtual machine. jUDDI also supports the RMI and SOAP protocols for configuring a server. To change the configuration, use `esb.juddi.client.xml` found at `jboss-as/server/default/deploy/jbossesb.sar/`.

The relevant configuration lines look something like this:

```
<proxyTransport>
   org.jboss.internal.soa.esb.registry.client.JuddiInVMTransport
</proxyTransport>
<custodyTransferUrl>
   org.apache.juddi.api.impl.UDDICustodyTransferImpl
```

```
  </custodyTransferUrl>
  <inquiryUrl>
    org.apache.juddi.api.impl.UDDIInquiryImpl
  </inquiryUrl>
  <publishUrl>
    org.apache.juddi.api.impl.UDDIPublicationImpl
  </publishUrl>
  <securityUrl>
    org.apache.juddi.api.impl.UDDISecurityImpl
  </securityUrl>
  <subscriptionUrl>
    org.apache.juddi.api.impl.UDDISubscriptionImpl
  </subscriptionUrl>
  <subscriptionListenerUrl>
    org.apache.juddi.api.impl.UDDISubscriptionListenerImpl
  </subscriptionListenerUrl>
  <juddiApiUrl>
    org.apache.juddi.api.impl.JUDDIApiImpl
  </juddiApiUrl>
```

`esb.juddi.client.xml` contains commented out settings for RMI and JAX-WS—if you want to change jUDDI to use one of these transports, you can simply comment out the InVM section and uncomment the pertinent transport section you wish to use.

Looking at jUDDI's database

Earlier in this chapter we mentioned that jUDDI supports multiple database providers for its database. Let's take a look at jUDDI's database and how it is created. The first time that you start up the AS server with JBoss ESB deployed, the database is automatically created. Note that, by default, the Hypersonic database is used by jUDDI (HSQLDB). This type of database is fine for learning about jUDDI, but it's not suitable for a production system where you want higher performance and scalability.

The manner in which the database is created is interesting. If you look in the `juddi-ds.xml` file in the `server/all/deploy/jbossesb-registry.sar/` directory, you'll see:

```
<?xml version="1.0" encoding="UTF-8"?>

<datasources>
  <local-tx-datasource>
    <jndi-name>juddiDB</jndi-name>
    <connection-url>
```

```
        jdbc:hsqldb:${jboss.server.data.dir}${/}hypersonic${/}juddiDB
    </connection-url>
    <driver-class>org.hsqldb.jdbcDriver</driver-class>
    <user-name>sa</user-name>
    <password></password>
    <min-pool-size>5</min-pool-size>
    <max-pool-size>20</max-pool-size>
    <idle-timeout-minutes>0</idle-timeout-minutes>
    <prepared-statement-cache-size>32</prepared-statement-cache-size>
    <depends>jboss:service=Hypersonic,database=juddiDB</depends>
  </local-tx-datasource>
  <mbean code="org.jboss.jdbc.HypersonicDatabase"
         name="jboss:service=Hypersonic,database=juddiDB">
    <attribute name="Database">juddiDB</attribute>
    <attribute name="InProcessMode">true</attribute>
  </mbean>
  <mbean code=
         "org.jboss.internal.soa.esb.dependencies.DatabaseInitializer"
          name="jboss.esb:service=JUDDIDatabaseInitializer">
    <attribute name="Datasource">java:/juddiDB</attribute>
    <attribute name="ExistsSql">select count from j3_publisher
    </attribute>
    <attribute name="SqlFiles">juddi-sql/hsqldb/import.sql
    </attribute>
    <depends>jboss.jca:service=DataSourceBinding,name=juddiDB
    </depends>
  </mbean>
</datasources>
```

The section that includes the `DatabaseInitializer` MBean is where the script that creates the database (`juddi-sql/hsqldb/import.sql`) is run. To use a database other than Hypersonic, you would edit this file and reference the database connection and driver properties. jUDDI includes database creation scripts for multiple databases under its `juddi-sql` directory.

Time for action – looking at the jUDDI registry database

Let's take a look at the database, specifically the services that are registered. Luckily, JBoss AS provides us with an easy tool to view the database through a UI.

1. Find the tool by going to `http://localhost:8080/jmx-console`.

2. In the console, select the **database=juddiDB,service=Hypersonic** service. Remember that the OOTB database for jUDDI is Hypersonic.

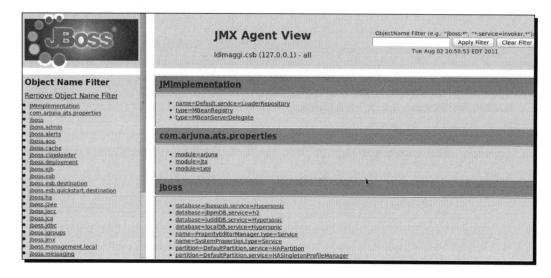

3. When the Database **MBean properties** are displayed, select the **StartDatabaseManager** operation and press the **Invoke** button:

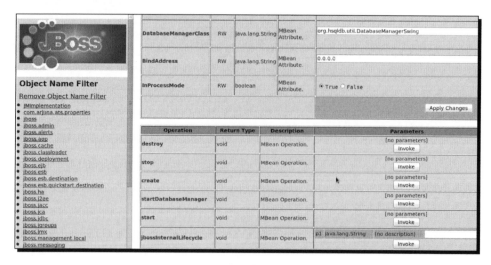

4. At this point the UI will open. Select **File | Connect**, and fill in the connection properties. The database URL should contain the same information as is displayed in the `juddi-ds.xml` file that we saw previously:

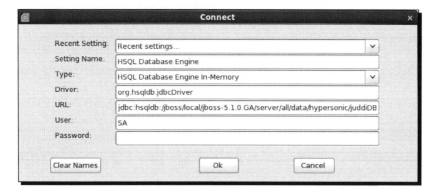

We'll explore the registry hierarchy after getting just a bit more background on how JBoss ESB uses the registry.

Other supported UDDI providers

Note that while jUDDI is the default UDDI provider for JBoss ESB, other UDDI providers are also supported. The following are some:

◆ **HP SOA Systinet**: JBoss ESB has been tested with Systinet 6.64

◆ **SOA Software Service Manager**: SOA Software's UDDI Server has been tested in conjunction with ESB using SOA Software Policy Server 6.0.1

Custom registry solutions

The ESB allows for custom non-UDDI registry solutions by providing a `org.jboss. soa.esb.services.registry.Registry` interface. By implementing that interface, developers can create any sort of registry implementation they want, and then specify it within their `jboss-esb.properties.xml` file in order to use it.

End-point reference

What is an EPR? EPR stands for end-point reference, it is basically an address that the ESB uses to send messages to. The endpoint reference is linked to a service and is stored within the registry. In each message sent by JBoss ESB, multiple EPRs are sent in the headers— where the message came from, where it is going to, where it should default to, and reply to.

What we've just described is somewhat abstract, but it is important to understand because this is the meat of what JBoss ESB stores in its registry.

Time for action – looking at EPRs

Now, let's take a look inside the registry to understand what is happening here.

1. Start by going to `http://localhost:8080/jmx-console`.

2. In the console, select the **database=juddiDB,service=Hypersonic service**:

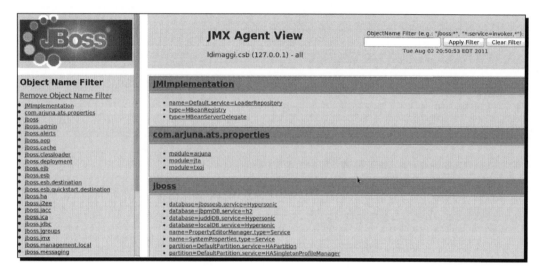

3. When the **Database MBean** properties are displayed, select the **StartDatabaseManager** operation and press the **Invoke** button:

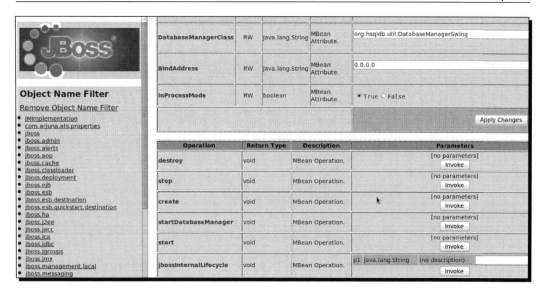

4. Type the following query into the textbox, and click on **Execute SQL**:

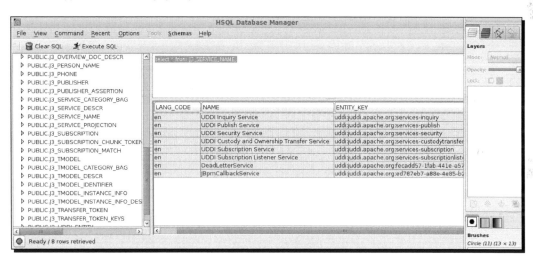

5. The previous query shows the names of the services that are registered by JBoss ESB. If we want to see the EPRs related to the services, we can type the following query into the textbox, and click on **Execute SQL**:

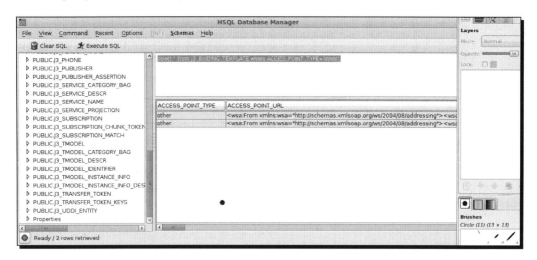

What you see here are two EPRs that are registered by default by JBoss ESB, one relating to the `CallbackQueue` and the other for the `DeadMessageQueue`.

JAXR—introducing the Java API for XML registries

What is JAXR? **JAXR**, or the **Java API for XML Registries** (JSR 93), is a way of interacting with various kinds of registries. It is meant to be an abstraction so that you can switch out different registry implementations (UDDI, ebXML, and so on) without having having to change your query code.

JAXR is notable in terms of JBoss ESB because it is used to query the registry. JBoss ESB uses Scout, the Apache JAXR implementation, on top of UDDI. For the purposes of this book, you should just know that this is an added layer of abstraction.

Federation

What is federation? When we speak of federation, we are talking about clusters of ESB servers. Users cluster ESB servers in order to eliminate a single point of failure—by using load balancing you can not only spread load across multiple ESB servers, but provide redundancy in case one of the servers goes down.

Federation in SOA is very similar to what the term means in terms of actual government—it is an organization of smaller groups wherein the smaller groups still have some autonomy. In terms of the registry, when we "federate" a service, or deploy it across a cluster of servers, the service may be deployed on several nodes, each of which is running its own registry, but is backed by a shared database. When a service is called by the `ServiceInvoker`, it may route a request to a server that is down, but then time out and resend the request to a server that is up, like service location.

Load balancing

Load balancing through `ServiceInvoker` allows the ESB to achieve fail-over for services. The `ServiceInvoker` does this by using different strategies to pick EPRs to invoke. You can choose one of the default load balancing strategies in JBoss ESB (round-robin, first-available, random, and so on) or develop your own and plug it into the configuration file.

You can choose a load balancing strategy by setting the `org.jboss.soa.esb.loadbalancer.policy` property within `jbossesb-properties.xml` to one of the following:

◆ `org.jboss.soa.esb.listeners.ha.RoundRobin`: a round-robin policy which alternates through a list of EPRs

◆ `org.jboss.soa.esb.listeners.ha.FirstAvailable`: a policy which chooses the first available EPR and then moves on to alternates if that one dies or becomes unavailable

◆ `org.jboss.soa.esb.listeners.ha.RandomRobin`: a policy that randomly chooses between different EPRs

Registry maintenance and performance

What can happen with a hard crash? As the ESB shuts down, the ESB unregisters endpoint references and services. When the ESB has finally shut down, it will have removed all ESB-related services and endpoints—therefore if you hard crash your server, your service will leave behind dead EPRs—EPRs that represent an endpoint from a previous session, that are no longer available.

One hard crash alone probably won't have much effect, but if you allow your system to hard crash a great deal, you'll continue to accrue dead EPRs. These extra EPRs can have a visible effect on your runtime performance. Your startup times will increase a great deal, the time that it takes to call a service with `ServiceInvoker` will increase—basically any EPR lookup will become slower and slower.

How can you stop these EPRs slowing down your ESB instance?

◆ The first way you can speed things up is with the brute force method. Stop your server, and completely clear your jUDDI database. On startup of the ESB, the tables and default data of the jUDDI database will be recreated and only the default endpoints and your current service endpoints will be registered. This will remove all duplicate and extraneous EPRs and lookup will be faster.

◆ The other method is a little easier. If you are using the `ServiceInvoker`, you can set the `org.jboss.soa.esb.failure.detect.removeDeadEPR` property, and when a stale EPR is selected, it will be removed. Note that there is a risk in using this property. If your service is slow to respond and times out, its EPR may be removed.

Registry interceptors

One other way of improving performance is by making use of registry interceptors. Registry interceptors catch registry requests and have the ability to handle them, modify results that come back from other interceptors or the registry itself, or simply pass the request along.

You can set registry interceptors in `server/[configuration]/deploy/jbossesb.sar/jbossesb-properties.xml`. This property lists the two registry interceptors provided by default by JBoss ESB:

◆ `org.jboss.internal.soa.esb.services.registry:InVMRegistryInterceptor` handles `InVMEprs` (EPRs representing InVM endpoints) by caching them and not passing requests on to subsequent EPRs.

◆ `org.jboss.internal.soa.esb.services.registry.CachingRegistryInterceptor:` maintains a cache for all EPRs, and additional properties controlling the behavior of the EPR cache can be found within the `jbossesb-properties.xml` file mentioned earlier.

Monitoring

jUDDI also has some simple monitoring abilities. As of JBoss ESB 4.10, jUDDI provided MBeans with details on how many queries were processed for every single API method, what the overall processing time was per method, and how many successful and failed queries were launched. These counts, while simple, give you the opportunity to see which API (Inquiry, Security, or Publish) and method-costly queries might be appearing on, and where the bulk of the queries and query time is spent.

Examining jUDDI query counts

With your ESB Server running, browse to `http://localhost:8080/jmx-console`, and then browse down to the **apache.juddi** section. A counter MBean is listed for each of the UDDI APIs; click on the **apache.juddi:counter=org.apache.juddi.api.impl.UDDIInquiryImpl** MBean.

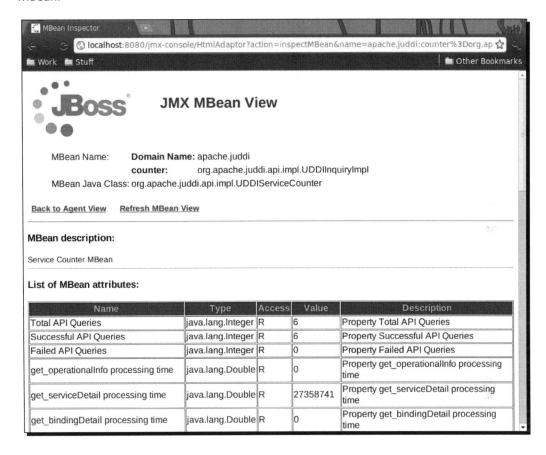

You should be able to see overall counts for the jUDDI Inquiry API (**Total API Queries**, **Successful API Queries**, and **Failed API Queries**) as well as similar counts broken down by each method within the UDDI Inquiry API (for example, `get_operationalInfo`). This should be useful in determining how frequently the registry is being called and how much time is spent in calling it.

Time for action – querying the UDDI server

To get a sense of UDDI, let's try sending some UDDI queries to JBoss ESB. For this exercise, you'll need to use JBoss ESB 4.10 on top of the JBoss 5.1.0.GA AS. There are instructions on setting up this scenario in *Chapter 1*. After setting that up, follow these steps:

1. To start, download a copy of SOAPUI (http://www.soapui.org—the free open source edition is all that is needed).

2. Run the soapui startup script (soapui.sh or soapui.bat, depending on your OS).

3. Next, we need to find the jUDDI services WSDL. Copy uddi-ws-3.1.0.jar from jboss-5.1.0.GA/server/default/deployers/esb.deployer/lib/ to a temporary location. Uncompress the file and create a new SOAPUI project (**File | New SOAPUI Project** in the SOAPUI menu) using the uddi_v3_service.wsdl file from the JAR you just uncompressed as the initial WSDL:

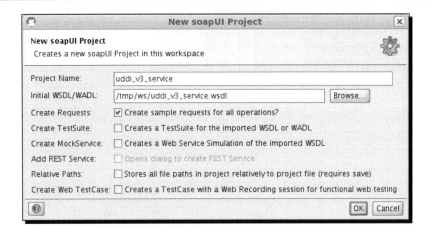

4. We'll try a simple query—scroll down to **UDDI_Security_SoapBinding**, and choose **get_AuthToken**. Double-click on the **Request 1** request to open it in the editor:

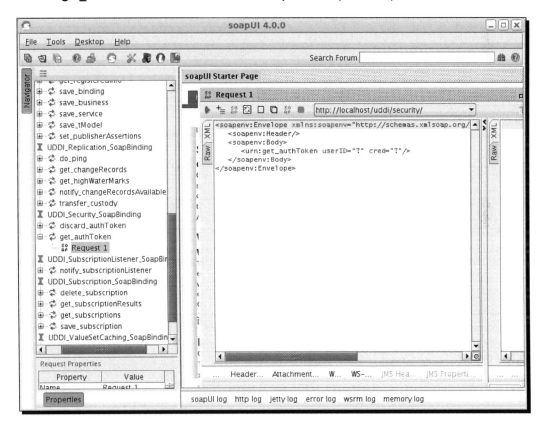

5. Change "?" in the userID="?" property to "root", and then change the "?" in the cred="?" property to "root" as well.

6. Select the dropdown box which contains the endpoint—it should by default say something like **http://localhost/uddi/security**—and choose **edit current**, enter your endpoint address, which is http://127.0.0.1:8080/juddiv3/services/ security?wsdl. You can look this up by using the JBoss WS console (http:// localhost:8080/jbossws) and then viewing the list of deployed services and searching for the Endpoint Address that corresponds to the jUDDI SecurityService:

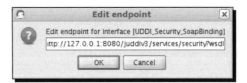

7. Press the green button, you should receive a response with an <authinfo> element that contains a generated authToken string.

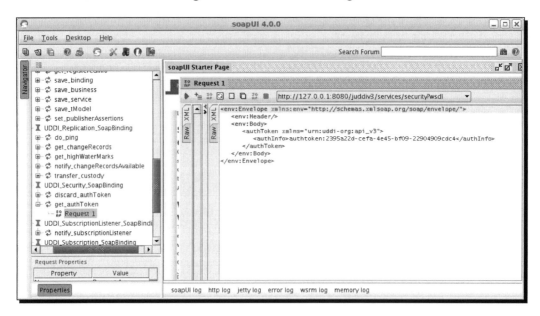

What just happened

You've just completed your first UDDI query using SOAPUI as a client and the jUDDI server that comes along with JBoss ESB. For more information on UDDI queries, a good starting point would be the jUDDI web site (http://juddi.apache.org) or the UDDI v3 specification (http://www.uddi.org/pubs/uddi_v3.htm).

Pop quiz

Before we move on, it's time to see what you've learned. Pencils ready? Let's begin!

1. What is federation?

   a. Clustering a service over multiple nodes to support failover

   b. Using multiple transports to relay a message

   c. Protecting a service with authentication

2. What is UDDI?

   a. Universal Description, Discovery, and Integration

   b. Universal Data Display Interface

   c. Unguarded Data Determination Invocation

3. What is JAXR?

   a. An abstraction on top of XML registries

   b. A new database

   c. A standard for federation

4. If your server suffers a hard crash, what might happen that would slow your services down?

   a. The logs fill up

   b. Stale EPRs might accumulate

   c. The database slows down with age

5. What is the purpose of a registry within an ESB?

   a. Tracking the endpoints of services at runtime

   b. Speeding up your service

   c. To track every invocation that occurs

6. How can I view my service data within the registry?

   a. Use a bean in the JMX Console

   b. Send a message

   c. Federation

7. What UDDI registry does JBoss ESB use by default? Can I use another implementation?

    a. jUDDI

    b. MUDDI

    c. PUDDI

8. What is an EPR?

    a. A runtime address of your service that the ESB sends messages to

    b. A standard for federation

    c. A way of invoking services

Chapter bibliography

Jamae, Javid and Johnson, Peter. JBoss in Action. : Manning, 2009.

Summary

We've covered several important concepts in this chapter:

- What is federation
- What the registry is used for
- What technologies and standards are behind Jboss ESB's registry
- How to perform a UDDI query on your registry
- How to view your service data within the registry

This information may help you debug future issues and gives you a better understanding of the underpinnings of JBoss ESB.

8
Integrating Web Services with ESB

In previous chapters we have covered the majority of the JBoss ESB core functionality, including services, out-of-the-box actions, gateways, and its registry. We are now going to cover another important aspect of an ESB, the ability to expose an ESB service as a web service and to consume an existing web service from within an ESB service.

A web service provides a standard mechanism through which one service can invoke a second, possibly remote, service without having to be concerned with any of the service implementation details, such as language and/or platform. The message exchange format is well defined as are the interactions which are allowed to occur between the client and server.

Web services enable many of the desirable attributes of an ESB service, such as loose coupling, and are likely to be present in many of the legacy services already existing within an organization.

In this chapter we will show how to:

♦ Export an ESB service as a web service

♦ Invoke an external web service

♦ Invoke a co-located web service

♦ Proxy a web service through the ESB, enabling interception and modification of the service invocation

So let's get on with it...

Preparing JBoss Developer Studio

The examples in this chapter are based on a standard ESB application template that can be found under the `Chapter8` directory within the sample download. We will modify this template application as we proceed through this chapter.

Before we start, please make sure that you have set up JBoss Developer Studio and **JBoss 5.1 Runtime** as described in *Chapter 2*.

Time for action – preparing the Chapter8 application

Before we can proceed with this chapter we must prepare the application and runtime environment.

The first task will be importing the example application into JBoss Developer Studio then we must modify the runtime configuration to allow us to run the Wise example which appears later in this chapter.

Import the `Chapter8` application into JBoss Developer Studio as follows:

1. Click on **File** menu and select **Import**.

2. Choose **Existing Projects into workspace** and select the folder where the book samples have been extracted.

3. Choose **Chapter8** project and click on **Finish**.

In order to execute the Wise example we will need to modify the runtime configuration to include the JDK tooling library, a requirement of Wise. Modify the runtime configuration as follows:

1. In JBoss Developer Studio, click **Window | Preferences**.

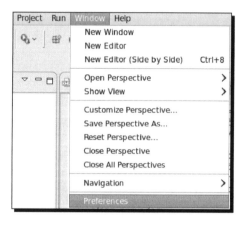

2. Select the **Installed JREs** and select the default JRE that is ticked and click on the **Edit** button:

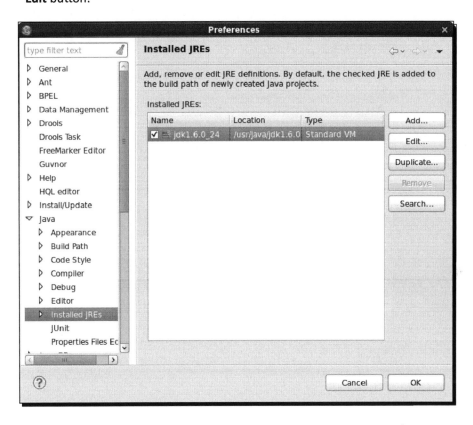

3. Click on the **Add External Jars** button and select the `tools.jar` file from the JDK directory. Your JAR listing should now show `tools.jar` as shown:

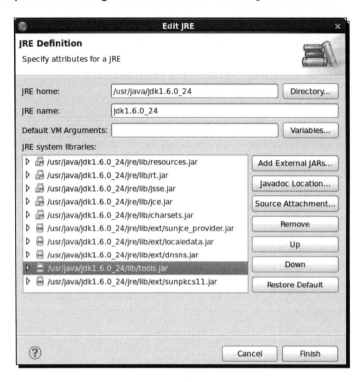

4. Click the **Finish** button and restart the **JBoss 5.1 Runtime** server.

What just happened?

We have imported the example application into JBoss Developer Studio, which we will use throughout the remainder of this chapter. We have also looked at the runtime configuration which is used to execute these examples, modifying it to include a necessary JAR for executing the example in the Wise section.

Time for action – switching consoles

When you are running the tests, you might notice that the console in JBoss Developer Studio sometimes will not show the output, but rather show the server's log output. This is due to the fact that JBoss Developer Studio displays both the server's log and the test output in one console window, showing only one at a time. This might confuse the reader to think that the test did not run. Here is a simple tip on how to switch between console outputs:

1. In JBoss Developer Studio, select the **Console** tab.

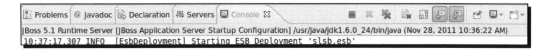

2. Notice the icon to the right that looks like the **Console** tab's icon with a downward pointing arrow ( ).

3. Click on that arrow and you will see there are two entries, one for the server and another for the test application:

4. Click on the required one and the **Console** tab will display the selected one's output.

What just happened?

We looked at the different consoles and discovered how to switch between them.

Exporting ESB services as a web service

Earlier in this book, in the Message validation section of *Chapter 3*, we described how it is possible to validate the request and response messages of a service by specifying the schema files which describe the XML format of the service request, response, and fault messages. What we didn't tell you at the time is that this same information can be used, by JBoss ESB, to automatically generate a web service endpoint to represent the ESB service (also known as an EBWS).

In order to validate the request and response messages it is necessary to explicitly enable the functionality by specifying the `validate` attribute on the `<actions>` element. As the desire to expose an ESB service through a web service is a common requirement, the opposite is true, the web service will be created by default unless it has been explicitly disabled by declaring the `webservice` attribute on the `<actions>` element to be `false`.

The schemas declared in the `inXsd`, `outXsd`, and `faultXsd` attributes of the `<actions>` element are used by JBoss ESB to generate a Web Services Description Language (WSDL) definition of the service, where the `inXsd` and `outXsd` attributes declare the message body contents of the request and response messages respectively and the `faultXsd` attribute declares the message body contents for all of the service fault messages.

JBoss ESB supports two Message Exchange Patterns (MEP) when declaring the service through WSDL, they are:

◆ In-Out, also known as `RequestResponse`

◆ In-Only, also known as `OneWay`

The choice of MEP is based on the existence of the `outXsd` attribute. If this attribute present then an In-Out MEP will be declared otherwise it will use an In-Only MEP.

The processing of an In-Only web service may be handled in an asynchronous manner, depending entirely on the SOAP stack being used, so that it allows the client invoker to continue without being delayed. An In-Out web service, on the other hand, will always be forced to wait for its response before it can continue.

Now take a look at the contents of the `esbcontent/META-INF/jboss-esb.xml` file for the `Chapter8` project, the relevant snippet of which is highlighted here:

```
<service category="Chapter8Sample"
         description="A template for Chapter8"
         name="Chapter8Service">
  <listeners>
    <jms-listener busidref="Chapter8EsbChannel"
                  name="Chapter8EsbListener"/>
  </listeners>
  <actions mep="RequestResponse" inXsd="BookServiceRequest.xsd"
           outXsd="BookServiceResponse.xsd">
    <action name="esbaction"
            class="org.jboss.soa.esb.samples.chapter8.MyAction"/>
  </actions>
</service>
```

Time for action – running the sample

Let's now deploy the sample and test it:

1. In JBoss Developer Studio, select the **Chapter8** project and click **Run | Run As | Run on Server**.

2. Click **Next**. A window with the project pre-configured to run on this server is shown. Ensure that project **Chapter8** selected and shown on the right-hand side:

3. Click **Finish**. The server's **Console** will display output similar to the following:

```
INFO   [TomcatDeployment] deploy, ctxPath=/Chapter8
INFO   [WSDLFilePublisher] WSDL published to: file:/home/book/
jboss-5.1.0.GA-esb4.10/server/default/data/wsdl/Chapter8.war/
Chapter8Sample/Chapter8Service.wsdl
INFO   [EsbDeployment] Starting ESB Deployment 'Chapter8.esb'
```

4. Select the `src` folder, expand it till the `TestWebService.java` file is displayed in the tree. Now click **Run | Run As | Java Application**.

5. The application **Console** will display the output as shown:

```xml
<?xml version="1.0" encoding="UTF-8"?>
<env:Envelope xmlns:env=
    "http://schemas.xmlsoap.org/soap/envelope/">
  <env:Header/>
  <env:Body>
    <ns2:getAuthorsResponse xmlns:ns2=
        "http://chapter8.samples.esb.soa.jboss.org/">
    <return>Charles Dickens</return>
    <return>Sir Arthur Conan Doyle</return>
    <return>Dan Brown</return>
    <return>Amish Tripathi</return>
    </ns2:getAuthorsResponse>
  </env:Body>
</env:Envelope>
```

What just happened?

By simply declaring the schemas for the service we were able to automatically create a web service endpoint for the ESB service. We then sent a SOAP request to this web service and received a SOAP response back, containing all the authors of the books which the service had in stock. Notice that the WSDL was auto-generated for us, based on the specified schemas, when the application was deployed.

Action implementation

Now that we have a better idea of how a web service is generated from the ESB service, let's examine at how it looks to the actions in the pipeline.

Earlier we stated that the schemas declare the XML format of their respective message bodies. What this means is that the message payload passed in to the service from the web service will be the XML representation of the SOAP body and that the service response payload must be the XML representation of the associated web service response.

The following listing of the `MyAction` class' process method shows how the payload contents can be manipulated in a straightforward manner. Note that the action expects the request to be in the form of an XML string and creates an XML string payload as a response.

```java
private String _books[] = new String[] {
    "Great Expectations", "Hound Of The Baskervilles",
    "The Da Vinci Code", "The Immortals Of Meluha" };
private String _authors[] = new String[] {
    "Charles Dickens", "Sir Arthur Conan Doyle",
    "Dan Brown", "Amish Tripathi" };

public Message process(Message message) throws Exception {
    String req = (String) message.getBody().get();
    StringBuffer resp = new StringBuffer();
    if (req.indexOf("getAuthors") > 0) {
        resp.append("<ns2:getAuthorsResponse
        xmlns:ns2=\"http://chapter8.samples.esb.soa.jboss.org/\">");
        for (String author : _authors) {
            resp.append("<return>")
                .append(author)
                .append("</return>");
        }
        resp.append("</ns2:getAuthorsResponse>");
    } else if (req.indexOf("getBooks") > 0) {
        resp.append("<ns2:getBooksResponse
        xmlns:ns2=\"http://chapter8.samples.esb.soa.jboss.org/\">");
        for (String book : _books) {
            resp.append("<return>")
                .append(book)
                .append("</return>");
```

```
        }
        resp.append("</ns2:getBooksResponse>");
    } else {
        resp.append("Unknown request!");
    }
    message.getBody().add(resp);
    return message;
}
```

Often it is desirable to transform the XML contents of the request and response into objects, in order to enable simpler processing or reuse of existing code or services. This can easily be achieved by introducing a transformation action into the exposed service pipeline, for example by using Smooks or XStream as was covered in *Chapter 4*, and then routing the message to a second service. This architecture may look like the following:

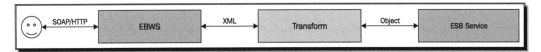

Note that the second ESB service can be directly consumed by other ESB services and also by the ESB service that is exporting the web service endpoint.

It is important to note that the WSDL generated by JBoss ESB, through this mechanism, will expose only one operation in the generated web service. If the service is intended to support multiple operations then this must be reflected in the schemas used to generate the request and response WSDL. The contents of the request body can then be used to determine which operation should be invoked.

Have a go hero – introduce a transformer

Modify the `TestWebService.java` file to retrieve the books. Update `MyAction` to perform fault handling. Go ahead and add a Smooks transformer after the `MyAction` configuration and try to remove the `MyAction` process methods' XML String code.

Securing EBWS

An ESB service exported through a web service endpoint can be secured through the usual service security mechanism, specified through configuration of the `<security>` element within the service definition. As with any other service you will need to specify the `moduleName` and `rolesAllowed` attributes to control how the authentication and authorization occurs.

The web service endpoint will extract the security credentials from the incoming SOAP request, identified within the request through the `security` SOAP header. The web service endpoint will recognize the `UsernameToken` element, the `BinarySecurityToken` element (for X.509/Kerberos and others), and **Security Assertion Markup Language (SAML)** assertions.

Specifying the security configuration will ensure that access to the web service will be authenticated and secure.

Here is a sample configuration that can be used to secure connections to EBWS. The sample shows a security module allowing access from users having either the `thosewhohaveaccesstows` or `moreroleswithaccess` role.

```
<service category="SecuredSample" name="SecuredService">
  <security moduleName="SomeSecurityModule"
       rolesAllowed="thosewhohaveaccesstows, moreroleswithaccess"/>
  ...
</service>
```

Time for action – securing the sample

Let us now add the `security` element to the sample and test it:

1. In JBoss Developer Studio, open the `esbcontent/META-INF/jboss-esb.xml` file in **Source** mode.

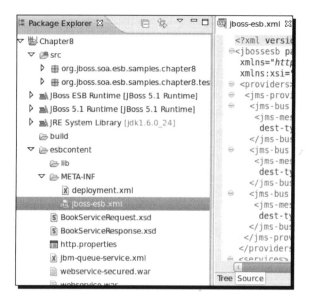

2. Add the highlighted section contents to the `service` in question:

```
<service category="Chapter8Sample"
        description="A template for Chapter8"
        name="Chapter8Service">
  <security moduleName="JBossWS" rolesAllowed="friend"/>
  <listeners>
    <jms-listener busidref="Chapter8EsbChannel"
                 name="Chapter8EsbListener"/>
  </listeners>
  <actions inXsd="BookService.xsd" mep="RequestResponse"
          outXsd="BookService.xsd">
    <action class="org.jboss.soa.esb.samples.chapter8.MyAction"
           name="esbaction"/>
  </actions>
</service>
```

3. Click the **Save** button and the modified application should now be deployed in the server.

4. Select the `src` folder, expand it till the `TestWebService.java` file is displayed in the tree. Now click **Run | Run As | Java Application**:

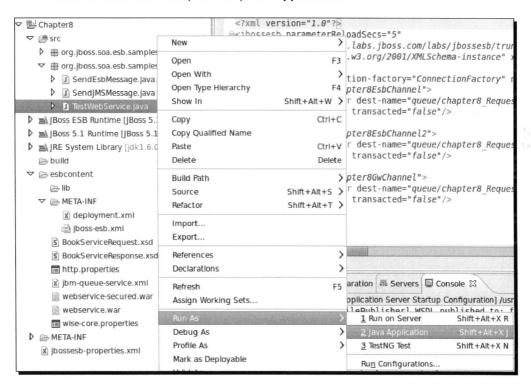

5. You will see the following output in the test **Console**:

```
java.io.IOException: Server returned HTTP response code: 500
for URL: http://localhost:8080/Chapter8/ebws/Chapter8Sample/
Chapter8Service
...
<?xml version="1.0" encoding="UTF-8"?>
<error>java.io.IOException: Server returned HTTP response code:
500 for URL: http://localhost:8080/Chapter8/ebws/Chapter8Sample/
Chapter8Service
</error>
```

6. Open the server **Console** and this error log should display:

```
ERROR [ActionProcessingPipeline] SecurityService exception :
org.jboss.soa.esb.services.security.SecurityServiceException:
Service 'Chapter8Service' has been configured for security but no
AuthenticationRequest could be located in the Message Context.
Cannot authenticate without an AuthenticationRequest.
...
ERROR [BaseWebService] org.jboss.soa.esb.couriers.
FaultMessageException: org.jboss.soa.esb.services.security.
SecurityServiceException: Service 'Chapter8Service' has been
configured for security but no AuthenticationRequest could be
located in the Message Context. Cannot authenticate without an
AuthenticationRequest.
```

7. Modify the main method within `TestWebService` to replace the input as follows:

```
public static void main(String[] args) throws Exception {
    String serviceURL = "http://localhost:8080/Chapter8/ebws/
        Chapter8Sample/Chapter8Service";
String input = "<soapenv:Envelope" +
  " xmlns:soapenv=\"http://schemas.xmlsoap.org/soap/envelope/\"" +
  " xmlns:chap=\"http://chapter8.samples.esb.soa.jboss.org/\"" +
  " xmlns:wsse=\"http://schemas.xmlsoap.org/ws/2002/04/secext\">" +
  "    <soapenv:Header>" +
  "        <wsse:Security>" +
  "            <wsse:UsernameToken>" +
  "                <wsse:Username>kermit</wsse:Username>" +
  "                <wsse:Password>thefrog</wsse:Password>" +
  "            </wsse:UsernameToken>" +
  "        </wsse:Security>" +
  "    </soapenv:Header>" +
  "    <soapenv:Body>" +
  "        <chap:getAuthors/>" +
  "    </soapenv:Body>" +
  "</soapenv:Envelope>";

    String response = invokeWebService(serviceURL, input);
```

8. Click the **Save** button, select the `TestWebService.java` file, click **Run | Run As | Java Application**.

9. You will see the following output in the test **Console**:

```
<?xml version="1.0" encoding="UTF-8"?>
<env:Envelope xmlns:env="http://schemas.xmlsoap.org/soap/
envelope/">
<env:Header/>
<env:Body>
<ns2:getAuthorsResponse
   xmlns:ns2="http://chapter8.samples.esb.soa.jboss.org/">
<return>Charles Dickens</return>
<return>Sir Arthur Conan Doyle</return>
<return>Dan Brown</return>
<return>Amish Tripathi</return>
</ns2:getAuthorsResponse>
</env:Body>
</env:Envelope>
```

What just happened?

We configured a security domain to enforce authentication for our EBWS service, choosing the `JBossWS` domain included as part of the `JBossWS` stack, and required all authenticated users to have the friend role in order to invoke the service. The client code was then modified to include the `UsernameToken` WSSE (Web Service Security Extension) header, enabling access to the service. If the service was to be invoked without credentials then the processing of the service pipeline would result in an exception being raised.

Other security mechanisms

In the previous example we used the `UsernameToken` option of WS-Security, however this results in the username and password being transferred in clear text. In production usage it is advisable to use the `BinaryToken` or **SAML** capabilities coupled with a secure transport. Readers are encouraged to look at WS-Security specifications, obtainable from the OASIS Web Services Security Technical Committee (`http://www.oasis-open.org/committees/tc_home.php?wg_abbrev=wss`), for usage and sample SOAP request/responses for these mechanisms.

ESB web service client

A common requirement when integrating services is often the ability to invoke existing web services. These web services may be internally developed, perhaps by a different team in your organization, or even external services, such as invoking the search API of your favorite search engine provider. This is where the ESB SOAPClient actions come into the picture, two implementations which take different approaches to invoking web services.

We will look at each of them more deeply in the following sections.

soapUI client

The first SOAP client action we will look at is based on the soapUI tool (http://www.soapui.org/), a popular Open Source testing tool which enables SOAP invocations using a template approach. The soapUI library generates a template based on the WSDL definition of the required operation, which is then populated by injecting parameters from the associated ESB message.

Before we go into further detail of the mapping, let's pause to take a quick look at this in action.

A typical configuration of using org.jboss.soa.esb.actions.soap.SOAPClient is shown:

```
<action name="soapui-client-action"
        class="org.jboss.soa.esb.actions.soap.SOAPClient">
  <property name="wsdl" value="http://localhost:8080/Chapter8/ebws/
            Chapter8Sample/Chapter8Service?wsdl"/>
  <property name="SOAPAction" value="getBooks"/>
</action>
```

Time for action – ESB SOAP client

We exported an ESB service as a web service in the previous section. Let us now invoke that web service with another ESB service.

1. In JBoss Developer Studio, open the esbcontent/META-INF/jboss-esb.xml file in **Source** mode.

2. Append the following service definition to the <services> tag.
    ```
    <service category="Chapter8Sample" description=""
             name="Chapter8WSClient">
      <listeners>
        <jms-listener busidref="Chapter8EsbChannel2"
    ```

```
                    name="Chapter8EsbListener"/>
    </listeners>
    <actions mep="RequestResponse">
      <action name="requestAction"
        class="org.jboss.soa.esb.samples.chapter8.MyRequestAction"/>
      <action class="org.jboss.soa.esb.actions.soap.SOAPClient"
            name="soapui-client-action">
        <property name="wsdl" value="http://localhost:8080/Chapter8/
                ebws/Chapter8Sample/Chapter8Service?wsdl"/>
        <property name="SOAPAction" value="Chapter8ServiceOp"/>
      </action>
    </actions>
  </service>
```

3. Click the **Save** button and the modified application should now be deployed in the server.

4. Select the `src` folder, expand it till the `SendEsbMessage.java` file is displayed in the tree. Now click **Run | Run As | Java Application**:

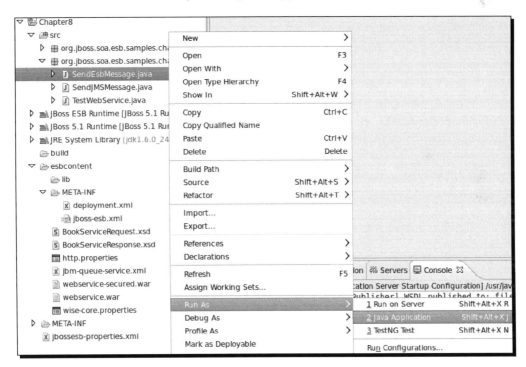

5. The server **Console** will display the output as follows:

```
INFO  [STDOUT] (Thread-46) Progress: 1 - Caching definition
from url [http://localhost:8080/Chapter8/ebws/Chapter8Sample/
Chapter8Service?wsdl]

...
```

6. The test **Console** will display the output as follows:

```
<env:Envelope xmlns:env='http://schemas.xmlsoap.org/soap/
envelope/'><env:Header></env:Header><env:Body><ns2:getAutho
rsResponse xmlns:ns2='http://chapter8.samples.esb.soa.jboss.
org/'><return>Charles Dickens</return><return>Sir Arthur Conan
Doyle</return><return>Dan Brown</return><return>Amish Tripathi</
return></ns2:getAuthorsResponse></env:Body></env:Envelope>
```

What just happened?

We deployed an ESB service with the ability to invoke an external web service. Note that the configuration of the pipeline contains a request mapper called `MyRequestAction`, used to convert the incoming message into a `Map` for populating the SOAP request template.

Have a go hero – quickstarts

Have a look at the `webservice_consumer1` quickstart. Examine the configuration and the usage of the `MyRequestAction` class.

Request processing

As mentioned previously the soapUI version of `SOAPClient` generates a template based on the WSDL definition for the appropriate service operation, which is then populated from a set of parameters extracted from the current ESB message.

The SOAP parameters for the template are defined within a map that resides in the payload location of the ESB message, the keys of the map entries specifying the template location of their associated values. There are two choices when specifying values:

- **Individual text values based on their explicit location**: For this choice each value must be explicitly configured within the payload parameter map with the key for each entry consisting of the concatenation of the local names of each element starting with the first element within the SOAP body. For example the value represented by the key `processOrder.order.id` would be used to populate the `id` element nested within the `order` and `processOrder` elements.

- ◆ **A single object instance representing all contents**: For this second choice a single object instance would be placed within the map to represent the contents of the SOAP body, with each nested value being taken from the object by following the normal java bean naming conventions. For example an instance of `ProcessOrderRequest`, located within the parameter map with a key of `processOrder`, would populate the order id by invoking the `getOrder().getId()` methods and converting the result to a string.

 The naming convention used in each choice follows the notation defined as part of the Object-Graph Navigational Language (OGNL) expression language for accessing properties of java objects. See `http://incubator.apache.org/ognl/` for more information.

Request transformations

The soapUI codebase creates a template based on the WSDL of the target web service which is then populated using the parameters extracted from the ESB message. This template, and its population, focus on the contents of the SOAP envelope's `Body` element but do not support creation of elements within the SOAP envelope's `Header` element.

In order to attach SOAP headers to the request it is necessary to transform the populated message before it is sent to the target web service. This can be achieved by including a Smooks transformation in the configuration of the action, using the `smooksTransform` parameter.

An example of this configuration is as follows:

```
<action name="soapui-client-action"
        class="org.jboss.soa.esb.actions.soap.SOAPClient">
    <property name="wsdl" value="http://localhost:8080/Chapter8/ebws/
            Chapter8Sample/Chapter8Service?wsdl"/>
    <property name="SOAPAction" value="getBooks"/>
    <property name="smooksTransform" value="smooks-transform.xml"/>
</action>
```

Have a go hero – SOAP request header transformation

Add a Smooks transformation to create SOAP headers as part of the request.

You can see the effect on the resulting request contents by specifying an extra entry into the parameter map, using the `dumpSOAP` key. The existence of this key will cause the integration code to display the raw template and the populated template for the request on the server console.

Response processing

The SOAP response from the web service can be processed in one of three ways, the result of which will be stored as the payload of the resulting ESB message:

- As a string containing the raw SOAP response message (the default)
- As a map containing the explicit element values, keyed using the same OGNL notation as used in the request processing
- As an Object Graph created and populated by the XStream toolkit

OGNL

In order to return a map containing the contents of the SOAP response message using the OGNL notation it is necessary to configure an additional property on the SOAPClient action. This property, responseAsOgnlMap, must be configured with the value true.

The following is an example of receiving our sample's response as an OGNL map:

```
<action name="soapui-client-action"
        class="org.jboss.soa.esb.actions.soap.SOAPClient">
  <property name="wsdl" value="http://localhost:8080/Chapter8/ebws/
                    Chapter8Sample/Chapter8Service?wsdl"/>
  <property name="SOAPAction" value="Chapter8ServiceOp"/>
  <property name="responseAsOgnlMap" value="true"/>
</action>
```

Have a go hero – OGNL response

Go ahead and set the responseAsOgnlMap property to true and see how the response looks on the test **Console**. Take a look at the webservice_consumer2 quickstart and familiarize yourself with the OGNL notation. Change the request map of the quickstart so that it uses explicit locations instead of an object instance.

XStream

XStream (http://xstream.codehaus.org/) is an Open Source library which supports the serialization and deserialization of XML to and from Java Objects. When used through the SOAPClient it supports the deserialization of the SOAP response into a Java object which is then returned through the ESB message payload.

In order to use the XStream functionality it is necessary to define a responseXStreamConfig action property containing the appropriate mappings. Here is an example of how our getAuthorsResponse SOAP envelope can be converted into a List<String> object.

```
<action name="soapui-client-action"
        class="org.jboss.soa.esb.actions.soap.SOAPClient">
  <property name="wsdl" value="http://localhost:8080/Chapter8/ebws/
                  Chapter8Sample/Chapter8Service?wsdl"/>
  <property name="SOAPAction" value="Chapter8ServiceOp"/>
  <property name="responseXStreamConfig">
    <alias name="getAuthorsResponse" class="java.util.ArrayList"
          namespace="http://chapter8.samples.esb.soa.jboss.org/"/>
    <alias name="return" class="java.lang.String" namespace=""/>
  </property>
</action>
```

Have a go hero – XStream conversion

Go ahead and add the highlighted section above to the sample and see how it changes the response output.

The Wise SOAPClient

The second SOAPClient action is based on **Wise (Wise Invokes Services Easily)**, a JBoss Open Source project (http://www.jboss.org/wise) which handles most of the necessary interactions of dealing with the JAX-WS APIs and proxies.

The goal of Wise is to make your life easier by automatically processing a web service's WSDL to generate the client-side proxy classes, select the appropriate services and endpoints, and enable the invocation of the operations by mapping an object model that you define to the JAX-WS objects needed to perform the operation. The result is that you can access a web service without having to generate the classes yourself.

A typical configuration sample would be like this:

```
<action name="soap-wise-client-action"
        class="org.jboss.soa.esb.actions.soap.wise.SOAPClient">
  <property name="wsdl" value="http://localhost:8080/Chapter8/ebws/
                  Chapter8Sample/Chapter8Service?wsdl"/>
  <property name="SOAPAction" value="getBooks"/>
</action>
```

Time for action – Incorporating the Wise SOAP Client

Let us modify our sample to use the Wise SOAPClient now. Follow these steps:

1. In JBoss Developer Studio, open the esbcontent/META-INF/jboss-esb.xml file in **Source** mode.

2. Replace the following code:

```
<action name="soapui-client-action"
        class="org.jboss.soa.esb.actions.soap.SOAPClient">
  <property name="wsdl" value="http://localhost:8080/Chapter8/
                ebws/Chapter8Sample/Chapter8Service?wsdl"/>
  <property name="SOAPAction" value="Chapter8ServiceOp"/>
</action>
```

With the followingcode:

```
<action class="org.jboss.soa.esb.actions.soap.wise.SOAPClient"
        name="soap-wise-client-action">
  <property name="wsdl"
            value="http://localhost:8080/BookService?wsdl"/>
  <property name="SOAPAction" value="getBooks"/>
  <property name="EndPointName" value="BookServicePort"/>
</action>
```

3. Click the **Save** button, and the modified application should now be deployed in the server.

4. Select the src folder, expand it till the SendEsbMessage.java file is displayed in the tree. Now click **Run | Run As | Java Application**.

   The server **Console** will display the output as below:

```
INFO  [STDOUT] (pool-41-thread-1) Request map is:
{getAuthors=null}

INFO  [STDOUT] (pool-41-thread-1) parsing WSDL...

INFO  [STDOUT] (pool-41-thread-1) generating code...

INFO  [STDOUT] (pool-41-thread-1) org\jboss\soa\esb\samples\
quickstart\webservice_consumer_wise\generated\BookService.java

INFO  [STDOUT] (pool-41-thread-1) org\jboss\soa\esb\samples\
quickstart\webservice_consumer_wise\generated\BookServiceService.
java

INFO  [STDOUT] (pool-41-thread-1) org\jboss\soa\esb\samples\
quickstart\webservice_consumer_wise\generated\GetAuthors.java
```

```
INFO   [STDOUT] (pool-41-thread-1) org\jboss\soa\esb\samples\
quickstart\webservice_consumer_wise\generated\GetAuthorsResponse.
java

INFO   [STDOUT] (pool-41-thread-1) org\jboss\soa\esb\samples\
quickstart\webservice_consumer_wise\generated\GetBooks.java

INFO   [STDOUT] (pool-41-thread-1) org\jboss\soa\esb\samples\
quickstart\webservice_consumer_wise\generated\GetBooksResponse.
java

INFO   [STDOUT] (pool-41-thread-1) org\jboss\soa\esb\samples\
quickstart\webservice_consumer_wise\generated\ObjectFactory.java

INFO   [STDOUT] (pool-41-thread-1) org\jboss\soa\esb\samples\
quickstart\webservice_consumer_wise\generated\package-info.java
```

The test **Console** will display the output as shown:

```
{result=[Great Expectations, Hound Of The Baskervilles,
The Da Vinci Code, The Immortals Of Meluha]}
```

What just happened?

We used the Wise SOAPClient to invoke a web service. Note that we are using WSDL from a different service than the soapUI example and that the processing of the WSDL results in the automatic generation of the appropriate Java client proxy classes. This stub generation will only happen once with all subsequent requests using the cached WSDL and the pre-compiled Java classes. This "on the fly" compilation is the reason that the tools.jar file was added at the beginning of the chapter to your JRE library list.

Have a go hero – Wise properties

Take a look at the wise-core.properties file in the esbcontent directory of the Chapter8 project, you will find a wise.tmpDir property which specifies the location of the temporary files generated by Wise. By default this will be /tmp on Mac and Linux and <ESB server drive>:/tmp on Windows.

Now take a look at the Wise generated files. Modify the SOAPAction and see if you can invoke the getAuthors method.

Request and response processing

The request parameters for the Wise SOAPClient are configured as a map in the payload of the incoming ESB message. The contents of this map can take one of two forms:

◆ A map of parameters where the key of each entry is the name of the SOAP parameter as declared within the WSDL

- ◆ A general map of parameters that can be transformed into the map required by the specific operation through a Smooks transformation. The Smooks transformation will be responsible for translating the incoming Map into the correct model required by the invocation of the SOAP operation.

The response will be stored in a map which will contain all the parameters that are returned as part of the SOAP invocation, the key for each entry being the name of the SOAP parameter as it is declared in the WSDL. This will include the result of the operation as well as the values associated with any in/out or out parameters defined in the WSDL for the operation. This map will be stored in the ESB message payload as a result of this action.

As with the request parameters, it is also possible to transform the response into a different Java model using a Smooks transformation. The map containing the transformed objects will, in that case, be stored in the ESB message payload instead of the original result of the SOAP invocation.

Transformations on the request and response objects are declared within the configuration by specifying the SmooksRequestMapper and SmooksResponseMapper action properties respectively. These properties will each reference a Smooks configuration which will be used to transform one Java model into another. Here is a sample from the quickstarts:

```
<action name="soap-wise-client-action"
        class="org.jboss.soa.esb.actions.soap.wise.SOAPClient">
  <property name="wsdl" value=
  "http://127.0.0.1:8080/Quickstart_webservice_consumer_wise2/
PingWS?wsdl" />
  <property name="SOAPAction" value="pingComplexObject"/>
  <property name="EndPointName" value="PingWSPort"/>
  <property name="SmooksRequestMapper"
            value="smooks-request-config.xml"/>
  <property name="SmooksResponseMapper"
            value="smooks-response-config.xml"/>
  <property name="LoggingMessages" value="false" />
  <property name="serviceName" value="PingWS"/>
</action>
```

As with the soapUI SOAPClient it is possible to further transform the SOAP request to add custom SOAP headers or to further manipulate the SOAP body before the invocation of the web service. Here is another sample from the quickstarts:

```
<action name="soapui-client-action"
        class="org.jboss.soa.esb.actions.soap.wise.SOAPClient">
  <property name="wsdl" value="http://127.0.0.1:8080/
Quickstart_webservice_consumer_wise3/HelloWorldWS?wsdl" />
  <property name="SOAPAction" value="sayHello"/>
  <property name="EndPointName" value="HelloWorldPort"/>
```

```
    <property name="LoggingMessages" value="true" />
    <property name="smooks-handler-config"
            value="smooks-handler.xml"></property>
        <property name="serviceName" value="HelloWorldWS"/>
</action>
```

Have a go hero – Smooks configurations

Take a look at the quickstarts `webservice_consumer_wise`, `webservice_consumer_wise2`, `webservice_consumer_wise3`, and `webservice_consumer_wise4`. Familiarize yourself with the approach these quickstarts apply.

Custom handlers

The Wise `SOAPClient` also supports the configuration of JAX-WS handlers, both `LogicalHandler` and `SOAPHandler`, which can enable additional processing of the incoming and outgoing messages. A sample configuration will look like this:

```
<action class="org.jboss.soa.esb.actions.soap.wise.SOAPClient"
        name="soap-wise-client-action">
    <property name="wsdl"
            value="http://localhost:8080/BookService?wsdl"/>
    <property name="SOAPAction" value="getBooks"/>
    <property name="EndPointName" value="BookServicePort"/>
    <property name="custom-handlers"
            value="org.jboss.soa.esb.samples.chapter8.MyLogHandler"/>
</action>
```

A simple implementation of this type of handler is shown:

```
package org.jboss.soa.esb.samples.chapter8;

import java.util.Collections;
import java.util.HashSet;
import java.util.Set;

import javax.xml.namespace.QName;
import javax.xml.ws.handler.MessageContext;
import javax.xml.ws.handler.soap.SOAPHandler;
import javax.xml.ws.handler.soap.SOAPMessageContext;

public class MyLogHandler implements SOAPHandler<SOAPMessageContext> {
    private static Set<QName> headers;

    static {
```

```java
        HashSet<QName> set = new HashSet<QName>();
        headers = Collections.unmodifiableSet(set);
    }

    public Set<QName> getHeaders() {
        return headers;
    }

    public void close(MessageContext messageContext) {
    }

    public boolean handleFault(SOAPMessageContext smc) {
        return true;
    }

    public boolean handleMessage(SOAPMessageContext msgContext) {
        System.out.println(msgContext.getMessage());
        return true;
    }

}
```

Have a go hero – using a custom handler

Go ahead and add the previous code to the `src` folder and configure the Wise `SOAPClient` to use this custom handler. Do you see the SOAP message being printed out on the server console?

Co-located web services

The two actions we have covered so far have discussed the invocation of remote web service endpoints, but what if the endpoint is deployed within the same server? We can still use the previous actions to invoke the endpoints but this will incur a cost, both from the network access at the transport layer and from any resource pooling on the receiving side.

The `SOAPProcessor` action provides a simple, optimized mechanism which allows the invocation of a web service within the same server but without taking any additional performance hit.

SOAPProcessor

The ability to invoke co-located web services lies within the `org.jboss.soa.esb.actions.soap.SOAPProcessor` action class. The input to this action is an ESB message which contains the raw SOAP request as its payload, allowing the indirect invocation of the web service through any listeners configured on the service.

In addition to providing indirect access to the web service endpoint, the `SOAPProcessor` action will also expose a WSDL if the service contains a HTTP or **JBoss Remoting** gateway, allowing the service to act as a proxy for the target web service.

A minimal configuration using this action would look like this:

```
<action name="JBossWSAdapter"
        class="org.jboss.soa.esb.actions.soap.SOAPProcessor">
  <property name="jbossws-context" value="webservice_war"/>
  <property name="jbossws-endpoint" value="BookService"/>
</action>
```

The properties which can be configured are as follows:

- `jbossws-endpoint`: The name of the JBoss WS endpoint that the `SOAPProcessor` is exposing. This property is required.

- `jbossws-context`: The name of the web service's deployment context. This property is optional.

- `rewrite-endpoint-url`: The default action, when exposing the WSDL through one of the gateways, is to rewrite the URL so that it appears to come from the gateway's endpoint. Sometimes this behavior is undesirable, for example when the web service container has already been configured to override the endpoint to that of a load balancer. Setting this to `false` disables the rewriting capabilities.

Time for action – incorporating a SOAPProcessor client

We will now modify the sample to use `SOAPProcessor`:

1. In JBoss Developer Studio, open the `esbcontent/META-INF/jboss-esb.xml` file in **Source** mode.

2. Replace the following code:
   ```
   <action name="requestAction"
    class="org.jboss.soa.esb.samples.chapter8.MyRequestAction"
    />
   <action class="org.jboss.soa.esb.actions.soap.wise.SOAPClient"
   name="soap-wise-client-action">
   ```

```
<property name="wsdl"
        value="http://localhost:8080/BookService?wsdl"/>
<property name="SOAPAction" value="getBooks"/>
<property name="EndPointName" value="BookServicePort"/>
</action>
```

With the following code:

```
<action class="org.jboss.soa.esb.actions.soap.SOAPProcessor"
        name="JBossWSAdapter">
  <property name="jbossws-endpoint" value="BookService"/>
  <property name="jbossws-context" value="BookService"/>
</action>
<action name="print-after"
        class="org.jboss.soa.esb.actions.SystemPrintln">
  <property name="message"
            value="AFTER invoking jbossws endpoint"/>
</action>
```

3. Add another listener to this service:

```
<service category="Chapter8Sample" description=""
        name="Chapter8WSClient">
  <listeners>
    <jms-listener busidref="Chapter8EsbChannel2"
                  name="Chapter8EsbListener"/>
    <jms-listener busidref="Chapter8GwChannel"
                  name="Chapter8GwListener"
                  is-gateway="true"/>
  </listeners>
```

4. Click the **Save** button and the modified application should now be deployed in the server.

5. Select the src folder, expand it till the SendJMSMessage.java file is displayed in the tree. Now click **Run | Run As | Java Application**:

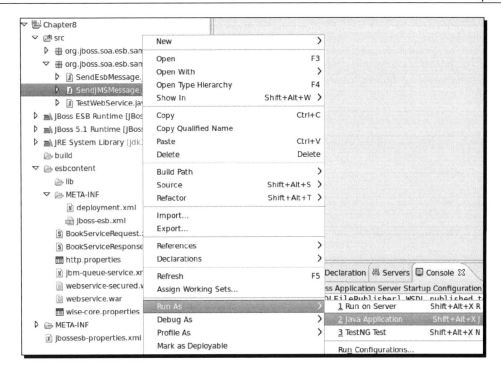

6. The server **Console** will display the output as shown:

```
INFO   [STDOUT] AFTER invoking jbossws endpoint:
INFO   [STDOUT] [<env:Envelope xmlns:env='http://schemas.xmlsoap.
org/soap/envelope/'><env:Header></env:Header><env:Body><ns2:get
BooksResponse xmlns:ns2="http://chapter8.samples.esb.soa.jboss.
org/"><return>Great Expectations</return><return>Hound Of The
Baskervilles</return><return>The Da Vinci Code</return><return>The
Immortals Of Meluha</return></ns2:getBooksResponse></env:Body></
env:Envelope>].
```

What just happened?

We used `SOAPProcessor` to invoke the web service. We used a JMS queue to send a SOAP message. Notice that `SendJMSMessage.java` uses the gateway queue to send the SOAP message.

```
QueueConnectionFactory qcf = (QueueConnectionFactory) tmp;
conn = qcf.createQueueConnection();
que = (Queue) iniCtx.lookup("queue/chapter8_Request_gw");
replyQueue =
    (Queue) iniCtx.lookup("queue/chapter8_Request_esb2_reply");
```

Notice we also removed the `MyRequestAction` from the pipeline.

Have a go hero – co-located services

Use other gateways like HTTP or File to send the SOAP requests. Route the response to another ESB service and write the contents to a file. Look at the `webservice_wssecurity` and `webservice_wsaddressing` quickstarts for usage of these advanced features.

Web service proxies

Another useful capability of JBoss ESB is to act as a proxy for existing web services. There are a number of reasons why this could be desirable, including controlling access to the service, modifying request and/or response invocations, redirecting requests to different versions of the web service, exposing a subset of the functionality and more. JBoss ESB forms a bridge between the client and the web service, reducing the coupling between the two endpoints. This reduced coupling increases the flexibility inherent in the system, allowing it to adapt to changes as and when they arise.

SOAPProxy

There are a number of parameters that can be specified with the SOAPProxy action:

- `wsdl`: a mandatory URL representing the WSDL for the original service
- `wsdlTransform`: an optional transformation resource that can be applied to the original WSDL before publishing
- `wsdlCharset`: an optional parameter specifying the character set of the original WSDL, if necessary

A basic example configuration would look like the following:

```
<action class="org.jboss.soa.esb.actions.soap.proxy.SOAPProxy"
        name="proxy-action">
  <property name="wsdl"
            value="http://localhost:8080/BookService?wsdl"/>
</action>
```

Time for action – incorporating SOAPProxy into the application

We will now modify the current example to use SOAPProxy:

1. In JBoss Developer Studio, open the `esbcontent/META-INF/jboss-esb.xml` file in **Source** mode.

2. Replace the following code:

```
<action class="org.jboss.soa.esb.actions.soap.SOAPProcessor"
        name="JBossWSAdapter">
  <property name="jbossws-endpoint" value="BookService"/>
  <property name="jbossws-context" value="BookService"/>
</action>
```

With this code:

```
<action class="org.jboss.soa.esb.actions.soap.proxy.SOAPProxy"
        name="proxy-action">
  <property name="wsdl" value=
  "internal://jboss.ws:context=BookService,endpoint=BookService"/>
</action>
```

3. Click the **Save** button and the modified application should now be deployed in the server.

4. Select the `src` folder, expand it till the `SendJMSMessage.java` file is displayed in the tree. Now click **Run | Run As | Java Application**.

The server **Console** will display the output as below:

```
INFO   [STDOUT] AFTER invoking jbossws endpoint:

INFO   [STDOUT] [<env:Envelope xmlns:env='http://schemas.xmlsoap.
org/soap/envelope/'><env:Header></env:Header><env:Body><ns2:get
BooksResponse xmlns:ns2="http://chapter8.samples.esb.soa.jboss.
org/"><return>Great Expectations</return><return>Hound Of The
Baskervilles</return><return>The Da Vinci Code</return><return>The
Immortals Of Meluha</return></ns2:getBooksResponse></env:Body></
env:Envelope>].
```

What just happened?

We used `SOAPProxy` to invoke the web service. We used a JMS Queue to send a SOAP message.

Have a go hero – advanced use cases for SOAPProxy

Have a look at `webservice_proxy_routed` and `webservice_proxy_versioning` quickstarts to see how those are configured and work.

Tweaking HttpClient

The soapUI `SOAPClient` and `SOAPProxy` actions use Apache Commons `HttpClient` in order to invoke the SOAP operation, it is common practice to specify a `property` file which can be used to alter the behavior, for example by specifying security-related configuration or details of a proxy.

Both of these actions allow the location of this property file to be configured as a parameter, however there is a difference in how this is done. Let's take a look at the ways these properties can be specified.

SOAPClient

This action allows a custom tag `<http-client-property>` to specify the configuration through a `file` attribute or explicitly through `http-client-property` properties.

The `file` attribute can refer to a configuration through:

- A path on the local file system
- An absolute resource path accessible from the deployment's `ClassLoader`
- A URL referencing a remote resource

The following configuration shows a reference to a resource which is included in the deployment:

```
<action name="soapui-client-action"
        class="org.jboss.soa.esb.actions.soap.SOAPClient">
  <property name="wsdl" value=
"http://localhost:8080/Chapter8/ebws/Chapter8Sample/
Chapter8Service?wsdl"/>
  <property name="SOAPAction" value="Chapter8ServiceOp"/>
  <http-client-property name="file" value="/http.properties"/>
</action>
```

Individual properties can also be set as follows:

```
<action name="soapui-client-action"
        class="org.jboss.soa.esb.actions.soap.SOAPClient">
  ...
  <property name="http-client-properties>
    <http-client-property name="http.proxyHost" value="esbhost"/>
    <http-client-property name="http.proxyPort" value="808"/>
  </property>
</action>
```

SOAPProxy

The SOAPProxy action allows the `file` attribute to be set via the `<property>` tag. A sample configuration is shown:

```
<action class="org.jboss.soa.esb.actions.soap.proxy.SOAPProxy"
        name="proxy-action">
  <property name="wsdl" value=
    "internal://jboss.ws:context=BookService,endpoint=BookService"/>
  <property name="file" value="/http.properties"/>
</action>
```

Sample properties

The following are some common properties specified in the `HttpClient` properties file:

```
# See:
# - http://wiki.jboss.org/wiki/Wiki.jsp?page=HttpRouter and
# - http://wiki.jboss.org/wiki/Wiki.jsp?page=HttpClientFactory

# Configurators
#configurators=HttpProtocol,AuthBASIC
configurators=HttpProtocol,AuthNTLM

# HttpProtocol config
#protocol-socket-factory=org.apache.commons.httpclient.contrib.ssl.
StrictSSLProtocolSocketFactory
protocol-socket-factory=org.apache.commons.httpclient.contrib.ssl.
EasySSLProtocolSocketFactory
#protocol-socket-factory=org.jboss.soa.esb.http.protocol.
SelfSignedSSLProtocolSocketFactoryBuilder
#protocol-socket-factory=org.jboss.soa.esb.http.protocol.
AuthSSLProtocolSocketFactoryBuilder
keystore=@keystore@
keystore-passw=@keystore.password@
truststore=@keystore@
truststore-passw=webservice_proxy_security_pass

# Connection config
max-connections-per-host=5

# HttpProtocol config
http.proxyHost=192.168.1.3
http.proxyPort=808

# AuthNTLM config
ntauth-username=JBOSSTEST
```

```
ntauth-password=JBOSSPASS
ntauthscope-host=ESBHOST
ntauthscope-port=80
ntauthscope-domain=JBOSS

# AuthBASIC config
auth-username=kermit
auth-password=thefrog
authscope-host=localhost
authscope-port=8443
authscope-realm=webservice_proxy_security
```

Custom configurator

The SOAPProxy action can make use of an HttpClient to invoke a remote endpoint.
Occasionally it may be necessary to extend the configuration of this client class and enable
some features which are not directly exposed by JBoss ESB. This can be achieved through
the inclusion of a custom configurator, a simple class which can initialize the HttpClient
programmatically using the properties supplied to the action.

The following shows how to implement a simple configurator which does nothing more than
log the fact that it has been invoked:

```
# Configurators
configurators=HttpProtocol, org.jboss.soa.esb.samples.chapter8.
MyConfigurator
```

The code for this configurator is shown here:

```
package org.jboss.soa.esb.samples.chapter8;

import org.apache.commons.httpclient.HttpClient;
import org.jboss.soa.esb.http.Configurator;
import org.jboss.soa.esb.ConfigurationException;

import org.apache.log4j.Logger;
import java.util.Properties;

public class MyConfigurator extends Configurator {

    private Logger log = Logger.getLogger(MyConfigurator.class);

    public void configure(HttpClient httpClient,
            Properties properties) throws ConfigurationException {

        System.out.println("MyConfigurator:: just logging entries!");
    }
}
```

Have a go hero – using a custom configurator

Go ahead and add the previous code to the `src` folder and configure the soapUI's `SOAPClient` to use this custom configurator. Do you see the message being printed out on the server **Console**?

SOAPProxy security pass through

When proxying a web service it is often necessary to consider the security requirements of the HTTP transport of the proxied service; with the `SOAPProxy` action there are two alternatives for specifying the basic authentication credentials of that connection:

◆ The credentials are provided by the client of the ESB service

◆ The `SOAPProxy` action will specify them directly

This behavior is controlled through the inclusion of the `clientCredentialsRequired` property on the action. By default this property has the value `true`, requiring that all necessary credentials will be provided by the client of the ESB service, however setting this to `false` will cause the `SOAPProxy` action to ignore any client credentials in favor of those within its `HttpClient` properties file.

The following is a sample configuration when using this property:

```
<action class="org.jboss.soa.esb.actions.soap.proxy.SOAPProxy"
        name="proxy-action">
  <property name="wsdl" value=
"internal://jboss.ws:context=BookServiceSecured,endpoint=BookServiceS
ecured"/>
  <property name="file" value="/http.properties"/>
  <property name="clientCredentialsRequired" value="false"/>
</action>
```

Cleaning up deployments

In JBoss Developer Studio expand the `esbcontent` folder of `Chapter8`. You will see there is another war file named `webservice-secured.war`. This is the service that we will use in the next section:

1. Rename the `webservice.war` file to "webservice.war.bak".

2. We will need to create a new File Filter to clean up our previous deployment, the details for which we first covered in the *Chapter 5* section entitled *Creating File Filters*.

   Create a filter, as shown in that section, then continue to complete the details.

3. In the **New File Filter** dialog, enter **Name** as "WSDLs", **Root Directory** as "server/${jboss_config}/data/wsdl" and **Includes** as "**/*.wsdl".

4. Click on **OK** and there should be an entry for **WSDLs**.

5. Expand to see the **webservice.war** folder, right-click on it and click **Delete File**.

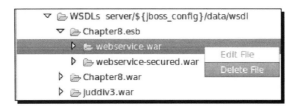

Time for action – SOAPProxy security pass through

Let us now proxy the secured web service using SOAPProxy passing in the authentication credentials from a properties file:

1. In JBoss Developer Studio, open the `esbcontent/META-INF/jboss-esb.xml` file in **Source** mode.

2. Replace the following code:

```
<action class="org.jboss.soa.esb.actions.soap.proxy.SOAPProxy"
        name="proxy-action">
  <property name="wsdl" value=
"internal://jboss.ws:context=BookService,endpoint=BookService"/>
</action>
```

With this code:

```
<action class="org.jboss.soa.esb.actions.soap.proxy.SOAPProxy"
        name="proxy-action">
  <property name="wsdl" value=
"internal://jboss.ws:context=BookService,endpoint=BookService "/>
  <property name="file" value="/http.properties"/>
  <property name="clientCredentialsRequired" value="false"/>
</action>
```

3. Click the **Save** button and the modified application should now be deployed in the server.

4. Select the `src` folder, expand it till the `SendJMSMessage.java` file is displayed in the tree. Now click **Run | Run As | Java Application**.

The server **Console** will display the output as shown:

```
INFO   [STDOUT] AFTER invoking jbossws endpoint:
```

```
INFO   [STDOUT] [<env:Envelope xmlns:env='http://schemas.xmlsoap.
org/soap/envelope/'><env:Header></env:Header><env:Body><ns2:get
BooksResponse xmlns:ns2="http://chapter8.samples.esb.soa.jboss.
org/"><return>Great Expectations</return><return>Hound Of The
Baskervilles</return><return>The Da Vinci Code</return><return>The
Immortals Of Meluha</return></ns2:getBooksResponse></env:Body></
env:Envelope>].
```

What just happened?

We used `SOAPProxy` to invoke a BASIC secured web service. We used a JMS queue to send a SOAP message. We passed the security credentials from an `HttpClient` properties file.

Have a go hero – security pass through

Look at the contents `http.properties` file. Modify the `clientCredentialsRequired` property to `true` and see what is displayed on the server **Console**. Execute the `webservice_proxy_security` quickstarts to see how SSL and BASIC are both configured together.

Summary

We learned a lot in this chapter about web service integration. Specifically, we covered:

◆ How to automatically export ESB services through a web service endpoint

◆ How to invoke externally hosted web services using SOAPClients

◆ How to invoke co-located web services using SOAPProcessor

◆ How to proxy another web service so that the internal details of this web service is not exposed to the outside world or on to the bus

◆ How to pass through credentials for proxied web services

We also discussed briefly about OGNL and XStream configurations, how to tweak HttpClient properties, an HttpClient custom handler and a JAXWS custom handler.

Now that you have been introduced to the core concepts and features of JBoss ESB you should have a better understanding of how to develop loosely coupled, robust, scalable, distributed enterprise SOA Services and clients.

But this book is just a starting point. There are many other areas which can be covered in order to expand your knowledge, such as clustering and load balancing, that we have not had the time to delve into. You are encouraged to explore the JBoss ESB site, ask questions on the forums and, perhaps, help others by answering their queries.

In the final section we have gathered together some additional resources that we think will be of interest to you, helping to enrich your knowledge of this and other JBoss projects. Happy reading and merry coding!

A
Where to go Next with JBoss ESB?

This book describes the core capabilities of JBoss ESB, and how you can apply them in building your own services and applications. For all its functions, JBoss ESB does not exist in a vacuum, however. One of JBoss ESB's great strengths is its wealth of integrations with supporting tools and other JBoss technologies. We've briefly referred to some of these integrations (for example, as in *Chapter 4* where we describe JBoss ESB's library of OOTB actions, including actions that support the integration of JBoss ESB with other JBoss projects). This appendix expands on the discussion of JBoss ESB's integrations with other JBoss technologies and tools and how you can use them with JBoss ESB.

Creating service definitions with the JBDS ESB editor

The "heart" of the configuration of a JBoss ESB based application is the set of services and providers that you define in the application's `jboss-esb.xml` file. If your application makes use of multiple services (and their actions and listeners) and providers, then this file can grow quite large and can be troublesome to maintain by editing its raw XML. JBDS, however, includes a GUI based ESB editor that makes it much easier to create and maintain an application's configuration in the `jboss-esb.xml` file.

To invoke the editor, simply double-click on an application's `jboss-esb.xml` file in JBDS. The editor looks like this (note that we'll use the "helloworld" quickstart's `jboss-esb.xml` file as an example):

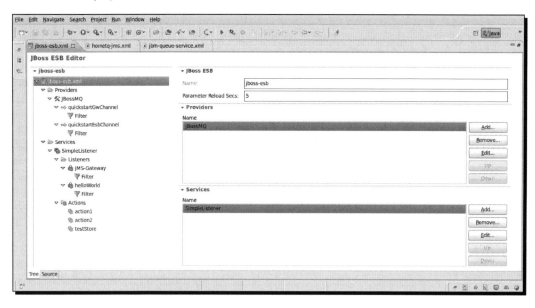

The major configuration elements of a JBoss ESB application are its **providers** and its **services**. To define a new service, the editor presents you with a drop-down list of all the supported provider types:

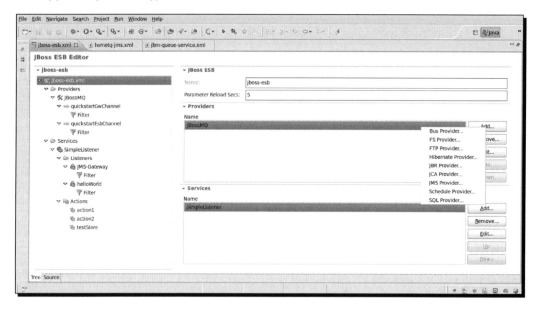

A service performs its tasks through the actions that you define. For out-of-the-box actions implemented by JBoss ESB, the editor presents you with a drop-down list of the full set of supported actions:

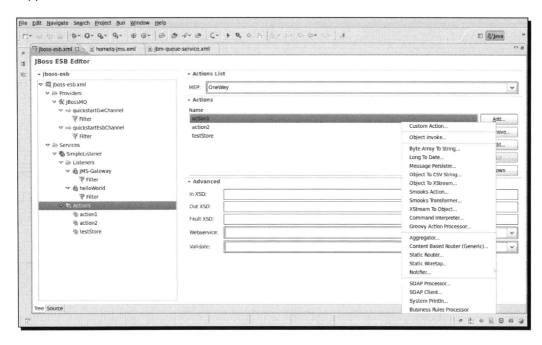

You can edit the properties for these OOTB actions in the editor. For example:

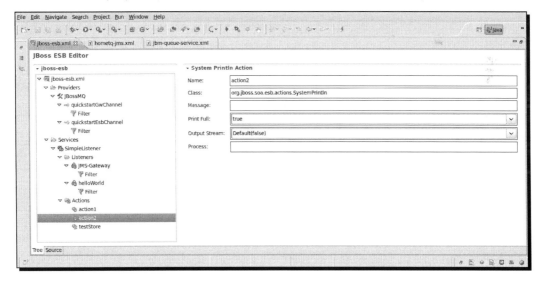

Custom actions that you create still require you to write the custom code for the actions. The ESB editor enables you to view and modify the action properties. For example:

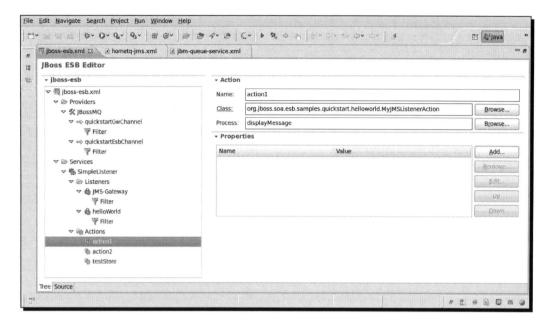

Using other UDDI providers (HP Systinet and SOA Software Service Manager)

As mentioned in *Chapter 7*, JBoss ESB supports other UDDI providers as a registry provider. Other than jUDDI, the two other UDDI implementations that have been tested with JBoss ESB are HP Systinet (version 6.64):

```
http://www8.hp.com/us/en/software/software-product.
html?compURI=tcm:245-936884
```

And SOA Software ServiceManager (version 6.0.1):

```
http://www.soa.com/products/service_manager/
```

Documents with details on integrating one of these providers are available at the JBoss ESB documentation page:

```
http://www.jboss.org/jbossesb/docs
```

Using other JBoss project technologies

We've discussed several times in this book how JBoss ESB enables you to re-use existing code by creating services that "plug" into the ESB instead of having to reinvent the wheel in your applications. JBoss ESB's integrations with other JBoss technologies serve a similar role in that they enable your services to take advantage of the unique capabilities provided by these technologies, without your having to recreate those capabilities in your own code.

JBoss Drools and rules-based services

What do we mean when we talk about "rules-based" programming?

Rules-based programming involves defining decision points that are controlled by rules. This is similar to other types of programming, but what makes rules-based programming different is that you separate the rules-related decision points from other programming logic. This may sound like a hair-splitting difference, but it's a big deal because:

◆ By separating these rules from your application's business logic code, you can enable your programmers to concentrate on the code and your business process people, who are probably not programmers, to concentrate on the business process rules. This separation makes the development, and equally importantly, the maintenance over time of the whole application easier.

◆ Additionally, while it is possible for you to hand code all the rules-handling code yourself (are you getting a mental picture of lots of very big nested if-then-else statements yet?), a dedicated rules engine that can process rules-based programs is going to be able execute rules more efficiently. This means that your rules-based application will not only be easier to maintain, it will also run faster.

All of which leads us to JBoss Drools. (`http://www.jboss.org/drools`)

Drools is sometimes thought of as a rules-based programming language and runtime engine, but it's really more than that. Drools is a unified and fully integrated solution for **Business Rules**, **Business Processes Management**, **Task Planning**, and **Event Processing**. The JBoss Drools project is organized into sub-projects, each of which handles one technology. The Drools "Expert" sub-project covers the rules-based programming that you can use in the JBoss ESB-Drools integration. The Expert sub-project includes the Rules API, the Rules engine, and Eclipse-based editing and debugging tools.

Now, don't panic! Just because the sub-project's name is "Expert" doesn't mean that you have to be an expert to learn how to program in Drools. What does a Drools rule look like? Let's take a look at a rule.

Rules are written in the Drools Rule Language. The file extension for a Drools rule file is
`.drl` This language is generic in nature, so that it can handle rules for a large variety of
applications. This rules language can also be extended to handle specific types of rules
applications such as accounting, medical, and so on. These extensions are referred to as
Domain Specific Languages (DSL).

Now, every rule follows a basic form. There's a left-hand side (LHS) and a right-hand side
(RHS). The left side defines the `when` clause, in other words the condition that causes the
rule to execute. And, the right side defines the `then`, in other words, the consequences of
the rule being executed. Here's a simple example of a rule:

```
rule "a simple rule"
    when (LHS)
        you need a rules-based app
    then (RHS)
        build it with JBossDrools!
```

Just like any other programming language, in order for a rule to do something useful, it
needs access to information to process. How does a rule access information? Through
Drools' working memory. The way it works is that information in the form of Java beans is
loaded into working memory. Drools refers to these beans as "facts"—since in the real world
your memory is full of facts too. Facts are typically packaged and distributed in Java jar files.
By using Java beans as facts, Drools is able to access the data elements in facts through the
beans' getter and setter methods.

When and if a rule is executed depends on the state of things in working memory. Changes in
working memory resulting from facts being inserted into working memory, changing or being
updated in working memory, or being removed from working memory, can cause the rules'
`when` conditions to become `true` and the result in one or more rules being executed.

The determination as to when a rule is executed is a major difference between rules-based
programming in Drools and procedural programming. How does Drools decide which rule
to run first when conditions in working memory satisfy multiple rules' LHS conditions? The
Drools rules runtime engine does not decide which rules to run based on a hard-coded
sequence of rules. What the rules engine does instead is it adds each rule with a matching
condition rule to its "agenda" of rules to run. If the agenda includes more than one rule, then
the rules engine has to perform conflict resolution on the rules to decide on the sequence in
which the rules should be run. The rules engine performs this conflict resolution based on a
combination of factors including:

- How often the rule has fired in the past. If the rule has been run many times in the past, then it is likely that it should be run often in the future too.

- The rule's complexity. If a rule is more complex, then the rule engine is more likely to consider applying it to the current condition.

- The order in which the rules were loaded into working memory.

- The salience of the rule. You define a Rule's salience (importance) as a property and assign it a numeric value when you write a rule.

- Invoking rules from a JBoss ESB service in the SOA platform, more recent rules are given precedence.

The JBoss ESB-Drools integration enables you to access rules from your service's actions. There are two JBoss ESB classes that support this:

- `org.jboss.soa.esb.actions.BusinessRulesProcessor`

- `org.jboss.soa.esb.actions.DroolsRuleService`

The `BusinessRuleProcessor` (this is sometimes referred to as "BRP") class uses rules loaded from rules files. This works well for relatively simple rules services. But, loading lots of rules from lots of files can be hard to maintain and makes for inefficient processing.

This service uses the `RuleAgent` class (`org.drools.agent.RuleAgent`) to either access packages of rules from files, or, to handle a more complex environment, where you want to use large numbers of complex rules services, and hundreds or even thousands of rules, `DroolsRuleService` is the better choice. In a large scale implementation such as this, you would not keep the rules in a correspondingly large number of standalone files. Instead, you would use a **Business Rules Management System (BRMS)** such as Drools Guvnor (`http://www.jboss.org/drools/drools-guvnor.html`).

Guvnor makes it easier to handle a production environment and a large number of rules (and large numbers of people writing rules) by implementing a central repository (backed by a database) for rules, with a web-based rules authoring interface that provides import/export/archiving functions, audit trails for changes made to rules, an error log to help debug problems, automated test development and execution, rule status tracking, and version control. Guvnor makes it easier for business rules expert non-programmers to create rules and for administrators to maintain large numbers of rules and manage multiple users.

Here's what Guvnor looks like:

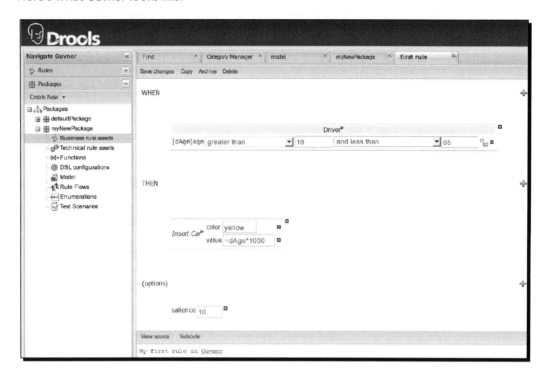

JBoss ESB supports rules services that are either stateless or stateful. In the stateless model, messages sent to the services contain all the facts to be inserted into the rules engine's working memory, before the rules are executed. In the stateful model, where the execution of the rules may take place in a session over an extended time period, several messages may be sent to a rule service, and the rules may fire and update either the message or the facts until a final message causes the service to end the session.

To see the JBoss ESB-Drools integration in action, take a look at any of the quickstarts whose names begin with "business_ruleservice" or review the JBoss ESB-Drools integration in the JBoss ESB Programmers' guide:

```
http://docs.jboss.org/jbossesb/docs/4.10/manuals/html/Programmers_
Guide/index.html
```

In the `business_rules_service` JBoss ESB quickstart, a business order placement system is simulated. Part of this system assigns a sales discount percentage to incoming customer orders, customer status (gold, platinum, and so on) and order priority.

The action that invokes the rules processor looks like this:

```
<action class="org.jboss.soa.esb.actions.BusinessRulesProcessor"
        name="BRP">
  <property name="ruleSet" value="MyBusinessRules.drl" />
  <property name="ruleReload" value="true" />
  <property name="object-paths">
    <object-path esb="body.orderHeader" />
    <object-path esb="body.customer" />
  </property>
</action>
```

Here's a fragment of the rules file (`MyBusinessRules.drl`) that is referenced in the action. Note that the `salience` value of the logging rule is lower than that of the customer order processing rules (as order processing is more time critical than logging). Also note how using Drools enables you to move the business process rules definitions out of your application programs and into a separate rules file.

The syntax of the rules follow the when/then model we discussed previously. The net result of the execution of these rules is to define the appropriate customer discount based on the customer status and order priority included in the messages processed by the ESB services.

```
rule "Logging"
salience 10
when
    order: OrderHeader()
    customer: Customer()
then
    System.out.println("Customer Status: " + customer.getStatus());
    System.out.println("Order Total: " + order.getTotalAmount());
end

rule "Customer Platinum Status"
salience 20
when
    customer: Customer(status > 50)
    order: OrderHeader(orderPriority == 3)
then
    System.out.println("Platinum Customer - High Priority -
                        Higher discount");
    order.setOrderDiscount(8.5);
end

rule "Customer Gold Status"
salience 20
```

```
when
    customer: Customer(status > 10, status <= 50)
    order: OrderHeader(orderPriority == 2)
then
    System.out.println("Gold Customer - Medium Priority -
                           discount ");
    order.setOrderDiscount(3.4);
end
```

JBoss Riftsaw and BPEL services

JBoss ESB's support for web services is described in detail in *Chapter 8*. This support is augmented by the JBoss ESB integration with the JBoss' open source BPEL engine, RiftSaw (`http://www.jboss.org/riftsaw`). RiftSaw enables you to integrate BPEL processes (which are exposed as web services).

There are a couple of set-up tasks that you have to perform before you can use Riftsaw with JBoss ESB, they are:

◆ Install RiftSaw and deploy it to your JBoss AS Server

◆ Install the BPEL Process Editor into JBDS

Let's install RiftSaw first. To do this, follow these steps: the entire set-up process is documented in the RiftSaw Getting Started Guide (`http://docs.jboss.org/riftsaw/releases/2.3.0.Final/gettingstartedguide/html/`)—we're covering the steps that will work for the JBoss AS server and JBoss ESB installation used throughout the book.

1. Create a directory where you can build RiftSaw, and set it as the current working directory:

   cd /opt/local; mkdir riftsaw ; cd riftsaw

2. Download the RiftSaw 2.3.0 source from:

   `http://downloads.jboss.org/riftsaw/releases/2.3.0.Final/riftsaw-2.3.0.Final-src.zip`

3. Unzip the source file:

   unzip riftsaw-2.3.0.Final-src.zip

4. Change your current working directory to the RiftSaw installation directory:

   cd /opt/local/riftsaw-2.0-SNAPSHOT/install

5. Build RiftSaw:

   mvn clean install -P docs

6. Edit the RiftSaw `deployment.properties` file and set `org.jboss.esb.server.home=/opt/local/jboss-5.1.0.GA` and `org.jboss.esb.home=/opt/local/jbossesb-4.10`.

7. Stop the AS server.

8. Deploy RiftSaw:

   `ant deploy`

9. Restart the AS server.

10. Finally, you should see the RiftSaw quickstarts were installed into `/jboss/local/riftsaw/riftsaw-2.3.0.Final/samples/`

Next, you should install the BPEL Process Editor into JBDS.

Strictly speaking, installing the BPEL editor is an optional step, but it's a tool that will make your life a lot easier (Easier than trying to create and maintain BPEL process definitions by editing raw XML, that is). The tool is a visual editor for BPEL processes. It's not installed into the default JBDS download, but it's easy (and of course, it's also free) to install it. The installation steps are as follows:

1. Open up JBDS and select **Help | Install New Software**, then select **Available Sites** and then **JBoss Developer Studio 4.0 Extras -https://devstudio.jboss.com/updates/4.0/extras/**:

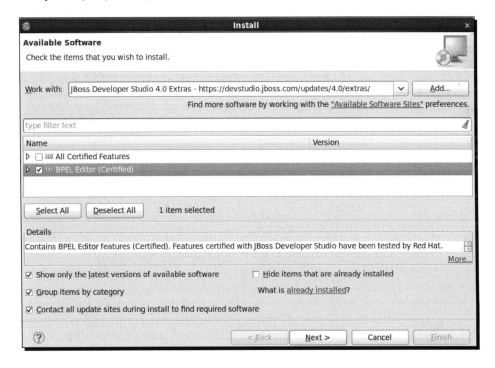

2. Then select the BPEL editor:

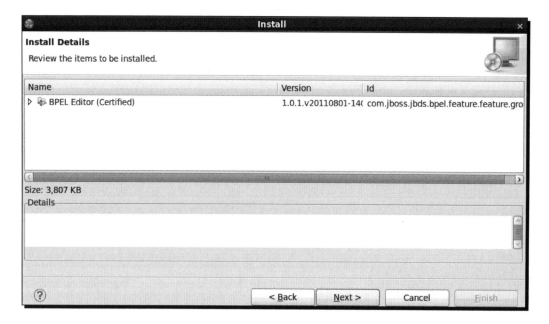

The editor displays and enables you to edit BPEL process files graphically:

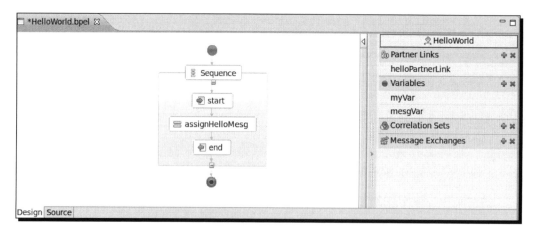

Note that the JBoss ESB-RiftSaw integration is similar to the JBoss ESB-JBPM integration (explained in a different section of this appendix), with one important difference. When we're dealing with BPEL, which means dealing with web services, all communication is synchronous and follows a request-response pattern. This makes the RiftSaw-JBoss ESB integration simpler than the corresponding JBPM-JBoss ESB integration in that just one message exchange pattern (MEP) is supported. The JBoss ESB-RiftSaw integration supports two types of operations:

- **Orchestrating ESB services from BPEL in Riftsaw to the ESB**: "Orchestration"? What's orchestration? Sorry, it's another term that's become a buzzword. Orchestration got its name as it is similar to the way that an orchestra conductor leads and directs the members of the orchestra. In contrast, "choreography" refers to programs or processes operating as equal partners, just like a well-rehearsed dance team. In the context of JBoss ESB and RiftSaw, "orchestration" refers to an integration of multiple computer programs or software processes, where the programs do not operate as co-equal peers, but rather one of them directs the operation of the other. Orchestration enables a BPEL process to combine with JBoss ESB services, but maintain control over the combination of services and the process.

  Orchestration with RiftSaw is actually very simple as from the ESB's point of view, the BPEL process is just another web service. This means that the ESB is able to receive messages from a RiftSaw BPEL process just as it would from any other web service.

- **Making calls from the ESB to a RiftSaw BPEL process definition**: There are two ways to do this, as follows:

  - First, as we just mentioned, as far as JBoss ESB is concerned, a RiftSaw BPEL process is a web service. Accordingly, a JBoss ESB service can just invoke a RiftSaw BPEL process just like any other web service that exposes a WSDL definition.

  - Second, JBoss ESB includes an OOTB action that is used to directly invoke a RiftSaw BPEL process. The `org.jboss.soa.esb.actions.bpel.BPELInvoke` OOTB action can be used if RiftSaw is running in the same Java VM as the JBoss ESB and if the BPEL process to be invoked is also deployed to the local RiftSaw instance. In addition, the `BPELInvoke` action lets you specify not just the RiftSaw process to be invoked, but also the specific operation that you want to execute within that process.

In the `esb_helloworld` quickstart, the following action invokes the BPEL process: Remember, that as far as the ESB is concerned, the BPEL process is just another web service that is accessed through its WSDL.

```
<action name="action2"
        class="org.jboss.soa.esb.actions.bpel.BPELInvoke">
   <property name="service" value="{http://www.jboss.org/bpel/
                        examples/wsdl}HelloService"/>
   <property name="operation" value="hello" />
   <property name="requestPartName" value="TestPart" />
   <property name="responsePartName" value="TestPart" />
</action>
```

And, here's the corresponding service definition in the WSDL:

```
<wsdl:service name="HelloService">
  <wsdl:port name="HelloPort" binding="tns:HelloSoapBinding">
    <soap:address location="http://localhost:8080/
                  Quickstart_bpel_hello_worldWS"/>
  </wsdl:port>
</wsdl:service>
```

JBoss jBPM and Business Process Management

Just as "middleware" can be a confusing term, "Business Process Management (BPM)" can also be an overused and misunderstood term. What it really comes down to is a systematic approach to defining, reviewing, and ultimately making business processes more effective. One of JBoss ESB's most powerful integrations is with JBoss jBPM. This integration enables you to connect your business processes to ESB services.

Before we describe this integration, how it works, and how you can use it, we have to be certain that we understand the definition of a "business process". In the context of Business Process Management, a process is not an active, executing program or application. We're talking about the process by which your business performs operations to fulfill a business requirement. For example, a business process can define the tasks that a business performs to execute a retail sale, request that a credit account be opened, restock a supply warehouse, or send bills to customers. The means that your business uses to perform these tasks can be manual, mechanical, involve software, or be a combination of all these approaches.

jBPM is the JBoss open source BPM framework. jBPM provides an Eclipse-based development environment, an administrative console, and a workflow management system. In jBPM, processes are defined in a Java-like Process Definition Language (**jPDL**). The jBPM development also includes a Graphical Process Design tool (**GPD**) that enables you to design your processes visually. Note that the process has a start and an end, references to multiple services, and transitions between states, based on the results of operations, including conditional operations.

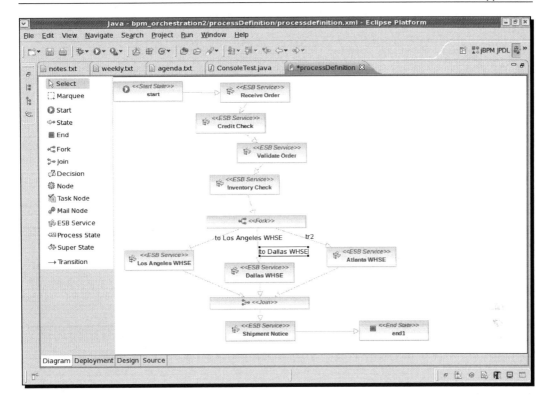

Finally, since a business process can be "long-running", where humans and computers often have to wait for something to happen (such as waiting for a credit application to be approved), jBPM includes a process engine runtime (this must be deployed to an application server) that is able to maintain a process state (in a database) while it runs and waits.

The JBoss ESB-jBPM integration supports two types of operations:

◆ Calling a jBPM process from an ESB service

◆ Orchestrating ESB services from a jBPM process

Orchestration enables a jBPM process to combine with JBoss ESB services, but maintain control over the combination of services and the process.

To see the JBoss ESB-jBPM integration in action, take a look at any of the quickstarts whose names begin with "bpm" or review the JBoss ESB-jBPM integration in the JBoss ESB Programmers' guide:

```
http://docs.jboss.org/jbossesb/docs/4.10/manuals/html/Programmers_
Guide/index.html
```

Calling a jBPM process from a JBoss ESB service uses the `org.jboss.soa.esb.services.jbpm.actions.BpmProcessor` action. Under the covers, this action uses the jBPM command API to execute three possible operations:

- `NewProcessInstanceCommand`: This creates a new `ProcessInstance` using a process definition that has already been deployed to jBPM. The process instance is left in the start state so that tasks referenced by the start node are executed.

- `StartProcessInstanceCommand`: This is the same as `NewProcessInstanceCommand`, except that the process instance that is created is moved from the start position to the first node in the process graph.

- `CancelProcessInstanceCommand`: This cancels a process instance.

All of these operations require ESB `action` attributes such as a process ID to be defined. The `action` definitions that call the jBPM process can also specify additional information in action configuration properties. For example, the `esbToBpmVars` property defines the variables that are to be extracted from the message from the ESB and set in the jBPM context.

In the `bpm_orchestration2` JBoss ESB quickstart, a jBPM process is used to simulate a sales order processing system. The following action is used to start a new jBPM process (after that process has been previously deployed), to pass the process variables, and to map these variables from information extracted from the messages the JBoss ESB service processes to the jBPM process variables:

```
<action name="start_a_new_process_instance"
        class="org.jboss.soa.esb.services.jbpm.actions.BpmProcessor">
  <property name="command" value="StartProcessInstanceCommand" />
  <property name="process-definition-name"
            value="bpm_orchestration2Process"/>
  <property name="esbToBpmVars">
    <mapping esb="eVar1" bpm="counter"  value="45" />
    <mapping esb="BODY_CONTENT" bpm="theBody" />
  </property>
</action>
```

Using Maven with JBoss ESB

Most of the examples that we have gone through so far have used Apache ant to compile and package JBoss ESB archives. Maven is another very popular build tool. You can use Maven as an alternative to ant to build, compile, and package your archives, and also run your JBoss ESB tests.

Compiling with Maven

The source of JBoss ESB is built with `ant`, which means that no list of dependencies for the `jbossesb-rosetta.jar` file exists, and this presents a problem for compiling your own custom actions, listeners, and notifiers. The `jbossesb-rosetta.jar` file, which contains all the code which you must extend from is not hosted in a public maven repository. In order to be able to compile, you'll have to locate the `jbossesb-rosetta.jar` file and treat it as a third-party JAR and install it into your local maven repository manually. This will install it locally, but if you try to build your project on another machine, remember that you will want to install it manually on that machine as well.

Then you'll want to create a `pom` for yourself—the following example sets the compiler to JDK 1.5 and includes a number of important dependencies for compiling custom actions. You can use it as an example if you wish to compile your custom actions or gateways inside your Maven build:

```xml
<?xml version="1.0" encoding="UTF-8"?>
<project xmlns="http://maven.apache.org/POM/4.0.0"
         xmlns:xsi="http://www.w3.org/2001/XMLSchema-instance"
         xsi:schemaLocation="http://maven.apache.org/POM/4.0.0
             http://maven.apache.org/maven-v4_0_0.xsd">
  <modelVersion>4.0.0</modelVersion>
  <packaging>jar</packaging>
  <groupId>com.packtpub</groupId>
  <artifactId>jbossesb-example</artifactId>
  <version>1.0</version>
  <name>JBoss ESB Maven Example</name>
  <description>JBoss ESB Maven Example</description>
  <url>http://www.packtpub.com/</url>
  <properties>
    <jbossesb.version>4.10</jbossesb.version>
  </properties>
  <build>
    <pluginManagement>
      <plugins>
        <plugin>
          <groupId>org.apache.maven.plugins</groupId>
          <artifactId>maven-compiler-plugin</artifactId>
          <configuration>
            <source>1.5</source>
            <target>1.5</target>
          </configuration>
        </plugin>
      </plugins>
    </pluginManagement>
```

```
        <plugins>
        </plugins>
    </build>
    <dependencies>
        <dependency>
            <groupId>junit</groupId>
            <artifactId>junit</artifactId>
            <version>4.5</version>
            <scope>test</scope>
        </dependency>
        <dependency>
            <groupId>commons-logging</groupId>
            <artifactId>commons-logging-api</artifactId>
            <version>1.1</version>
        </dependency>
        <dependency>
            <groupId>org.jboss.soa.esb</groupId>
            <artifactId>rosetta</artifactId>
            <version>4.10</version>
        </dependency>
        <dependency>
            <groupId>log4j</groupId>
            <artifactId>log4j</artifactId>
            <version>1.2.14</version>
        </dependency>
    </dependencies>
</project>
```

ESB packaging with Maven

You can use the JBoss packaging plugin to package an ESB archive. The ESB packaging plugin contains a number of configuration options which allow the user to configure the archive name, whether the archive is exploded or not, the locations of the deployment descriptor and deployment file, and what artifacts to include within the archive. Documentation can be found at `http://mojo.codehaus.org/jboss-packaging-maven-plugin/esb-mojo.html`.

The following is an example of a `pom.xml` file using the packaging plugin to package an ESB archive. This example can be used as a template in order to create your own maven `pom` files to package your ESB archives.

```
<?xml version="1.0" encoding="UTF-8"?>
<project xmlns="http://maven.apache.org/POM/4.0.0"
        xmlns:xsi="http://www.w3.org/2001/XMLSchema-instance"
        xsi:schemaLocation="http://maven.apache.org/POM/4.0.0
```

```
                http://maven.apache.org/maven-v4_0_0.xsd">
<modelVersion>4.0.0</modelVersion>
<packaging>jboss-esb</packaging>
<groupId>com.packtpub</groupId>
<artifactId>jbossesb-example</artifactId>
<version>1.0</version>
<name>JBoss ESB Maven Example</name>
<description>JBoss ESB Maven Example</description>
<url>http://www.packtpub.com/</url>
<properties>
  <jbossesb.version>4.10</jbossesb.version>
</properties>
<build>
  <pluginManagement>
    <plugins>
      <plugin>
        <groupId>org.apache.maven.plugins</groupId>
        <artifactId>maven-compiler-plugin</artifactId>
        <configuration>
          <source>1.5</source>
          <target>1.5</target>
        </configuration>
      </plugin>
    </plugins>
  </pluginManagement>
  <plugins>
    <plugin>
      <groupId>org.codehaus.mojo</groupId>
      <artifactId>jboss-packaging-maven-plugin</artifactId>
      <version>2.2</version>
      <extensions>true</extensions>
      <executions>
        <execution>
          <id>jboss-esb</id>
          <phase>package</phase>
          <goals>
            <goal>esb</goal>
          </goals>
          <configuration>
            <deploymentDescriptorFile>
              src/main/resources/META-INF/jboss-esb.xml
            </deploymentDescriptorFile>
            <excludeAll>true</excludeAll>
          </configuration>
```

```
            </execution>
          </executions>
        </plugin>
      </plugins>
    </build>
    <dependencies>
      <dependency>
        <groupId>junit</groupId>
        <artifactId>junit</artifactId>
        <version>4.5</version>
        <scope>test</scope>
      </dependency>
      <dependency>
        <groupId>commons-logging</groupId>
        <artifactId>commons-logging-api</artifactId>
        <version>1.1</version>
        <scope>provided</scope>
      </dependency>
      <dependency>
        <groupId>org.jboss.soa.esb</groupId>
        <artifactId>rosetta</artifactId>
        <version>4.10</version>
        <scope>provided</scope>
      </dependency>
      <dependency>
        <groupId>log4j</groupId>
        <artifactId>log4j</artifactId>
        <version>1.2.14</version>
        <scope>provided</scope>
      </dependency>
    </dependencies>
  </project>
```

How to test your ESB services

Now that you have created ESB services, how do you test them? Actions themselves are generally easily testable—create a message with some test data, and you can simulate the effect of executing a single action. What is more complex is integration testing—testing your complete action chain and testing your service through the listeners and providers that you set up within your configuration file. In the following section, we'll discuss how to perform this sort of integration test so that you can add it into your build process.

Testing a single action

Actions alone are generally easily testable. You can create a message with some test data, invoke the action's process method upon the message, and then make comparisons with the resulting message or check for exceptions.

```
package org.jboss.soa.esb.samples.quickstart.helloworld;
import junit.framework.TestCase;
import org.jboss.soa.esb.actions.SystemPrintln;
import org.jboss.soa.esb.helpers.ConfigTree;
import org.jboss.soa.esb.message.Message;
import org.jboss.soa.esb.message.format.MessageFactory;

public class SimpleJUnitTestCase extends TestCase {
    private static final String MESSAGE_STRING = "helloworld";
    public void testSystemPrintln() throws Exception {
        Message message = MessageFactory.getInstance().getMessage();
        message.getBody().add(MESSAGE_STRING);
        ConfigTree config = new ConfigTree("config");
        SystemPrintln spl = new SystemPrintln(config);
        Message result = spl.process(message);
        String resultString = (String) result.getBody().get();
        assertEquals(MESSAGE_STRING, resultString);
    }
}
```

This code gives the following output:

```
junit:
    [junit] Running org.jboss.soa.esb.samples.quickstart.helloworld.
            SimpleJUnitTestCase
    [junit] Testsuite: org.jboss.soa.esb.samples.quickstart.helloworld.
            SimpleJUnitTestCase
    [junit] Message structure:
    [junit] [helloworld].
    [junit] Tests run: 1, Failures: 0, Errors: 0, Time elapsed: 0.4 sec
    [junit] Tests run: 1, Failures: 0, Errors: 0, Time elapsed: 0.4 sec
    [junit] ------------- Standard Output ---------------
    [junit] Message structure:
    [junit] [helloworld].
    [junit] ------------- ---------------- ---------------
    [junit]
    [junit] Testcase: testSystemPrintln took 0.198 sec


BUILD SUCCESSFUL
Total time: 2 seconds
```

AbstractTestRunner

Do you want to be able to execute your action chain via the service invoker in tests? AbstractTestRunner allows you to do that, without the overhead of starting a container. In order to use AbstractTestRunner, you specify your ESB configuration files (jboss-esb.xml and jbossesb-properties.xml), and AbstractTestRunner will take care of setting up the registry and controller.

AbstractTestRunner is included inside the test-util.jar in the ESB binary distribution. If you are using ant, simply add it to your <junit/> classpath. If you are using Maven, install it locally into your repository:

```
mvn install:install-file -Dfile=test-util.jar -DgroupId=org.jboss.soa.esb
\ -DartifactId=test-util -Dversion=4.10 -Dpackaging=jar
```

Once installed, add org.jboss.soa.esb:test-util as a dependency with test scope. The following HelloWorldTest class makes an anonymous instance of the AbstractTestRunner class, invokes the run() method, and sets the service config to the helloworld-jboss-esb.xml configuration.

The test method is where we use ServiceInvoker. ServiceInvoker invokes the FirstServiceESB:SimpleListener service with a message containing "helloworld". The test method is invoked when the testRunner object executes the run() method.

```
package org.jboss.soa.esb.samples.quickstart.helloworld;
import junit.framework.TestCase;
import org.jboss.soa.esb.testutils.AbstractTestRunner;
import org.jboss.soa.esb.client.ServiceInvoker;
import org.jboss.soa.esb.message.Message;
import org.jboss.soa.esb.message.format.MessageFactory;
import org.jboss.soa.esb.actions.ActionProcessingException;


public class HelloWorldTest extends TestCase {
    public void test_async() throws Exception {
        AbstractTestRunner testRunner = new AbstractTestRunner() {
            public void test() throws Exception {
                ServiceInvoker invoker =
                    new ServiceInvoker("FirstServiceESB",
                                            "SimpleListener");
                Message message =
                    MessageFactory.getInstance().getMessage();
                message.getBody().add("helloworld");

                message = invoker.deliverSync(message, 10000);

                // Insert code here to verify your results
```

```
                  assertEquals("helloworld", message.getBody().get());
              }
         }.setServiceConfig("helloworld-jboss-esb.xml");

         testRunner.run();
    }
}
```

Below is the configuration for our `AbstractTestRunner` example. The following action chain prints the message using the `SystemPrintln` action and stores the message in `TestMessageStore`:

```xml
<?xml version = "1.0" encoding = "UTF-8"?>
<jbossesb xmlns="http://anonsvn.labs.jboss.com/labs/jbossesb/
          trunk/product/etc/schemas/xml/jbossesb-1.0.1.xsd"
          xmlns:xsi="http://www.w3.org/2001/XMLSchema-instance"
          xsi:schemaLocation="http://anonsvn.labs.jboss.com/labs/
            jbossesb/trunk/product/etc/schemas/xml/jbossesb-1.0.1.xsd
            http://anonsvn.jboss.org/repos/labs/labs/jbossesb/trunk/
            product/etc/schemas/xml/jbossesb-1.0.1.xsd"
          parameterReloadSecs="5">

    <providers>
      <jms-provider name="JBossMQ"
                    connection-factory="ConnectionFactory">
        <jms-bus busid="quickstartGwChannel">
          <jms-message-filter dest-type="QUEUE"
              dest-name="queue/quickstart_helloworld_Request_gw"/>
        </jms-bus>
        <jms-bus busid="quickstartEsbChannel">
          <jms-message-filter dest-type="QUEUE"
              dest-name="queue/quickstart_helloworld_Request_esb"/>
        </jms-bus>

      </jms-provider>
    </providers>

    <services>
      <service category="FirstServiceESB"
               name="SimpleListener"
               description="Hello World">
        <listeners>
          <jms-listener name="JMS-Gateway"
                        busidref="quickstartGwChannel"
                        is-gateway="true"/>
```

```
          <jms-listener name="helloWorld"
                      busidref="quickstartEsbChannel"
      </listeners>
      <actions mep="OneWay">
        <action name="action1"
              class="org.jboss.soa.esb.samples.quickstart.
                    helloworld.MyJMSListenerAction"
              process="displayMessage"/>
        <action name="action2"
              class="org.jboss.soa.esb.actions.SystemPrintln">
          <property name="printfull" value="false"/>
        </action>
        <!-- The next action is for Continuous
            Integration testing -->
        <action name="testStore"
              class="org.jboss.soa.esb.actions.TestMessageStore"/>
      </actions>
    </service>
  </services>
</jbossesb>
```

AbstractTestRunner is a great way to test your actions in combination with others in an action chain, but if you want to use your full ESB configuration—using providers and listeners—you'll have to run an in-container test (see the Arquillian section).

TestMessageStore

If you want to test the aggregated results of your action chain, you have to store the result message somewhere. JBoss ESB provides an org.jboss.esb.actions. TestMessageStore action which logs the message result and any exceptions thrown.

TestMessageStore is very important for the situation in which you want to test in a container against your deployed services. In this situation, you need to be able to receive the exceptions in the chain and the result message, the TestMessageStore action allows you to store both. In the tests that validate the quickstart examples within the JBoss ESB project, a small MBean is created which stores a TestMessageStoreSink that can be queried through JMX. This allows the tests to check results on the server itself without having to worry about receiving the results from a file or checking the server log file, where timing or permissions issues can lead to tests going astray.

In order for you to access `TestMessageStore`, you most likely need to reproduce the sort of MBean that JBoss ESB uses internally for its integration tests. Download the `esb` source and examine:

- `qa/quickstarts/src/org/jboss/soa/esb/server/`
  `QuickstartMessageStoreImplMBean.java`
- `qa/quickstarts/src/org/jboss/soa/esb/server/`
  `QuickstartMessageStoreImpl.java`
- `qa/quickstarts/src/org/jboss/soa/esb/server/`
  `QuickstartMessageStore.java`
- `qa/quickstarts/resources/server/META-INF/jboss-service.xml`

If you compile the three sources and `jboss-service.xml` into an SAR, you can deploy it and then start querying the MBean for results once you have invoked your service. The `qa/quickstarts/src/org/jboss/soa/esb/quickstart/test/` tests within the JBoss ESB source are very good examples of how to access the MBean and retrieve message results.

Once that is working, the `TestMessageStore` action is inserted in the action chain of your jboss-esb.xml configuration.

```
<actions>
  <action name="action2"
          class="org.jboss.soa.esb.actions.SystemPrintln">
    <property name="printfull" value="false"/>
  </action>
  <!-- The next action is for Continuous Integration testing -->
  <action name="testStore"
          class="org.jboss.soa.esb.actions.TestMessageStore"/>
</actions>
```

After invoking your service, you should see your action chain execute, and a log message that shows that your message was added into `TestMessageStoreSink` (output from the helloworld quickstart shown):

```
01:17:44,937 INFO   [STDOUT] TestMessageStoreSink: Adding message: Hello
World
```

Arquillian

Once you build an ESB archive, you also want to test it. Unit tests are excellent for testing your business logic, but you also want to test how your services work when your archive is deployed to a container. What's the easiest way to deploy, run tests, and then subsequently undeploy all of your test resources? All sorts of issues lurk here—how do you tell whether the container or your archive is fully deployed and ready to test? How do you ensure your archive and resources are fully removed and undeployed by the time your next test runs?

Arquillian (http://www.jboss.org/arquillian/) is a test framework that focuses on making container deployment very easy within your tests. It allows you to test within an embedded or a remote container. In terms of testing JBoss ESB, Arquillian only supports testing services in a remote container, but it is a big advantage in integration testing your ESB archives because it manages the container lifecycle for you.

In this first example, we have a previously built ESB archive. In order for Arquillian to deploy it, it needs to be created through **ShrinkWrap** (http://www.jboss.org/shrinkwrap), so we wrap it in a file, we import it as a **ZipFile** object and create it as a **JavaArchive** object. Arquillian will now deploy it during the execution of the test.

```
package org.jboss.soa.esb;

import java.io.File;
import java.util.zip.ZipFile;

import org.jboss.arquillian.api.Deployment;
import org.jboss.arquillian.junit.Arquillian;
import org.jboss.shrinkwrap.api.ShrinkWrap;
import org.jboss.shrinkwrap.api.importer.ZipImporter;
import org.jboss.shrinkwrap.api.spec.JavaArchive;
import org.junit.Test;
import org.junit.runner.RunWith;

@RunWith(Arquillian.class)
public class ArquillianBinaryTest {
    private static final String ESB_LOCATION =
                "/src/jbossesb/product/samples/quickstarts/
                 helloworld_book/build/QuickStartHelloWorld.esb";

    @Deployment(testable=false)
    public static JavaArchive createTestArchive() throws Exception {
        File file;
        ZipFile existingZipArchive = null;
        file = new File(ESB_LOCATION);
        existingZipArchive = new ZipFile(file);
        return ShrinkWrap.create(JavaArchive.class, "test.esb")
            .as(ZipImporter.class)
            .importZip(existingZipArchive)
            .as(JavaArchive.class);
    }

    @Test
    public void testMethod() throws Exception {
        // Insert your test logic and execution here
    }
}
```

The second Arquillian example shows how to create our deployment as a ShrinkWrap archive. We import the necessary configuration and descriptor files as well as a custom action, and then the resulting archive is deployed through ShrinkWrap. This is a great option to take if you want to test alternative configurations.

```java
package org.jboss.soa.esb;
import java.io.File;

import org.jboss.arquillian.api.Deployment;
import org.jboss.arquillian.junit.Arquillian;
import org.jboss.shrinkwrap.api.ShrinkWrap;
import org.jboss.shrinkwrap.api.asset.FileAsset;
import org.jboss.shrinkwrap.api.spec.JavaArchive;
import org.jboss.soa.esb.samples.quickstart.helloworld.
MyJMSListenerAction;
import org.junit.Test;
import org.junit.runner.RunWith;

@RunWith(Arquillian.class)
public class ArquillianTest {


    @Deployment(testable=false)
    public static JavaArchive createTestArchive() throws Exception {
        return ShrinkWrap.create(JavaArchive.class, "test.esb")
            .add(new FileAsset(new File("jbm-queue-service.xml")),
                "jbm-queue-service.xml")
            .addClass(MyJMSListenerAction.class)
            .addAsManifestResource("jboss-esb.xml")
            .addAsManifestResource("deployment.xml");
    }

    @Test
    public void testMethod() throws Exception {
        // Insert your test logic and execution here
    }
}
```

Cargo

Cargo (http://cargo.codehaus.org/) is an alternative to using Arquillian. Cargo is a set of build tools which allow you to control a Java container as part of your Maven or ant build cycle. You can start a container pre-test, deploy your ESB archive, and then run tests, either using ServiceInvoker or one the listeners that you have set up (file, JMS, and so on) to test your application.

There are multiple ways you can deploy your newly built ESB archive to the Cargo-controlled container that you are testing. You can copy the archive directly into the `deploy` directory as part of the build, and then clean up by deleting it once your tests are finished. Alternatively if you are using Maven, you can use the jboss-maven-plugin's `jboss:hard-deploy/hard-undeploy` goal to copy it to the `deploy` directory. Finally, you can use Cargo to either locally or remotely deploy to your container using the `cargo:deploy` goal.

Chapter bibliography

- http://soa.dzone.com/articles/jbossesb-drools-integration
- http://soa.dzone.com/news/impatient-start-jboss-riftsaw-0
- http://soa.dzone.com/news/bpel-esb-and-back-introduction
- http://soa.dzone.com/news/esb-bpel-continuing-riftsaw
- http://planet.jboss.org/post/hanging_together_on_the_soa_platform_introduction_to_the_esb_jbpm_integration

B

Pop-quiz Answers

Chapter 1

1. True.

2. Server, binary, and source.

3. False, although commercial support is available.

4. False, leaving a detailed post with attached files and configuration information is preferred.

5. A set of configurations and services to start up at runtime.

6. Copy one of the existing profiles to another name in `<jboss-as>/server`. You would want to make a copy to be able to refer to the original configuration files and to start over again without having to reinstall in case something went wrong.

7. False! They contain valuable information.

8. MBeans are managed beans that abstract objects and monitor and display attributes of services, as well as provide methods for controlling them.

Chapter 2

1. (c) In the `quickstarts.properties` file

2. (a) `deployment.xml`

3. (c) The **Add and Remove** feature in JBDS

4. (a) In the `readme.txt` files

5. (c) By using the JBoss AS admin console

Chapter 4

1. (b) The `process` method.
2. (c) With content-based routing.
3. (b) A notifier OOTB action.
4. (b) A converter/transformer.
5. (a) `SOAPProcessor`.

Chapter 7

1. (a) Clustering a service over multiple nodes.
2. (a) Universal Description, Discovery, and Integration.
3. (a) Abstraction on top of XML registries.
4. (b) Stale EPRs might accumulate.
5. (a) Tracking the endpoints of a service at runtime.
6. (a) Use an MBean in the JMX console.
6. (a) jUDDI.
7. (a) A runtime address.

Index

Symbols

.ear, Java archives **33**
.esb, Java archives **33**
.jar, Java archives **33**
.sar, Java archives **33**
.war, Java archives **33**
<actions> tag **190**
<activation-config> element **198**
<camel-gateway> element **189**
<groovy-listener> element **194**
<http-bus> element **187**
<jbr-bus> element **192**
<jbr-provider> element **192**
<listeners> tag **185, 193**

A

action chain
  about **121**
  sample **121, 122**
action class **120**
actions
  about **119**
  types, custom actions **120, 123**
  types, out-of-the-box actions **120**
Address already in use exceptions **39**
admin console
  accessing **50**
  URL **39**
affiliated registries **204**
allowedPorts attribute **184**
ant deploy command **138**

ant runtest command **49, 139, 145**
ant sendesb **49**
Arquillian
  about **284, 285**
  example **285**
a ZipFile **284**

B

Bean Scripting Framework. *See* **BSF**
boot.log **35**
BPEL processes
  JBoss Riftsaw **146**
BPEL services **268-270**
BRMS **265**
BSF
  URL **132**
bus
  graphical representation **150**
Business Process Management
  about **145**
  CancelProcessInstanceCommand **145**
  NewProcessInstanceCommand **145**
  StartProcessInstanceCommand **145**
Business Rules **263**
Business Rules Management System. *See* **BRMS**
ByteArrayToString action **135**

C

camel gateway
  about **188**
  provider configuration **188**

quickstart, running 189
Cargo 285
Class not found (CNF) exceptions 39
Client API
  UDDI Subscription Listener API set 205
  UDDI Value Set Caching API set 205
clientCredentialsRequired property 253
co-located web services
  custom handlers 244
  SOAPProcessor 245
compose method 178
composite services
  about 112
  service chaining 112
  Service Continuations 114
ConfigProperty annotation
  configuring, elements used 127
ConfigTree
  using, for JBoss ESB configuration 95
ConfigTree annotation 128
ConfigTree parameter 99, 128
custom actions
  about 120, 123
  annotations, using 127, 128
  JavaBean actions 126
  lifecycle actions 123-125
custom actions, annotations used
  about 127, 128
  ConfigProperty annotation, configuring 127
  lifecycle annotations 128
  Process methods, defining 129, 130
custom registry solutions 209

D

database, jUDDI
  about 206, 207
  registry database, examining 208, 209
decompose method 178
deploy directory 286
destroy methods 123
displayMessage method 91, 125
Drools 146
Drools Guvnor 265
DSL 264

dynamic method
  about 105
  multiple process methods 106

E

EBWS
  other security mechanisms 233
  securing 229, 230
  security element, adding to 230-233
End-point reference. See EPR
Endpoint References 150
Enterprise Service Bus. See ESB
EPR
  about 210-212
  cleaning 214
ESB
  about 77
  building blocks, actions 119
  message structure, examining 80
ESB-aware provider 46
ESB runtime
  setting up, in JBDS 63-68
ESB services
  exporting, as web service 225, 226
  testing 278
ESB services, exporting as web service
  about 225
  actions, implementing 228, 229
  sample, running as 226, 227
  transformer, adding 229
ESB services test
  AbstractTestRunner 280-282
  Arquillian 283-285
  Cargo 285
  single action, testing 279
  TestMessageStore 282, 283
esbToBpmVars property 274
ESB-unaware provider 46
ESB web service client
  about 234
  ESB SOAP client 234
  SOAPUI client 234
  Wise SOAPClient 239
Event Processing 263

exceptions
Address already in use exceptions 39
Class not found (CNF) exceptions 39
Illegal state exceptions 39
Java not found exceptions 39

F

faultXsd attribute 225
federation 212, 213
file attribute 250
File gateway
about 182
using 182, 183
file provider
structure 173
using 173
FTP gateway
about 189
quickstart, running 189
FTP provider 171, 172
functional groups, OOTB
BPEL Processes 132
Business Process Management 131
EJBs 131
Miscellaneous 132
notifiers 131
routers 131
Rules Services 131
scripting 131
smooks message fragment processing 131
transformers/Converters 131
web services/SOAP 131

G

gateway
about 176
behavior 177
messages, composing 177
getContext() method 94
Graphical Process Design tool (GPD) 272
Groovy gateway
about 194
variables 194
groovy_gateway quickstart 195
Groovy script 194
Guvnor 265, 266

H

HP Systinet 262
HttpClient
custom configurator 252, 253
sample properties 251, 252
SOAPClient 250
SOAPProxy 251
tweaking 250
HTTP gateway
about 184
asynchronous behavior, using 187
HTTP bus 187
HTTP provider 187
minimal configuration 184, 185
using 185, 186
HTTP provider
about 187
configuration 187
configuring 188
exception element 187

I

Illegal state exceptions 39
Initialize methods 128
invmLockStep attribute 165, 170
inVMLockStepTimeout attributes 170
InVM message delivery
controlling 164
lock-step delivery, using 165-168
inVMPassByValue property 163
InVM threads
about 168
listener threads, increasing 168, 170
InVM transport
about 157, 158
body address, examining 163
caveats 162
GLOBAL attribute 157
NONE attribute 157
optimization 162
transactions 158
Invoke button 210
is-gateway attribute 189

J

JAAS 117
Java API for XML Registries. *See* JAXR
Java archives
  .ear 33
  .esb 33
  .jar 33
  .sar 33
  .war 33
  about 284
Java Authentication and Authorization Service.
        See JAAS
Java-like Process Definition Language (jPDL) 272
Java Management Extension (JMX) console 37
Java Message Service API 171
Java not found exceptions 39
JAXR 212
JBDS
  about 54, 78, 151, 179, 222
  Chapter3 app, opening 78, 79
  Chapter8 application, preparing 222-224
  consoles, switching 224
  downloading 54
  ESB runtime, setting up 63-68
  File Filter, creating 151-153
  installing 55-60
  running 60-62
  quickstart, deploying 70-73
  using, to run quickstart 68, 70
JBDS ESB editor
  configuration elements, providers 260
  configuration elements, services 260
  invoking 260
  service definitions, creating 259-262
JBoss 5.1 Runtime 78, 179, 222
JBoss 5.1 Runtime server 224
JBoss Application Server. *See* JBoss AS
JBoss AS
  downloading 25-28
  installing 25-28
  JBoss ESB, deploying 30-32
JBoss Developer Studio. *See* JBDS
JBoss Drools 263, 264

JBoss ESB
  bus 150
  core capabilities 259
  deploying, to JBoss AS 30-32
  deployment files 46
  distribution, selecting 28, 29
  documentation page 262
  downloading 24, 25
  Drools integration 266
  Helloworld quickstart 47
  installation, testing 34
  issues, handling 39
  Maven, using 274
  quickstart, deploying 48
jbossesb-4.10-src.zip 29
jbossesb-4.10.zip
  about 29
  contents, reviewing 30
  Contributors.txt 30
  docs 30
  install 30
  javadocs 30
  JBossEULA.txt 30
  lib 30
  README_FIRST.txt 30
  samples 30
  xml 30
JBoss ESB archive
  admin console, accessing 50
  deploying, remotely 50
  deployment, performing 51, 52
JBoss ESB classes 265
JBoss ESB configuration
  ConfigTree, using 95
JBoss ESB configuration, ConfigTree used
  about 95
  attributes, accessing 96, 98
  ConfigTree hierarchy, traversing 96
  property configuration, in jboss-esb.xml file 95
JBoss ESB, distribution
  jbossesb-4.10-src.zip 29
  jbossesb-4.10.zip 29
  jbossesb-server-4.10.zip 29
  selecting 29
JBossESB-Drools integration 265

JBoss ESB-jBPM integration
in action 273
operations 273
JBoss ESB-RiftSaw integration
operations 270, 271
jbossesb-server-4.10.zip 29
JBoss ESB services
actions 119
jboss-esb.xml file 259
JBoss project technologies
about 263
BPEL services 268-270
JBoss Drools 263, 264
JBoss jBPM 272
JBoss Riftsaw 268
rules-based programming 263
JBoss Remoting 245
JBoss Remoting gateway
about 192
asynchronous JBR, using 194
asyncResponse property 192
provider configuration 192
serviceInvokerTimeout property 192
synchronous property 192
using 193
JBoss Riftsaw
about 146
web services, using 146
JBoss WS console 218
jbossws-context property 245
jbossws-endpoint property 245
JCA gateways
about 198
using 198
JMS gateway
about 180
using 180, 181
JMS provider
using 171
jUDDI
characteristics 205
monitoring abilities 214
query counts, examining 215
UDDI server, querying 216-218
URL 205
websites 218

K

key
dumpSOAP key 237
keyedReference validation 205

L

lifecycle methods 100, 101
listeners 46
load balancing 213
lock-step delivery 164
logs
application, deployment in server log 36
boot.log 35
files 35
finding 35
server.log 35
LongToDateConverter action 135

M

Managed Beans (MBeans) 38
Maven
compiling with 275, 276
ESB packaging 276, 278
JBoss ESB, using 274
maxThreads property 168
MBean
examining 38
MEP
about 106, 226
OneWay 107
RequestResponse 107
routing information 107
undefined 107
mep attribute
about 107
OneWay MEP 107
RequestResponse MEP 107
value specified 107
mep property 122
message body
about 84
body contents 88
header 89

main payload 85
main payload, examining 85-88
named objects 85
message composing
example 178, 179
steps 178
message context
about 93
printing 94
Message Exchange Pattern. *See* **MEP**
message header
about 89
additional contents 93
correlation 90
EPRs 90
examining 91, 92
information, routing 89, 90
MessageID 90
message identity 90
RelatesTo 90
service actions 91
message inflow 198
Message Oriented Middleware. *See* **MOM**
MessagePayloadProxy class 135
message structure, ESB
applications, deploying 84
attachment 80
body 80, 84
context 80, 93
examining 80
header 80, 89
loosely coupled 80
message, examining 80
messages, implementing 84
printing 81-83
properties 80
reusable 80
self contained 80
validation 94
message validation
about 94
enabling 95
MOM 108
MyAction class 106
MyAction lockStepAction method 168

N

New File Filter dialog 254
NewProcessInstanceCommand 145
Nodes
about 204
Inquiry API set 204
Publication API set 204
Replication API set 204
Security Policy API set 204
notifiers
about 144, 176
behavior 177
NotifyConsole 144
NotifyFiles 144
NotifyFTP 144
NotifyQueues 144
NotifySQLTable 144
NotifyTopics 144
working 144, 145

O

Object-Graph Navigational Language. *See* **OGNL**
ObjectInvoke ction 135
ObjectToCSVString action 135
ObjectToXStream action 135
OGNL 238
OGNL notation 238
OOTB
about 131
BPEL processes 146
Business Process Management 145
Drools 146
EJBs, invoking 133
functional groups 131
notifiers 144
scripting 132
Transformers/converters 135
web services 134
Organization for the Advancement of Structured Information Standards 203
org.jboss.soa.esb.actions.annotation.OnException annotation 131
org.jboss.soa.esb.actions.annotation.OnSuccess annotation 130

org.jboss.soa.esb.actions.annotation.Process
annotation 129

org.jboss.soa.esb.client.ServiceInvoker utility
class 108

org.jboss.soa.esb.configure.ConfigProperty
annotation 127

org.jboss.soa.esb.failure.detect.removeDeadEPR
property 214

org.jboss.soa.esb.http.HttpRequest.getRequest()
188

org.jboss.soa.esb.lifecycle.annotation.Destroy
annotation 128

org.jboss.soa.esb.lifecycle.annotation.Initialize
annotation 128

org.jboss.soa.esb.loadbalancer.policy property
213

Out-of-the-box. *See* **OOTB**

outXsd attributes 225, 226

P

PersistAction action 135
printLine() method 97
printMessage() method 97
process attribute 121
processException method 102
processing methods
  about 102
  AbstractActionPipelineProcessor method 105
  exceptions, examining 103-105
processSuccess method 102, 130
profile
  modifying 33
provider configuration
  about 170
  file provider 173
  FTP provider 171
  JMS provider 171
  SQL provider 172
providers
  about 44
  attributes 45
  busid 45
  message filter 45
  name 45

Q

quickstart
  example programs 42
  examples 42

R

Red Hat Enterprise Linux (RHEL) 54
registry
  about 202-204
  actions 202
  diagram 202
  hard crash 213
registry interceptors
  about 214
  setting 214
responseAsOgnlMap property 238
rewrite-endpoint-url property 245
RiftSaw
  about 268
  installing 268, 269
  of set-up tasks 268
rolesAllowed attributes 229
routers
  actions, ContentBasedRouter 141
  actions, JMSRouter 140
  actions, Aggregator 140
  actions, EchoRouter 140
  actions, HttpRouter 140
  actions, StaticRouter 141
  actions, StaticWiretap 141
  content-based routing, implementing 142, 143
RuleAgent class 265
rules-based programming 263
run() method 280

S

SAML 230
SAML capabilities 233
scripting
  actions 132
  GroovyActionProcessor 132
  ScriptingActio 132
Security Assertion Markup Language. *See* **SAML**

security context
about 117
encrypted authentication request 117
encrypted, pre-authenticated principal 117
server.log 35
service
binding template 204
business entity 203
business services 203
category 46
description 46
name 46
technical data models 204
service chaining
about 112, 113
more services, adding 114
Service Continuations
benefits 114, 115
ServiceInvoker
about 108
asynchronous delivery 109
exceptions, examining 110, 111
MEPs, experimenting with 112
sync delivery, experimenting with 112
synchronous delivery 109
transport mechanism 108
service pipeline
about 99
lifecycle methods 99-101
processing methods 101, 102
ShrinkWrap 284
Smooks
about 136
quickstart, running 138, 139
routers 140
transformation types, enrichment 136
transformation types, Java Binding 136
transformation types, Message Splitting 136
transformation types, persistence 136
transformation types, Templating 136
transformation types, validation 137
using, situations 137
SmooksAction action 136
SOAPProcessor
about 245
jbossws-context property 245

jbossws-endpoint property 245
rewrite-endpoint-url property 245
SOAPProcessor client, incorporating 245, 247
SOAPProxy
deployments, cleaning up 254, 255
incorporating, into application 248, 249
security pass through 253-256
SOAPProxy action 253
SOAPUI
URL 216
SOAPUI client
about 234
ESB SOAP client 234-236
OGNL 238
request processing 236, 237
request transformations 237
response processing 238
XStream conversion 238
soapUI tool 234
SOA Software ServiceManager 262
SQL gateway
about 195
using 195-198
SQL provider
configuration 172, 173
StartProcessInstanceCommand 145
statusCode attribute 185
synchronousTimeout property 184

T

Task Planning 263
TestMessageStore action 283
transactions, InVM transport
non transacted InVM listener 162
testing 159-162
transactions
about 115, 116
atomicity 115
consistency 115
durability 116
isolation 116
Transformers/converters
about 135
ByteArrayToString 135
LongToDateConverter 135

ObjectInvoke 135
ObjectToCSVString 135
ObjectToXStream 135
PersistAction 135
Smooks 136
SmooksAction 136
XStreamGToObject 135
transportGuarantee attribute 187
transport mechanism, ServiceInvoker
(JMS) InVM 108
about 109
File/FTP/FTPS/SFTP 108
Java Message Service 108
SQL 108
Transport providers
about 154
file provider, using 155-157
InVM transport 157, 158
temp file contents, examining 157

U

UDDI
about 203
building blocks 203
Client API 205
Node API 204
services 203
UDDI providers
HP SOA Systinet 209
HP Systinet 262
SOA Software Service Manager 209, 262
UDDI v3 specification 218
UDP gateway
about 189
configuration 190
handlerClass attribute 190
Host attribute 190
Port attribute 190
using 190-192
Uniform Resource Identifier. *See* **URI**
Uniform Resource Name. *See* **URN**
Universal Description, Discovery,
and Integration. *See* **UDDI**
URI 90
urlPattern attribute 184
URN 90

V

validate attribute 94, 225

W

W3C WS-Addressing specification 89
webservice attribute 225
web service proxies
about 248
SOAPProxy 248
web services
ESB services, exporting as 225, 226
integrating, with ESB 221
quickstart, running 134
SOAPClient 134
SOAPProcessor 134
WISE SOAPClient 134
when clause 264
Wise SOAPClient
about 239
custom handlers 243, 244
incorporating 240, 241
request processing 241-243
response processing 241-243
Wise (Wise Invokes Services Easily) 239

X

XML Schema Document. *See* **XSD**
XSD 94
XStream 238

Thank you for buying
JBoss ESB *Beginner's Guide*

About Packt Publishing

Packt, pronounced 'packed', published its first book "*Mastering phpMyAdmin for Effective MySQL Management*" in April 2004 and subsequently continued to specialize in publishing highly focused books on specific technologies and solutions.

Our books and publications share the experiences of your fellow IT professionals in adapting and customizing today's systems, applications, and frameworks. Our solution based books give you the knowledge and power to customize the software and technologies you're using to get the job done. Packt books are more specific and less general than the IT books you have seen in the past. Our unique business model allows us to bring you more focused information, giving you more of what you need to know, and less of what you don't.

Packt is a modern, yet unique publishing company, which focuses on producing quality, cutting-edge books for communities of developers, administrators, and newbies alike. For more information, please visit our website: www.packtpub.com.

About Packt Open Source

In 2010, Packt launched two new brands, Packt Open Source and Packt Enterprise, in order to continue its focus on specialization. This book is part of the Packt Open Source brand, home to books published on software built around Open Source licences, and offering information to anybody from advanced developers to budding web designers. The Open Source brand also runs Packt's Open Source Royalty Scheme, by which Packt gives a royalty to each Open Source project about whose software a book is sold.

Writing for Packt

We welcome all inquiries from people who are interested in authoring. Book proposals should be sent to author@packtpub.com. If your book idea is still at an early stage and you would like to discuss it first before writing a formal book proposal, contact us; one of our commissioning editors will get in touch with you.

We're not just looking for published authors; if you have strong technical skills but no writing experience, our experienced editors can help you develop a writing career, or simply get some additional reward for your expertise.

JBoss AS 7
Configuration, Deployment, and Administration

Build a fully-functional, efficient application server using JBoss AS

Francesco Marchioni

JBoss AS 7 Configuration, Deployment and Administration

ISBN: 978-1-84951-678-5   Paperback: 380 pages

Build a fully-functional, efficient application server using JBoss AS

1. Covers all JBoss AS 7 administration topics in a concise, practical, and understandable manner, along with detailed explanations and lots of screenshots

2. Uncover the advanced features of JBoss AS, including High Availability and clustering, integration with other frameworks, and creating complex AS domain configurations

3. Discover the new features of JBoss AS 7, which has made quite a departure from previous versions

Drools Developer's Cookbook

Over 40 recipes for creating a robust business rules implementation by using JBoss Drools rules

Lucas Amador

Drools Developer's Cookbook

ISBN: 978-1-84951-196-4   Paperback: 273 pages

Over 40 recipes for creating a robust business rules implementation by using JBoss Drools rules

1. Master the newest Drools Expert, Fusion, Guvnor, Planner and jBPM5 features

2. Integrate Drools by using popular Java Frameworks

3. Part of Packt's Cookbook series: each recipe is independent and contains practical, step-by-step instructions to help you achieve your goal.

Please check **www.PacktPub.com** for information on our titles

[PACKT] open source *
PUBLISHING
community experience distilled

Java EE 6 with GlassFish 3 Application Server

ISBN: 978-1-849510-36-3   Paperback: 488 pages

A practical guide to install and configure the GlassFish 3 Application Server and develop Java EE 6 applications to be deployed to this server

1. Install and configure the GlassFish 3 Application Server and develop Java EE 6 applications to be deployed to this server

2. Specialize in all major Java EE 6 APIs, including new additions to the specification such as CDI and JAX-RS

3. Use GlassFish v3 application server and gain enterprise reliability and performance with less complexity

4. Clear, step-by-step instructions, practical examples, and straightforward explanations

Application Development for IBM WebSphere Process Server 7 and Enterprise Service Bus 7

ISBN: 978-1-847198-28-0   Paperback: 548 pages

Build SOA-based flexible, economical, and efficient applications for IBM WebSphere Process Server 7 and Enterprise Service Bus 7

1. Develop SOA applications using the WebSphere Process Server (WPS) and WebSphere Enterprise Service Bus (WESB)

2. Analyze business requirements and rationalize your thoughts to see if an SOA approach is appropriate for your project

3. Quickly build an SOA-based Order Management application by using some fundamental concepts and functions of WPS and WESB

Please check **www.PacktPub.com** for information on our titles

Printed in Great Britain
by Amazon.co.uk, Ltd.,
Marston Gate.